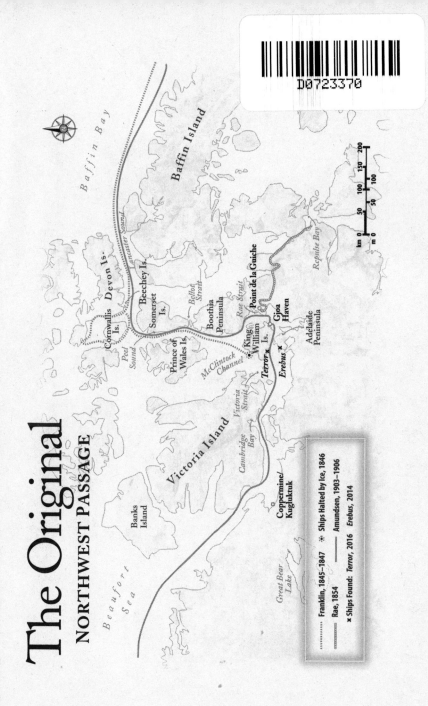

The Original
NORTHWEST PASSAGE

Baffin Bay

Baffin Island

Baffin Bay

Lancaster Sound

Devon Is.

Cornwallis Is.

Beechey Is.

Somerset Is.

Bellot Strait

Boothia Peninsula

Rae Strait

Point de la Guiche

Gjoa Haven

Peel Sound

Prince of Wales Is.

King William Is.

Terror

Erebus

Adelaide Peninsula

Repulse Bay

McClintock Channel

Victoria Strait

Victoria Island

Cambridge Bay

Banks Island

Beaufort Sea

Great Bear Lake

Coppermine/ Kugluktuk

km 0   50   100   150   200

m 0   50   100

Franklin, 1845–1847   ☀ Ships Halted by Ice, 1846

Rae, 1854   —— Amundsen, 1903–1906

✕ Ships Found: *Terror, 2016   Erebus, 2014*

D0723370

DEAD RECKONING

The Untold Story of the Northwest Passage

Ken McGoogan

HARPER **PERENNIAL**

Dedicated to

THE FORGOTTEN HEROES AND HEROINES
OF ARCTIC EXPLORATION

Published by Harper Perennial, an imprint of HarperCollins Publishers Ltd

First published by Patrick Crean Editions, an imprint of HarperCollins Publishers Ltd,
in a hardcover edition: 2017
This Harper Perennial trade paperback edition: 2018

HarperCollins books may be purchased for educational, business,
or sales promotional use through our Special Markets Department.

HarperCollins Publishers Ltd
Bay Adelaide Centre, East Tower
22 Adelaide Street West, 41st Floor
Toronto, Ontario, Canada
M5H 4E3

www.harpercollins.ca

Library and Archives Canada Cataloguing in Publication
information is available upon request.

ISBN 978-1-44344-127-8

Printed and bound in the United States of America

LSC/H 10 9 8 7 6 5 4 3 2 1

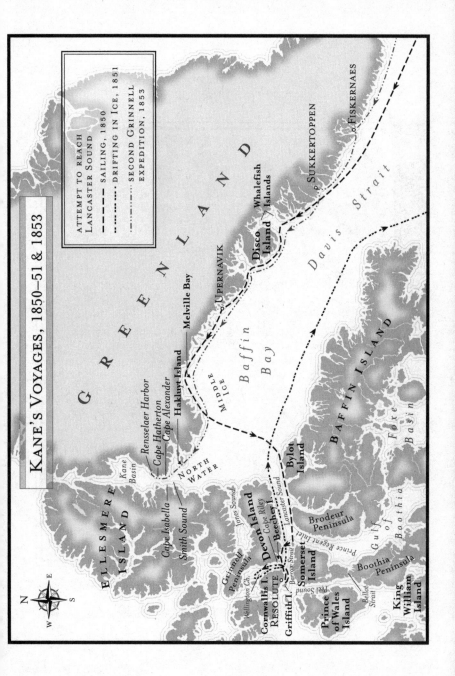

KANE'S VOYAGES, 1850–51 & 1853

ATTEMPT TO REACH
LANCASTER SOUND
— — — SAILING, 1850
· · · · · DRIFTING IN ICE, 1851
—··—··— SECOND GRINNELL
EXPEDITION, 1853

N
W   E
S

G R E E N L A N D

Rensselaer Harbor
Cape Hatherton
Cape Alexander
Hakluyt Island
Melville Bay
UPERNAVIK
Whalefish Islands
Disco Island
Davis Strait
SUKKERTOPPEN
FISKERNAES

Kane Basin
ELLESMERE ISLAND
Cape Isabella
Smith Sound
NORTH WATER
MIDDLE ICE
Baffin Bay
BAFFIN ISLAND
Foxe Basin

Jones Sound
Grinnell Peninsula
Wellington Ch.
Cornwallis I.
RESOLUTE
Devon Island
Cape Riley
Beechey I.
Griffith I.
Barrow Strait
Lancaster Sound
Bylot Island
Brodeur Peninsula
Prince Regent Inlet
Somerset Island
Peel Sound
Prince of Wales Island
Gulf of Boothia
Boothia Peninsula
Bellot Strait
King William Island

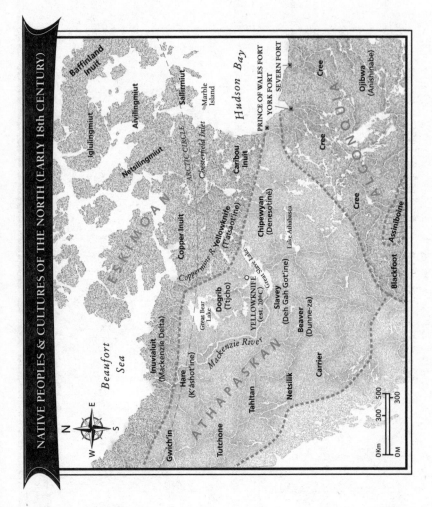

NATIVE PEOPLES & CULTURES OF THE NORTH (EARLY 18th CENTURY)

CONTENTS

Maps

Dead reckoning:

Dead reckoning is the process of determining one's present position by projecting course(s) and speed(s) from a known past position, and predicting a future position by projecting course(s) and speed(s) from a known present position . . .

—National Geospatial-Intelligence Agency

PROLOGUE

Challenging "Official" History

The discoveries of *Erebus* and *Terror* have sparked renewed interest in the history of Arctic exploration, and particularly in the long-lost expedition of Sir John Franklin. Even before archaeologists finished searching the ships, analysts went to work parsing the implications of the findings. Did early searchers misinterpret the one-page record found on the northwest coast of King William Island, where in 1848 Franklin's men landed after abandoning their ice-locked vessels? Did some sailors return and reboard? Did they drift south, or did they actively sail one or both ships? Does it matter? "Franklinistas" yearn for answers to such questions.

On the other hand, some thinkers have suggested that this single-minded focus, the "gravitational pull of the Franklin disaster," distorts our understanding of exploration history. In *Writing Arctic Disaster*, Adriana Craciun argues that Franklin made only a minor contribution to Arctic discovery. And she questions the wisdom of celebrating "a failed British expedition, whose architects sought to demonstrate the superiority of British science over Inuit knowledge."

This book, *Dead Reckoning: The Untold Story of the Northwest Passage*, sets out to navigate between extreme positions. It is a voyage of discovery. The late Pierre Berton established a point of departure, a known past position, with *The Arctic Grail*. But that work appeared in 1988—almost three decades ago. To determine our present position in these agitated seas, we must take into account everything we have learned since then—about climate change, for example, and the Inuit oral tradition. Berton begins his history in 1818, with a Royal Navy initiative, so signalling his acceptance of the orthodox British framing of the narrative. Since *The Arctic Grail* appeared, numerous Canadian authors have drawn attention to Inuit contributors. But until now, nobody has sought to integrate those figures into a sweeping chronicle of northern exploration.

To research *Dead Reckoning: The Untold Story of the Northwest Passage*, I have visited Scotland, England, Tasmania, Norway and the United States. In the Arctic, I have had the privilege of going out on the land with Inuk historian Louie Kamookak. And every summer since 2007, I have sailed in the Northwest Passage as a resource staffer with the travel company Adventure Canada. On board ship, when I wasn't giving talks, I learned from such Inuit culturalists as politician Tagak Curley, lawyer-activist Aaju Peter and singer-songwriter Susan Aglukark. I rubbed shoulders also with archaeologists, geologists, ornithologists, anthropologists, art historians and wildlife biologists. My voyaging immersed me in debates over climate change, adventure tourism and who controls the Northwest Passage.

The author in 1999, lugging a plaque to the John Rae cairn overlooking Rae Strait.

Along the way, I revelled above all in visiting historical sites. On one occasion, we chanced upon an impressive cairn in a bay off Boothia Peninsula, and I determined only later that it marked the grave of a cook who had sailed with Canadian explorer Henry Larsen. On another, we explored Rensselaer Bay on the Greenland coast, where Elisha Kent Kane spent two winters trapped in the ice. Back in 1999, years before these outings, I had gone north to locate

The Clipper Adventurer, *now called the* Sea Adventurer, *is an expeditionary cruise ship that sails frequently in the Northwest Passage.*

a cairn that explorer John Rae had built in 1854 and, with a couple of friends, ended up lugging an awkward plaque across bog and tundra.

That experience stayed with me. But I also vividly remember my initial Adventure Canada visit to Beechey Island, where in 1846 John Franklin buried the first three men to die on his final expedition. After going ashore in a Zodiac, we stood gazing at their graves while a bagpiper played "Amazing Grace" and giant flakes of snow softly fell and melted as they hit the ground. I felt moved by what I heard and saw—the skirling of the pipes, the desolate loneliness of the landscape. And yet, even after reading the wooden headboards, facsimiles of the originals, I felt more shaken by what I did not see—by the absence of ice.

At this time I was writing *Race to the Polar Sea*, and I knew we had arrived at Beechey Island two weeks later than Kane had in 1850. And yet, where his ship got frozen into pack ice, and he struggled through snow and ice when he stumbled ashore, I saw nothing around me but open water and naked rock and scree. As I stood at the three Franklin graves, I realized that climate change is bringing a centuries-old saga to an abrupt conclusion. And that nineteenth-century stories of Arctic exploration are more relevant than ever—irreplaceable touchstones that enable us to compare and contrast, and to grasp what the Northwest Passage is telling us.

In style and structure, *Dead Reckoning* is more literary than academic, more narrative than analytical—although, yes, I am bent on dragging Arctic discovery into the twenty-first century. By the time I set foot on Beechey, I had spent most of a decade researching and writing about northern exploration. Yet I was still meeting people who believed that John Franklin was "the discoverer of the Northwest Passage." In the twentieth century, even some Canadian historians followed their British counterparts in creating an "official" history that culminates not with the triumphant North-west Passage voyage of Amundsen, nor with the discovery of Rae Strait, which enabled the Norwegian explorer to succeed, but with Franklin's calamitous 1845 expedition.

Orthodox history nods grudgingly towards those non-British voyagers who cannot be completely ignored—men like Amundsen, Kane and Charles Francis Hall. Yet it continually shortchanges those highlighted by another book from the mid-1980s—*Company of Adventurers* by Peter C. Newman. Fur-trade explorers who made remarkable contributions by working with native peoples include

The Beechey Island gravesite. The three farthest headstones, which are replicas, mark the graves of the first crewmen to die (in 1846) during the last expedition led by John Franklin. The nearest grave is that of John Torrington, who died on January 1, 1846, at age twenty, on HMS Terror.

Samuel Hearne, Alexander Mackenzie and John Rae, the first great champion of Inuit oral history. A peerless explorer, Rae was defrauded of his rightful recognition after a campaign led by Lady Franklin, widow of Sir John. Ironically, she too looms large in these pages because she orchestrated an Arctic search that transformed the map of Canada's northern archipelago.

The twenty-first century demands a more inclusive narrative of Arctic exploration—one that accommodates both neglected explorers and forgotten First Peoples. With *Dead Reckoning: The Untold Story of the Northwest Passage,* I hope to restore the unsung heroes to their rightful eminence. Certainly, such British naval officers as Franklin, James Clark Ross and William Edward Parry risked starvation, hardship and often their very lives in a quest for glory at the top of the world. But they were far from alone. *Dead Reckoning* recognizes the contributions of the fur-trade explorers, and of the Dene, the Ojibway, the Cree and, above all, the Inuit, whose Thule ancestors have inhabited the Canadian Arctic for almost one thousand years. Were it not for the Inuit, John Franklin's ships would still be lying undiscovered at the bottom of the Arctic Ocean.

Part One

AN ARCTIC DREAMLAND

I.

Nightmares and Fever Dreams

A rchaeologists have identified several peoples who arrived in the Canadian Arctic before the time frame encompassed by this narrative. The Dorset crossed the Bering Land Bridge around 500 BC, for example, and the Thule, ancestors of contemporary Inuit, followed in the eleventh century AD. Vikings turned up early enough to interact with both Dorset and Thule. But the European idea of seeking a navigable Northwest Passage across the top of North America, that vision of discovery— that was born later, in England.

By the mid-1800s, when John Franklin occasioned what Adriana Craciun has called "the worst polar disaster in history, and the worst catastrophe in British exploration," European explorers had spent three centuries searching for the Northwest Passage. They had suffered scurvy, frostbite, amputation and starvation, and many had lost their lives in a hunt so difficult that its achievement promised fame, fortune and the love of women. Those who led the search frequently got caught up in a vision of extraordinary success, a fantasy of emerging from Arctic waters into the Pacific Ocean as the most heroic adventurers of their day.

In its particulars, the vision changed over the centuries. But in the mid-1500s, with Spanish and Portuguese galleons controlling southern trade routes to the fabled riches of Cathay (China and India) by way of the Cape of Good Hope or the Strait of Magellan, London merchants dreamed of locating a waterway that would enable them to sail, unaccosted, from the Atlantic Ocean to the Pacific. Such a discovery, they fervently believed, would make them wealthy beyond their wildest imaginings. Such riches would make them powerful. They would enjoy the love of beautiful women. In 1576, a consortium of English merchants called the Muscovy Company sent the veteran sailor Martin Frobisher to locate the elusive passage.

He had a reputation as a hard-driving man, but in *Martin Frobisher: Elizabethan Privateer*, author James McDermott reminds us that he averted more than one near-disaster at sea: "If Frobisher may be condemned for his autocratic and inflexible nature, he deserves also the credit for confronting . . . dangers with a single-mindedness that might have evaded more balanced temperaments."

A swashbuckling privateer, essentially a government-sanctioned pirate, Frobisher sailed north and west from England with three ships. Five weeks out, he lost two of them to a storm. In *Unknown Shore: The Lost History of*

Sir Martin Frobisher *by Cornelis Ketel, c. 1577.*

England's Arctic Colony, author Robert Ruby describes how the captain saved his own ship: "Frobisher himself grabbed the foresail and held on until the wind tore it away, along with the spar. Somehow he kept his footing. Crawling aft, he cut down the mizzenmast with an axe to reduce the storm's pressure on the ship—in those conditions, the less canvas, the better. He took charge, and imperiousness was his best quality."

Reduced to a single vessel, Frobisher sailed on. He sighted the coast of Labrador on July 28, and in mid-August reached land at what would one day be called Baffin Island, entering the mouth of the bay that now bears his name. With ice and wind discouraging any farther northward advance, he sailed west into this long narrow inlet towards present-day Iqualuit to see, as Ruby put it, "whether he might carry himself through the same into some open sea on the back side."

Now came the first of many cross-cultural misunderstandings that would mark the gradual elaboration of the Arctic map. Having determined that he had entered a bay and not a strait, Frobisher spotted a group of Inuit hunters on shore and welcomed one of them aboard his ship. Using sign language, he arranged to take a guided tour of the region. He sent the visitor ashore in a small boat with five of his men, warning them not to get too close to the other hunters. The crewmen, heedless, were taken captive.

After searching fruitlessly for several days, and with winter approaching, Frobisher took his would-be guide as a hostage (he soon died) and sailed for home. According to Inuit oral history, the five sailors lived among the locals for several years, but then put to sea from Baffin Island in a makeshift boat, never to be seen again.

Meanwhile, arriving in London in October 1576, Frobisher produced a chunk of hard black rock "as great as a half-penny loaf."

One of his men had picked it up, mistaking it for a piece of burnable coal. Four experts examined the rock, and one went along with the idea that it might contain gold. Frobisher and his backers, led by Michael Lok of the Muscovy Company, leveraged this assessment to gain financing for another voyage.

With the additional backing of Queen Elizabeth, and focused now on mining for precious metals, Frobisher sailed west across the Atlantic not once but twice more, in 1577 and 1578. On his second voyage, bringing a long-standing European tradition to the Arctic, and despite having encountered a handful of inhabitants, Frobisher claimed his "newly discovered" lands for England. Back home, Queen Elizabeth named the new territory Meta Incognita, or "the unknown limits."

On his final Arctic voyage, Frobisher sailed from Plymouth with fifteen ships—to this day, the largest Arctic expedition ever assembled. He intended to establish a mining colony of a hundred men. As he neared Baffin Island, ice and stormy weather wrecked one ship and drove him south into the mouth of a rushing tidal waterway that would later be named Hudson Strait. He sailed almost a hundred kilometres up this "mistaken strait," then turned back reluctantly and beat his way north.

By the time he reached Frobisher Bay, he had lost more ships and so much material that founding a settlement had become impossible. On Kodlunarn Island near the entrance to that inlet, he built a stone house whose ruins would be discovered, thanks to Inuit oral history, almost three hundred years later by the American Charles Francis Hall. Frobisher brought home a small mountain of black rocks this time, all of which would prove to be worthless. This debacle ruined Michael Lok, who published a denunciation entitled "The Abuses of Captayn Furbusher Agaynst the Companye, Ano 1578."

Undeterred, Frobisher sailed with Sir Francis Drake to the West Indies, and was later knighted for heroism in fighting the Spanish Armada in 1588. He died in 1594 after sustaining a gunshot wound while besieging a Spanish-held fortress near Brest.

Back in England, a less colourful but more meticulous navigator took up the search for the Northwest Passage in the late 1580s. John Davis crossed the Atlantic Ocean three times and produced the first coherent picture of the northeastern latitudes of North America, and of the west coast of Greenland. In 1585, he established friendly relations with a few Greenlandic Inuit before crossing the large strait that now bears his name. On the northeast coast of Baffin Island, Davis entered and began exploring Cumberland Sound. As winter came on, he ran out of time and departed for home, thinking that he might have discovered the entrance to the Passage.

The next year, he sailed again and skirted Baffin Island, but failed to penetrate Cumberland Sound or to make any new discoveries. In 1587, Davis tried a third time. He sailed north along the Greenland coast to a prominent headland near present-day Upernavik, and named it Sanderson's Hope. He met and made friends with a second group of Greenlandic Inuit.

After crossing Davis Strait, Davis revisited Cumberland Sound, but realized now that it provided no entrance to any northwest passage. Proceeding south, he noted the existence of Frobisher Bay without recognizing it as such, and then crossed the mouth of a "very great" inlet with a mighty tidal race—later, Hudson Strait.

Here, according to Canadian historian Leslie H. Neatby, Davis saw what he described as "the sea falling down into the gulf with a mighty overfall, and roaring, and with divers circular motions like whirlpools, in such sort as forcible streams pass through the arches of bridges." Such was the entrance to Hudson Strait at flood tide, when Atlantic waters poured westward into the massive bay, creating some of the highest tides in the world.

Despite his "great admiration" for this "furious overfall," Davis did not enter the strait. Probably this astute navigator had already decided, rightly, that any navigable passage would be found north of what would come to be called Baffin Island. He continued south along the coast of Labrador and then sailed home to England. In his journal, he wrote that, between Greenland and Baffin Island, "the Passage was free and without impediment toward the North."

After Davis, both English and Dutch explorers sought a route to the Orient through a northeast passage. This entailed venturing beyond Norway, through the Barents Sea, and then proceeding past the North Pole, where geographers posited the existence of the Open Polar Sea. Unfortunately, and despite these theories, voyagers kept finding their way blocked by pack ice.

But now Henry Hudson enters our tale. Over the centuries, the quest for a navigable northwest passage spawned numerous catastrophes. Expeditions led by Jens Munk and James Knight would end famously in disaster, and John Franklin would contribute two well-known calamities. Apart from the final Franklin tragedy, however, no dreadful demise looms larger in the popular imagination than that of Henry Hudson. The image of Hudson set adrift in a small boat with seven men and a youth, victims of mutiny in a forbidding seascape, haunts anyone awake to the nightmare history of Arctic exploration.

Caught up in the fever dream of discovering a Northwest Passage, Hudson feared nothing, took calculated risks, and regarded the merchants who financed his voyages as glorified clerks. In the early 1600s, he sought a northeast passage across the top of Russia and came within 1,070 kilometres of the North Pole before he was driven back by ice. Backed by the Dutch East India Company, the Englishman tried again in 1609, but encountered, as others had, impenetrable ice in the Barents Sea.

Deciding unilaterally that a northwest passage held more promise, he set aside his orders. He turned his ship around, sailed south past Greenland and then along the coast of North America, looking for that elusive entranceway. He passed Nova Scotia, visited the mouth of the Delaware River and then explored the Hudson River from present-day New York City to Albany. In sum, whenever it suited him, as author Douglas Hunter observes in *God's Mercies: Rivalry, Betrayal and the Dream of Discovery*, Hudson "egregiously defied his sailing directions" to venture where he thought best.

Henry Hudson was a younger contemporary of Elizabethan scientist William Gilbert, who in 1600 published a book, *De Magnete*, seeking to explain why mariners' compasses acted erratically when they sailed north—a phenomenon that would lead, two centuries later, to attempts to locate the ever-shifting north magnetic pole. Ten years after Gilbert's book appeared, and having gleaned what he could from that volume, Hudson embarked on what would prove to be his final voyage. He departed from London, a city of 200,000 that was spilling beyond its medieval walls.

British merchants, yearning to acquire spices from the Far East, were urging him to seek a passage through the "furious overfall" which had so impressed Frobisher and Davis. On April 17, 1610, Hudson sailed down the Thames in a small, seventy-ton wooden ship called *Discovery*. With him he brought twenty-one men and two boys, one of whom was his teenage son.

Seventeen months later, in September 1611, the *Discovery* arrived back in England carrying seven men and one boy, sole survivors of this latest voyage to the new world. Hudson and his son were not among those who returned, and the deck of the ship was stained with blood.

Like the later Franklin tragedy, the Hudson saga has inspired numerous interpretations. Only the eight survivors, obviously, could present a rendition of what had happened. They were all mutineers, or had at least gone along with a mutiny. They included the ship's navigator, Abacuk Pricket, who had kept a journal of the voyage that would be recognized as the most reliable source. Pricket identified Henry Greene and Robert Juet, both now conveniently dead, as instigators of the mutiny.

The trouble had begun less than one month out of port, off the coast of Iceland, when the volatile Greene, an early favourite of Hudson, got into a fight with the ship's surgeon, Edward Wilson, a superior officer. When Hudson chose to pardon this act of rebellion, first mate Robert Juet voiced his outrage. Hudson ignored all protest and sailed on.

Towards the end of June, having battled ice off the coast of Greenland, he guided the *Discovery* into the furious overfall. Here extraordinary tides, which can reach fifty or sixty feet, battered the ship with whirling chunks of ice. Despite dissension, and with some men clamouring to turn back, Hudson sailed on, hugging the coastline. Hudson Strait is 725 kilometres long, but eventually the ship emerged into a "great and whirling sea," where, to the amazement of the sailors, polar bears swam among the ice floes.

Robert Juet ridiculed the notion that a channel to the Orient might exist to the west, and Hudson responded with a lecture and charts that convinced nobody. After passing a towering cape he named Wolstenholme, Hudson sent a scouting party ashore. The men found abundant wildlife and an Inuit storehouse filled with food. They wanted to remain and clean the place out. But the strong-willed Hudson, believing he was nearing his geographical objective, insisted on departing immediately. He proceeded south into James Bay, but then sailed back and forth without finding any egress.

The crew became increasingly disgruntled. Robert Juet again ridiculed the captain, and this time Hudson accused him of disloyalty. Juet demanded a trial before the ship's company and got it. To his chagrin, several crewmen testified to his traitorous remarks. Hudson demoted Juet and several who had sided with him. He indicated that good behaviour could lead to reinstatement, but the lines were drawn. The new first mate was the superbly capable Robert Bylot.

Hudson explored James Bay through October, despite encroaching ice. By November 10, 1610, the *Discovery* was frozen fast near Charlton Island. Hudson began rationing food, and some crewmen grumbled about not having taken more from the storehouse at Cape Wolstenholme. One man died and a silly dispute over who should inherit his cape caused a rift between Hudson and his former protégé, Henry Greene. The captain then had an altercation with the ship's carpenter, Philip Staffe, over the building of a shelter in the freezing cold.

The ensuing winter brought blizzards, hunger and scurvy. As the ice began to recede, a native appeared. Hudson communicated a desire to trade and gave him a few trinkets. The man returned with skins and meat. But the English response proved too miserly to encourage further dealings, and the man never returned.

The warming spring weather opened the water to fishing. On the first day, the sailors netted more than five hundred fish. They rejoiced, but never did that well again, and food once more became scarce. Hoping to renew trade with the natives, Hudson took enough food for eight or nine days and, with a few men, went searching in the shallop—a risky decision that left an unruly crew in control of the *Discovery*. The local people wanted nothing to do with the interlopers, and at one point set the forest ablaze to discourage their approach.

Back on the ship, without explanation, Hudson now demoted that capable navigator Robert Bylot and promoted an illiterate in his place—a man who knew nothing of navigation, and so could not question his calculations. By this action, he took sole control of the ship's route. Having narrowly survived one horrendous winter locked in the ice of James Bay, he appeared bent on risking a second to continue seeking the Northwest Passage—and this, many of the men found unacceptable.

With the ice melting and the ship set to sail, Hudson decided to divide the remaining food and give each man his share. Some men devoured their two-week allotment in a day. Many suspected the captain of hoarding and playing favourites, and in this they would be proven correct. Hudson had suspicions of his own. He launched a search that turned up three dozen hidden "cakes" of food.

The situation exploded on June 23, 1611, a Saturday night, when Juet and Greene launched their mutiny. The journal-keeper, Abacuk Pricket, hedged and equivocated, telling them that even if they succeeded and reached home, then as mutineers they would hang. Greene said he would rather hang than starve. Juet swore that he would justify the mutiny to the authorities. Pricket claimed that he made the conspirators swear on a Bible that they would harm nobody.

In the morning, the mutineers seized Henry Hudson and his closest allies. They brought alongside the ship a small boat with oars and a sail. Into this, after some pushing and shoving, they forced

The Last Voyage of Henry Hudson, *painted by John Collier in 1881. In 1611, mutineers forced Hudson and eight allies—one of them his son, John—into a small boat and sailed away.*

Hudson and eight others, one of them his son, John Hudson. Two of those driven into the shallop were sick, and two pleaded unsuccessfully to remain with the *Discovery*. One man, Philip Staffe, the carpenter, refused to countenance the mutiny and was allowed to board the small boat with his chest, musket and an iron pot.

The mutineers cut the shallop loose, and then, shockingly, sailed away northward. Hudson and his friends, Pricket writes, were "without food, drink, fire, clothing, or other necessaries" in one of the most forbidding seascapes in the world. Those abandoned to the small boat broke out oars and rowed after the sailing ship, desperate to negotiate a return. But on seeing their persistence, the mutineers added sails and, swinging northeast, left the shallop far behind.

On the evening of June 26, thanks to the navigational skills of Robert Bylot, the *Discovery* reached Cape Wolstenholme at the western end of Hudson Strait. Nearby, during their inbound voyage, the men had raided that Inuit storehouse. This time, they encountered some apparently friendly hunters—doubtless those they had previously robbed. The next day, when they went ashore in a small boat to trade, they walked into an ambush. Two sailors were killed on shore. Others, wounded, made it back to the boat. But a hail of arrows killed Henry Greene, and three wounded sailors died back on board ship.

Only eight men and a cabin boy remained alive. Sick and starving, reduced to eating small birds, they had to travel through Hudson Strait and then cross the rolling Atlantic. Again, despite his rudimentary instruments, Robert Bylot proved equal to the navigational challenge. In mid-September, having first reached western Ireland, the mutineers arrived in London (one more having died).

Some citizens there, on learning what had transpired, demanded that the perpetrators be hanged. But both Bylot and Pricket claimed they had discovered a northwest passage. And Bylot, in particular, had gained crucial knowledge and demonstrated singular expertise. The mutineers went free. Eventually, merchants bent on locating that elusive Passage found a legal loophole. The survivors were charged not with mutiny but with murder, and then, of this, judged innocent.

Meanwhile, Robert Bylot proved useful. The year after he arrived home, sailing with captain Thomas Button, he re-entered Hudson Bay. The voyagers survived the harsh winter and charted most of the west coast of the Bay, including the mouth of the Churchill River. On his next voyage, sailing as captain of the *Discovery*, and backed by the Muscovy Company, Bylot proceeded through Hudson Strait and swung north to probe those waters. He was halted by pack ice at the eastern end of "Frozen Strait."

In 1616, forty years after Martin Frobisher's first voyage, Bylot sailed west yet once more. This time an accomplished pilot, William Baffin, came with him. Together, after voyaging north through Davis Strait, Bylot and Baffin mapped the contours of what came to be called Baffin Bay. They discovered the entrance to Smith Sound, the main gateway to the North Pole, and reached a northern latitude of almost 78°, which would stand as a record for 236 years. Finally, they discovered Lancaster Sound. This would prove to be the entrance to the Northwest Passage, though it failed to register with the navigators as such because of the icy conditions.

Back in England, armchair voyagers remained committed to finding the Passage. They expressed doubts about the Bylot-Baffin maps, and indicated as much on the charts they published. Two centuries later, when in 1818 Sir John Ross "rediscovered" Baffin Bay, he and others were astonished by the accuracy of the Bylot-Baffin maps. Most of the credit went to Baffin, ostensibly because he was the first to use lunar observations to calculate longitude, but probably because Bylot's reputation had been damaged by his involvement in the Hudson mutiny. Hudson himself, never seen again, became a first unhappy omen. Voyagers entered these northern waters at their peril.

2.

Catastrophe Engulfs Jens Munk

Despite what happened to Henry Hudson, explorers continued to seek an eastern entrance to the Northwest Passage through Hudson Bay. In 1619, soon after Robert Bylot and Thomas Button searched the Bay and found no way through, the Danish-Norwegian explorer Jens Munk, unconvinced, sailed into the Bay with sixty-four men in two ships. The *Unicorn*, a frigate, carried forty-eight men, and the sloop *Lamprey*, sixteen.

A veteran seaman at thirty-nine, Munk had been sailing since boyhood, and had served with distinction during a war against Sweden. More recently, as a result of a failed High Arctic whaling initiative, he had lost a fortune and no small amount of prestige. Munk sought the Northwest Passage as a way of restoring his damaged reputation. In this he anticipated John Franklin who, with much the same motive, would embark more than two centuries later. As we shall see, the catastrophes that engulfed the two expeditions would resonate in other ways.

Late in the summer of 1619, having sailed from Copenhagen and probed Frobisher Bay on Baffin Island, Munk beat his way through the treacherous Hudson Strait, which he called "Fretum Christian" after his sovereign, Christian IV. On the north shore of the strait, while hunting caribou on July 18, he had an ultimately friendly encounter with Inuit hunters.

In *The Journal of Jens Munk, 1619–1620*, translated into modern English by Walter Kenyon, we read that, having spotted the hunters from the *Unicorn*, Munk jumped into a boat with a few sailors. "When they saw that I intended to land," he writes, "they hid their weapons and other implements behind some rocks and just stood waiting." After landing, though the Inuit tried to stop him, Munk strode over, picked up the weapons, and examined them. "While I was looking them over," he notes, "the natives led me to believe that they would rather lose all their clothing and be forced to go naked than lose their weapons. Pointing to their mouths, they indicated that they used the weapons to procure their food." When Munk laid the weapons aside, "they clapped their hands, looked up to heaven, and seemed overjoyed."

Munk presented the hunters with knives and other metal goods. He gave a looking-glass to one man, who did not know what it was. "When I took it from him and held it in front of his face so that he could see himself, he grabbed the glass and hid it under his clothing." The hunters gave Munk numerous presents, including various kinds of birds and seal meat. "All the natives embraced one of my men," he added, "who had a swarthy complexion and black hair—they thought, no doubt, that he was one of their countrymen."

A few days later, returning to this harbour, Munk hoped to see more of the Inuit but encountered none. In typical European style, he erected a marker bearing "the arms of His Royal Majesty King Christian IV" and, because of the excellent hunting, named the harbour Reindeer Sound. Near the Inuit fishing nets, he left a few knives and trinkets. And then he resumed his difficult voyage into unknown waters, drifting "wherever the wind and the ice might carry us, with no open water visible anywhere."

With winter coming on, Munk managed to cross Hudson Bay, which he called "Novum Mare Christian." On September 7, he entered the estuary of the Churchill River "with great difficulty, because there were high winds, with snow, hail, and fog." Here, in "Jens Muncke's Bay," he sheltered his ships and settled in for winter. Some of the men had fallen ill, so he had them taken ashore. He built a fire to comfort the sick, but the party ended up huddling in tents through a terrible, two-day snowstorm.

Now came a moment worth noting. "Early the next morning," Munk writes, "a large white bear came down to the water's edge, where it started to eat a beluga fish that I had caught the day before. I shot the bear and gave the meat to the crew with orders that it was to be just slightly boiled, then kept in vinegar overnight. I even had two or three pieces of the flesh roasted for the cabin. It was of good taste and quite agreeable."

Munk sent men to investigate the surrounding woods. On September 19, after consulting with his officers, he sailed the *Unicorn* and the sloop upriver as far as possible. By October 1, he had both vessels secured and well protected. He had all the men take their meals on the *Unicorn* so as not to keep two galleys going at once. Soon he was making scientific observations and recording opinions on bird migrations and the origins of icebergs. Having always intended to live off the land, Munk encouraged his men to hunt the flocks of ptarmigan and partridge.

On November 21, Munk writes, "We buried a sailor who had been ill for a long time." This would prove a harbinger of things to come. On December 12, one of the two surgeons died: "We had to keep his body on the ship for two days because the frost was so severe that no one could get ashore to bury him." On Christmas Eve, as yet unconcerned, Munk gave the men "some wine and strong beer, which they had to boil as it was frozen." Over the next few days, the men played games to amuse themselves. "At the time," Munk writes, "the crew was in good health and brimming with excitement."

This stylized woodcut map of the estuary of the Churchill River, originally published by the Hakluyt Society in 1897, depicts the Jens Munk expedition soon after it arrived in 1619 to spend the winter. Here we see Munk's two ships on the west side of the harbour. In this bucolic representation, complete with two well-built houses, a few men are logging, two are returning from a hunt with dead caribou slung over their shoulders and several are preparing to bury one of their comrades—a dark omen of what is to come. According to the Historical Atlas of Manitoba, *this is the first large-scale map of a Manitoba locale. In 1783, after a French fleet destroyed the nearby Prince of Wales Fort, Samuel Hearne built Fort Churchill at this spot.*

The trouble began in earnest on January 10, when the priest and the remaining surgeon "took to their beds after having been ill for some time. That same day my head cook perished. And then a violent illness spread among the men, growing worse each day. It was a peculiar malady, in which the sick men were usually attacked by dysentery about three weeks before they died."

The healthy men, dwindling in numbers, continued to hunt and provide for the rest. But by January 21, thirteen men were down with the sickness, among them the sole remaining surgeon, "who was mortally ill by then." Munk pleaded with that man "if there was not some medicine in his chest that would cure the men, or at least comfort them. He replied that he had already used every medicine he had with him, and that without God's assistance he was helpless."

Two days later, one of the mates died after a five-month illness. That same day, "the priest sat up in his berth and preached a sermon, the last one he was ever to deliver in this world." Munk pleaded with the dying surgeon for advice, but received the same answer as before. By February 16, Munk writes, only seven men "were healthy enough to fetch wood and water and do whatever else had to be done on board." The following day, the death count reached twenty.

In his journal, Munk records death after death. The cold grew so severe that nobody could go ashore to fetch food or water. A kettle burst when the water inside turned to ice. Munk and his men had never experienced such a winter. Occasionally, someone would go ashore and shoot a few ptarmigan, providing a welcome addition to the larder. Some of the men "could not eat the meat," Munk writes, "because their mouths were so swollen and inflamed with scurvy, but they drank the broth that was distributed amongst them."

Late March brought better weather, but "most of the crew were so sick that they were both melancholy to listen to and miserable to behold." By now the illness was raging so violently "that most of those who were still alive were too sick even to bury the dead." Munk examined the contents of the surgeon's chest but could make no sense of what he found: "I would also stake my life on the opinion that even the surgeon did not know how those medicines were to be used, for all the labels were written in Latin, and whenever he wished to read one, he had to call the priest to translate it for him."

Munk writes that his "greatest sorrow and misery" started as March ended, "and soon I was like a wild and lonely bird. I was obliged to prepare and serve drink to the sick men myself, and to give them anything else I thought might nourish or comfort them." On April 3 the weather turned so bitterly cold that nobody could get out of bed: "nor did I have any men left to command, for they were all lying under the hand of God." By now, so few were healthy "that we could scarcely muster a burial party."

By Good Friday, besides Munk himself, only four men "were strong enough to sit up in their berths to hear the homily" marking the occasion. By this time, Munk writes, "I too was quite miserable and felt abandoned by the entire world, as you may imagine." Later in April, the weather improved enough that some men could crawl out of their berths and warm themselves in the sun: "But they were so weak that many of them fainted, and we found it almost impossible to get them back into bed."

Men continued to die, sometimes two or three a day. The living were now "so weak that we could no longer carry the dead bodies to their graves but had to drag them on the small sled that was used for hauling wood." By May 10, eleven men remained alive, all of them sick, including Munk. When two more men died, Munk writes, "only God can know the torments we suffered before we got them to their graves. Those were the last bodies that we buried." Those who died now remained unburied on the ship.

By late May, seven men lived on. Munk writes: "We lay there day after day looking mournfully at each other, hoping that the snow would melt and that the ice would drift away. The illness that had fallen upon us was rare and extraordinary, with most peculiar symptoms. The limbs and joints were miserably drawn together, and there were great pains in the loins as if a thousand knives had been thrust there. At the same time the body was discoloured as when someone has a black eye, and all the limbs were powerless. The mouth, too, was in miserable condition, as all the teeth were loose, so that it was impossible to eat."

Soon only four men remained alive, "and we just lay there unable to do a thing. Our appetites and digestions were sound, but our teeth were so loose that we could not eat." Dead bodies lay scattered around the ship. Two men went ashore and did not return. Munk managed to crawl out of his berth and spent a night on deck, "wrapped in the clothing of those who were already dead."

The next day, to his astonishment, he saw the two men who had gone ashore upright and walking around. They came across the ice and helped him ashore. Now, for some time, these three "dwelt under a bush on shore, where we built a fire each day." Whenever they found any greenery, they would dig it up and suck the juice out of its main root. Slowly, incredibly, the three began to recover. They went back aboard ship and found everyone dead. They retrieved a gun and returned to shore, where they shot and ate birds.

Gradually, the three survivors recovered. They reboarded the *Unicorn* and threw decomposing bodies overboard "because the smell was so bad that we couldn't stand it." Then, battling a plague of black flies, they stocked the smaller *Lamprey* with what food they would need to reach home. Finally, on July 16, Munk writes, "We set sail, in the name of God, from our harbour."

Such was the navigational skill of Jens Munk that, after battling fog, ice and gale-force winds, he guided the ship through the swirling currents of Hudson Strait and then across the stormy Atlantic. He and his two remaining men reached Norway in late September and their home port of Copenhagen on Christmas Day.

Most accounts of this disaster express wonder that cold and scurvy could take such a toll, wiping out sixty-two of sixty-five men. But an article by Delbert Young, published decades ago in the *Beaver* magazine, points to poorly cooked or raw polar-bear meat as the likely culprit. Soon after reaching land near present-day Churchill, Manitoba, Munk reported that at every high tide, white beluga whales entered the estuary. His men caught one and dragged it ashore.

Next day, as noted above, a "large white bear" turned up to feed on the whale. Munk shot and killed it. His men relished the bear meat. Again, Munk had ordered the cook "just to boil it slightly, and then to keep it in vinegar for a night." He had the meat for his own table roasted, and wrote that "it was of good taste and did not disagree with us."

As Delbert Young notes, Churchill sits at the heart of polar-bear country. Probably, the sailors ate a fair bit of polar-bear meat. During his long career, Munk had seen men die of scurvy and knew how to treat that disease. He noted that it attacked some of his sailors, loosening their teeth and bruising their skin. But when men began to die in great numbers, he was baffled. His chief cook died early in January, and from then on "violent sickness . . . prevailed more and more."

After a wide-ranging analysis, Young identifies the probable killer as trichinosis—a parasitical disease, unidentified until the twentieth century, which is endemic in polar bears. Infected meat, undercooked, deposits embryo larvae in a person's stomach. These tiny parasites embed themselves in the intestines. They reproduce, enter the bloodstream and, within weeks, encyst themselves in muscle tissue throughout the body. They cause the terrible symptoms Munk describes and, left untreated, can culminate in death four to six weeks after ingestion. Could trichinosis, induced by raw polar-bear meat, have later played a role in killing some of Franklin's men? To this we shall return.

After his disastrous misadventure in the North Country, incredibly, Jens Munk began planning another expedition to the same area, this time to establish a fur-trade colony. Not surprisingly, he found it impossible to attract financial backers or crew. He turned to naval activities, commanded fleets to protect Danish shipping and eventually served as an admiral in the Thirty Years War (1618–1648) that engulfed Central Europe.

3.

What Thanadelthur Made Possible

Half a century after the Jens Munk debacle, on May 2, 1670, England's King Charles II waved his magic wand and granted an exclusive trading monopoly over the Hudson Bay drainage basin to "the Governor and Company of Adventurers of England trading into Hudson Bay." His seven-thousand-word Royal Charter outlined the Company's rights and duties, which included an obligation to search for the Northwest Passage.

By the early 1700s, when the Hudson's Bay Company (HBC) began building Prince of Wales Fort at Churchill, Manitoba, three aboriginal peoples had for centuries been contending to control the mammal-rich hunting grounds to the west and north. These were the Cree, the Dene and the Inuit.

Roughly speaking, allowing for diversity as a result of intermarriages and adoptions, as well as occasional Assiniboine and Ojibway interlopers, some two thousand Swampy Cree made up the vast majority of the "Homeguard Indians" who had settled in the vicinity of HBC trading posts. These Algonquian-speaking people were Western Cree, as distinct from the Eastern Cree, who lived east of Hudson Bay. They were skilful hunters and discerning traders who demanded muskets that worked in winter, and enjoyed playing French traders against British ones. By the 1760s, the Western Cree numbered thirty thousand and ranged westward from Churchill to Lake Athabasca, which is located on the northern border between Saskatchewan and Alberta.

The lands north and west of this vast, Algonquian-speaking territory were dominated by the so-called "Northern Indians." These Dene, as they called themselves, spoke Athapaskan and had long been rivals and enemies of the Cree. They hunted and fished through most of present-day Northwest Territories, edging into what is now Nunavut.

Subgroups of the Dene were known then as Dogrib and Slavey (sometimes considered one) and Chipewyan, whose name derives from an Algonquian-Cree word referring to the wearing of beaver-skin shirts with backs that narrowed to a point at the bottom, as on a contemporary tailcoat. The Yellowknife or "Copper Indians," so called because they used copper tools, were a regional subgroup of the Chipewyan, who contested territories traditionally controlled by the Inuit.

Like the Cree, the Dene responded to the demands of the environment by functioning mainly as autonomous extended families. Local bands might include six to thirty hunters, or 30 to 140 persons. Such groupings were often culturally diverse as a result of intermarriages, adoptions and the practice of stealing wives.

In the treeless, frozen lands that lay still farther north, the Inuit extended across the Arctic from Alaska to Greenland. These "Esquimaux," as they were called, constituted a single people, as Knud Rasmussen would demonstrate early in the twentieth century. They could understand each other because they spoke related languages: Yup'ik in the west, Inuktitut in the east and Kalaallisut in Greenland.

The Inuit, armed only with harpoons and knives, found hunting walruses especially challenging in winter, when the crafty creatures made a habit of escaping down ice holes.

The Inuit hunted caribou, but also fish and sea mammals such as seals, walruses and beluga whales.

The Inuit sometimes came south to Churchill seeking wood and metal. But they did not enjoy friendly relations with the Dene, who were beginning to acquire European muskets and jealously guarded their role as fur traders. Such was the background against which, in the eighteenth century, two radically different Chipewyan-Dene individuals would play crucial roles in the European search for the Northwest Passage and what they called the "Far-Off Metal River," which today is known as the Coppermine. The first was a woman named Thanadelthur.

In the spring of 1713, a party of well-armed Cree attacked some Chipewyan-Dene and took three young women captive. That autumn, two of the females escaped and hurried westward, hoping to rejoin their people. They survived one winter, but then got lost. In the autumn of 1714, cold and hungry, and with one of them sick, they decided to retreat in the direction of a well-known Hudson's Bay Company post located a couple of hundred kilometres south of Churchill. This was York Fort, which would become York Factory when a chief factor was stationed there. One of the women died en route.

Five days later, on November 24, the other encountered some HBC men in the wilds. Seventeen-year-old Thanadelthur accompanied these men to York Fort. Governor James Knight, now in his seventies, and formerly the commander of a merchant fleet, quickly realized that she might prove useful. Because the Homeguard Cree were armed with more muskets, Chipewyan fur traders had ceased coming to HBC trading posts. Knight wanted to expand trade into the northwest, and was looking for an interpreter who could make peace between the two peoples.

The highly intelligent Thanadelthur could communicate readily with both Cree and Dene. Over the next few months, she also picked up English. And in June 1715, Knight sent her west on a peacemaking mission with William Stuart, an efficient HBC man, and 150 Homeguard Cree.

Knight commissioned Thanadelthur to inform the Chipewyan that the HBC would soon build a major fur-trading post at Churchill. In addition, because the governor was obsessed with rumours that deposits of copper and "yellow metal," or gold, existed far to the west, she was to inquire, off-handedly, about minerals. Setting out westward, the travellers ran into problems. The hunting was so poor that,

The multilingual Thanadelthur used her eloquence to create peace between traditional enemies. Ambassadress of Peace: A Chipewyan Woman Makes Peace with the Crees, *1715, oil on board, painted by Francis Arbuckle, 1952.*

as winter came on, the expedition had to separate into smaller groups.

One party of peacemakers encountered and massacred nine Chipewyans, though later the killers claimed self-defence. When Thanadelthur and Stuart came upon the scene, they were horrified. The young woman, determining that some surviving Chipewyan had headed west, told the innocent Cree with whom she had arrived to wait and, with a few men, set off in pursuit of the survivors. She came upon a few hundred Chipewyan who were gathering to seek revenge. Now she demonstrated her eloquence. Thanadelthur talked for hours and eventually persuaded the Chipewyan to return with her to meet the waiting Cree. They came. The two groups smoked the pipe of peace, and a few Chipewyan returned with Thanadelthur to York Fort, arriving in May 1716.

James Knight was thrilled with how, by "her perpetual talking," Thanadelthur had established peace between those ancient enemies, the Homeguard Cree and the Chipewyan-Dene. This informal treaty would open the far northwest to Knight himself. Later in the year, Thanadelthur welcomed the governor's idea of travelling to announce the building of an HBC post at Churchill, and so to solidify the new understanding. Then, around Christmas, she took sick. After a lingering illness, to Knight's dismay, she died on February 5, 1717.

In his Company journal, Knight wrote lamenting the loss of Thanadelthur's high spirit, firm resolution and great courage. But he carried on. The Chipewyan warriors she had brought to York Fort had carried knives and copper ornaments. As interpreter, Thanadelthur had relayed their understanding that copper and "yellow metal" could be found along "a far-off metal river."

Knight went ahead with plans to establish a trading post at the mouth of the Churchill River, to trade with the Chipewyan and possibly the Inuit. He spent a winter there, after constructing a rough, wooden fur-trading post near the former winter quarters of Jens Munk, a few kilometres upriver from where the HBC would later build Prince of Wales Fort.

Knight had long been intrigued by fanciful European maps that showed a northwest passage, identified as "the Strait" or "Straits of Anián," crossing the continent from north of California to the northeast corner of Hudson Bay. With Thanadelthur, he had asked the visiting Chipewyan-Dene to draw a map of the drainage basin of Hudson Bay. They produced one identifying seventeen rivers. The northernmost river, Knight believed, was the eastern mouth of the Strait of Anián, or the entrance to the Northwest Passage.

In September 1718, Knight sailed to England, bent on mounting an expedition to find the Strait of Anián and the gold and copper of the Far-Off Metal River. Having become a free agent, Knight negotiated the support of the Hudson's Bay Company. The governing committee agreed to send him to seek the elusive strait and passage through Hudson Bay at a latitude north of 64°. He would also expand trade, investigate the feasibility of establishing a whaling industry and discover the source of those nuggets of copper he had produced as evidence of the existence of precious metals at the mouth of a distant river.

On June 4, 1719, the aging but irrepressible Knight sailed from Gravesend, southeast of London on the River Thames. He left with forty men and two ships, the frigate *Albany* and the sloop *Discovery*. Knight and his men sailed into Hudson Bay and were never seen again by white men.

Three years later, in 1722, an HBC captain named John Scroggs made a perfunctory search of the northern reaches of Hudson Bay. He found some wreckage on Marble Island, twenty-five kilometres off the west coast near Chesterfield Inlet, and concluded that both of Knight's ships had sunk and "every man was killed by the Eskimos."

Scroggs produced no evidence. But his racist speculation would remain unchallenged for decades. Then the explorer Samuel Hearne, after visiting Marble Island three times, presented a radically different interpretation of what had happened to Knight. In *Journey to the Northern Ocean*, Hearne described finding guns, anchors, cables, bricks, a smith's anvil and the foundations of a house, as well as a number of graves. Hearne also discovered "the bottom of the ship and sloop, which lie sunk in about five fathoms of water, toward the head of the harbour."

He rejected the idea that the Inuit had anything to do with the demise of the expedition, noting that Knight and his men presented no threat. They were also far better armed than the Inuit and would have been invincible. Hearne writes that he interviewed Inuit eyewitnesses, who explained that sickness and famine decimated Knight's shipwrecked party. Only five sailors survived the first winter. The following summer, three of them died after eating raw whale blubber. The last two men, Hearne wrote, "though very weak, made a shift to bury" their comrades: "Those two survived many days after the rest, and frequently went to the top of an adjacent rock, and earnestly looked to the South and the East, as if in expectation of some vessels coming to their relief. After continuing there a considerable time together, and nothing appearing in sight, they sat down close together, and wept bitterly. At length one of the two died, and the other's strength was so far exhausted, that he fell down and died also, in attempting to dig a grave for his companion. The skulls and other large bones of those two men are now lying above-ground close to the house."

For more than two centuries, Hearne's reconstruction stood as definitive. Who could argue with eyewitnesses? And who could forget the distressing image of those final survivors, scanning the horizon for salvation? The only problem with this evocative rendition is that, two decades after he visited Marble Island, while sitting at his writing desk in London, Samuel Hearne invented it out of whole cloth. In *Dead Silence: The Greatest Mystery in Arctic Discovery*, authors John Geiger and Owen Beattie make this case at length. The end result, as they observe, was "the most haunting vision of failed discovery in the pageant of Arctic exploration."

From the vantage point of the twenty-first century, we can see that, while repudiating the racism of Scroggs's analysis, Hearne oversimplified the expedition's fate. Subsequent investigations suggest that Knight's two ships sustained heavy damage in the shallow, rocky harbour at Marble Island. The aging Knight may well have died during the ensuing winter, although the only graves ever found on the island were those of Inuit.

If Knight survived, the obsessive old man might have led his men ashore, then started overland for the Far-Off Metal River, only to perish in what he called "the Barrens." The most likely scenario, however, is that in the spring of 1720, with their ships incapacitated, Knight's surviving men piled into their open boats, started rowing towards Churchill, roughly five hundred kilometres south, and perished in the wind and the waves.

4.

Matonabbee Leads Hearne to the Coast

Roughly four decades after the death of Thanadelthur, a second outstanding "Northern Indian," a man named Matonabbee, began emerging into the saga of northern exploration. In the late 1750s, as an informal HBC ambassador in the tradition of Thanadelthur, Matonabbee reduced hostilities among the native peoples. Born around 1737, the son of a Chipewyan-Dene woman taken captive by the Cree, he had spent his youth in the Churchill area, shuttling among the English-speaking fur traders, the Cree and the Chipewyan. By the early 1760s, he had become a "leading Indian."

Matonabbee collected furs from Chipewyan-Dene far to the west, and led "gangs" in transporting them to Churchill (Prince of Wales Fort) before setting out again with trade goods. In the autumn of 1770, while returning to the Bay with a dozen men, beating south through cold and howling winds, Matonabbee was astonished to encounter an underdressed HBC man stumbling through the snow with a couple of Homeguard Cree.

Samuel Hearne, a strapping twenty-five-year-old, was equally stunned when Matonabbee addressed him in English. Hearne was

This portrait of Matonabbee (c. 1737–1782) by Ruth Jepson celebrates the Dene leader as a figure crucial to Samuel Hearne's epic journey. Without Matonabbee, the English explorer would never have established a first location in the southern channel of the Northwest Passage.

six feet tall, and this singular Chipewyan—"one of the finest and best proportioned men I ever saw"—was able to look him almost directly in the eye. When Matonabbee asked how he had fallen into such straits, the young explorer could hardly believe his ears. Could this be the native leader he had originally hoped to find? The one who had not only visited the Far-Off Metal River, but who had brought back copper from its banks?

Born in London in 1745, Samuel Hearne grew up with his widowed mother in Beaminster, Dorset, in South West England. In 1757, already a towering youth, Hearne had joined the Royal Navy under the protection of Samuel Hood, a famous fighting captain who later became First Lord of the Admiralty. As a "young gentleman" who walked the quarterdeck, Hearne served with Captain Hood through the Seven Years' War. He received an excellent eighteenth-century education while learning all he would ever need to know about chasing down and seizing enemy vessels.

In 1763, when the end of the war closed off any prospect of advancement, Hearne turned to the merchant marine. Early in 1766, seeking adventure and a chance to make his name, the young sailor joined the fur-trading Hudson's Bay Company, which was looking to expand into whaling. He signed on to serve as first mate on a whaling ship. During the next three years, while based at Prince of Wales Fort, Hearne demonstrated his navigational skills and began learning the languages of the native peoples with whom he came into contact—the Cree, the Dene and the Inuit.

The current HBC governor, Moses Norton, had fallen victim to the obsession of James Knight. He, too, wanted to lay hands on the fabled riches of the Far-Off Metal River. He hoped to accomplish this while answering critics who charged that the HBC was not fulfilling its charter obligations to explore the surrounding country-side. And in 1769, he offered young Hearne the chance to seek the Northwest Passage.

In November, Hearne set out from Churchill with some fellow traders. A guide named Chawhinahaw, paid to lead the party to Matonabbee, instead abandoned them to their own devices. Hearne made it back to Prince of Wales Fort and, in February 1770, set out again, travelling this time with two Homeguard Cree and a party of Dene led by Conneequese. After wending northwest for several months, and getting robbed by passing strangers, Hearne lost his quadrant in an accident. Unable to take the requisite readings, he started back to Churchill and ran into heavy weather. Reduced to shivering and floundering along without snowshoes, he met the one native leader who could appreciate not only how he had come to this, but what he intended still to accomplish.

Respected by both Cree and Dene, and able to move freely among them, Matonabbee knew how to travel in the North Country. He led an ever-changing retinue that included his five or six wives, who carried supplies, cooked meals, sewed clothing and made snowshoes. On December 7, 1770, two weeks after returning with Hearne to Prince of Wales Fort, Matonabbee led the young Englishman out of Churchill.

On this third sortie, the ex–Royal Navy man "went native."

Fitted out with a new quadrant and other supplies, Hearne meant to investigate the mouth of the Far-Off Metal River, and either to discover the Northwest Passage or else disprove its existence. "I was determined to complete the discovery," he wrote later, "even at the risk of life itself."

Matonabbee led the party northwest, following the caribou and buffalo. Hearne took notes as he travelled, and later described his harrowing adventure in a work universally recognized as a classic of exploration literature, and best known as *Journey to the Northern Ocean*. In it, Hearne described Matonabbee as easy, lively and agreeable in conversation, "but exceedingly modest; and at table, the nobleness and elegance of his manners might have been admired by the first personages in the world; for to the vivacity of a Frenchman, and the sincerity of an Englishman, he added the gravity and nobleness of a Turk; all so happily blended, as to render his company and conversation universally pleasing."

Matonabbee "was remarkably fond of Spanish wines," he added, "though he never drank to excess; and as he would not partake of spirituous liquors, however fine in quality or plainly mixed, he was always master of himself. As no man is exempt from frailties, it is natural to suppose that as a man he had his share; but the greatest with which I can charge him is jealousy, and that sometimes carried him beyond the bounds of humanity."

Travelling northwest, Hearne and his fellows lived a cycle of "either all feast, or all famine," frequently trekking two or three days on nothing but tobacco and snow water. Then someone would kill a few deer and everyone would gorge themselves. On one occasion Matonabbee ate so much that he fell ill and had to be hauled on a sledge. Hearne learned to eat caribou stomachs and raw muskox, and also to endure long fasts that caused him "the most oppressive pain."

He describes travelling through sparse woods comprising stunted pines, dwarf junipers, and small willows and poplars. The travellers followed deer through ponds and swamps, but would stop for days at a time when the hunting was good.

But Hearne's book is cherished, above all, for its vivid portrait of life among the Chipewyan-Dene of the eighteenth century: "It has ever been the custom for the men to wrestle for any woman to whom they are attached; and, of course, the strongest party always carries off the prize. A weak man, unless he be a good hunter and well-beloved, is seldom permitted to keep a wife that a stronger man thinks worth his notice: for at any time when the wives of those strong wrestlers are heavy-laden either with furs or provisions, they make no scruple of tearing any other man's wife from his bosom, and making her bear a part of his luggage.

"This custom prevails throughout all their tribes, and causes a great spirit of emulation among their youths, who are upon all occasions, from their childhood, trying their strength and skill in wrestling. This enables them to protect their property, and particularly their wives, from the hands of those powerful ravishers; some of whom make almost a livelihood by taking what they please from the weaker parties, without making them any return. Indeed, it is represented as an act of great generosity, if they condescend to make an unequal exchange; as, in general, abuse and insult are the only return for the loss which is sustained."

Scarcely a day would pass, Hearne adds, without such a wrestling match. "It was often very unpleasant to me," he writes, "to see the object of the contest sitting in pensive silence watching her fate, while her husband and his rival were contending for the prize. I have indeed not only felt pity for those poor wretched victims, but the utmost indignation, when I have seen them won, perhaps, by a man whom they mortally hated. On those occasions their grief and reluctance to follow their new lord has been so great, that the business has often ended in the greatest brutality; for, in the struggle, I have seen the poor girls stripped quite naked, and carried by main force to their new lodgings."

Later, Hearne notes, "I have throughout this account given the women the appellation of girls, which is pretty applicable, as the objects of contests are generally young, and without any family."

Although these eighteenth-century Northern Indians do not much resemble their contemporary descendants, and would happily rob their fellow travellers not only of their goods but even of their wives, Hearne writes that "they are, in other respects, the mildest tribe, or nation, that is to be found on the borders of Hudson's Bay: for let their affronts or losses be ever so great, they never will seek any other revenge than that of wrestling. As for murder, which is so common among all the tribes of Southern Indians, it is seldom heard of among them. A murderer is shunned and detested by all the tribe, and is obliged to wander up and down, forlorn and forsaken even by his own relations and former friends."

This peaceable approach did not extend to people of other nations, as Hearne would discover to his shock and horror. In May 1771, at a place called Clowey Lake, scores of Dene strangers, on learning that Matonabbee was bound for the Far-Off Metal River, attached themselves to his party. They did so "with no other intent," Hearne wrote later, "than to murder the Esquimaux, who are understood by the Copper Indians to frequent that river in considerable numbers."

During the past couple of years, while sailing up and down the west coast of Hudson Bay, Hearne had met numerous Inuit. He had mastered the rudiments of their language, and he knew the vast majority of them to be peaceful and good-hearted. At Clowey Lake, he urged his companions to approach these people in peace, as possible trading partners, and not with a view to waging war. The newly arrived Dene reacted with derisive fury, accusing Hearne of cowardice. Perhaps he was afraid to fight the Inuit?

Nearing the Far-Off Metal River, with the warriors clearly preparing an attack, Hearne tried again, and met the same response. He writes: "As I knew my personal safety depended in a great measure on the favourable opinion they entertained of me in this respect, I was obliged to change my tone, and replied, that I did not care if they rendered the name and race of the Esquimaux extinct; adding at the same time, that though I was no enemy of the Esquimaux, I did not see the necessity of attacking them without cause."

As the only European in the party, Hearne had no hope of averting what was coming. He talked with Matonabbee, but even that leader felt powerless to deflect "the current of a national prejudice which had subsisted between those two nations from the earliest periods, or at least as long as they had been acquainted with the existence of each other."

In June, leaving behind most of the women and children, Matonabbee and Hearne proceeded northwest with about sixty warriors from various groups, many of whom they had only just met. Trekking through rain, sleet and driving snow, they covered almost three hundred kilometres in sixteen days. With his quadrant, Hearne determined that he was roughly a thousand kilometres northwest of Churchill, although he had travelled more than twice that distance. The party pushed on, and after a final forced march of fifteen or sixteen kilometres, reached the Far-Off Metal River—today's Coppermine.

It looked nothing like the glorious waterway of legend. Fewer than two hundred metres across, and marked by rocks and shoals, it would never accommodate European ships. Indeed, even canoeists would find it hard to navigate. Hearne spent a couple of days surveying the river. Then, on July 17, 1771, he witnessed one of the most infamous actions in exploration history.

In my book *Ancient Mariner: The Amazing Adventures of Samuel Hearne, the Sailor Who Walked to the Arctic Ocean*, I devote several pages to analyzing how and why it happened. The bare facts are these. At one o'clock in the morning, after scouts had spotted about twenty Inuit camping by the river, the Dene warriors secretly assembled and waited until the Inuit had retired to their tents. Then they fell upon the sleeping innocents. Hearne writes: "In a few seconds the horrible scene commenced; it was shocking beyond description; the poor unhappy victims were surprised in the midst of their sleep, and had neither time nor power to make any resistance; men, women, and children, in all upwards of twenty, ran out of their tents stark naked, and endeavoured to make their escape; but the Indians having possession of all the landside, to no place could they fly for shelter. One alternative only remained, that of jumping into the river; but, as none of them attempted it, they all fell a sacrifice to Indian barbarity!"

Hearne goes into harrowing detail. "The terror of my mind," he concludes, "at beholding this butchery, cannot easily be conceived, much less described; though I summed up all the fortitude I was master of on the occasion, it was with difficulty that I could refrain from tears; and I am confident that my features must have feelingly expressed how sincerely I was affected at the barbarous scene I then witnessed." Hearne adds that even decades later he could not "reflect

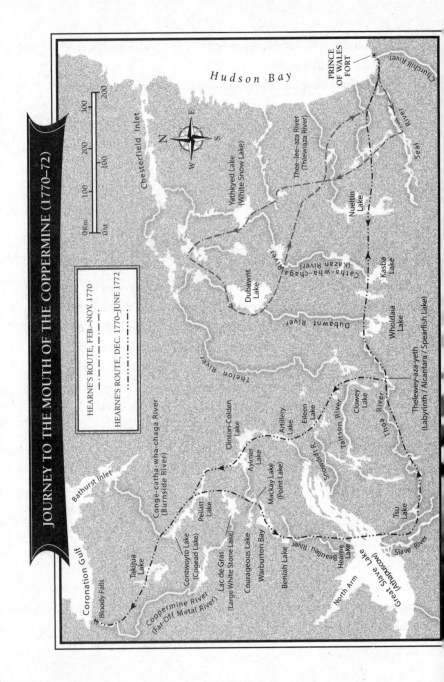

JOURNEY TO THE MOUTH OF THE COPPERMINE (1770–72)

Hudson Bay

Chesterfield Inlet

PRINCE OF WALES FORT

HEARNE'S ROUTE, FEB.–NOV. 1770

HEARNE'S ROUTE, DEC. 1770–JUNE 1772

Bathurst Inlet

Coronation Gulf

Bloody Falls

Takijua Lake

Contwoyto Lake (Cogead Lake)

Conge-catha-wha-chaga River (Burnside River)

Pellatt Lake

Lac de Gras (Large White Stone Lake)

Coppermine River (Far-Off Metal River)

Courageous Lake

Warburton Bay

Clinton-Colden Lake

Aylmer Lake

Mackay Lake (Point Lake)

Beniah Lake

Hearne Lake

North Arm

Great Slave Lake (Athapuscow)

Beaulieu River

Slave River

Tsu Lake

Snowdrift R.

Artillery Lake

Eileen Lake

Clowey Lake

Taltson River

Thoa River

Thelewey-aza-yeth (Labyrinth / Alcantara / Spearfish Lake)

Wholdaia Lake

Theton River

Dubawnt River

Dubawnt Lake

Catha-wha-chaga River (Kazan River)

Kasba Lake

Nueltin Lake

Yathkyed Lake (White Snow Lake)

Thee-lee-aza River (Thlewiaza River)

Seal River

Churchill River

0 Km   100   200   300
0 M   100   200

on the transactions of that horrid day without shedding tears." He named the site Bloody Falls. In 1996, Dene and Inuit representatives participated in a healing ceremony at the spot, and today it is a territorial park.

In 1771, after tracking the river north for another fifteen kilometres, Samuel Hearne became the first European to reach the Arctic Ocean. At present-day Kugluktuk, he established a first geographical point on the northern coast of North America—and, not incidentally, the first location along what would one day be recognized as the southern channel of the Northwest Passage.

During his pioneering trek, Hearne travelled 5,600 kilometres through uncharted territory, mostly on foot, occasionally by canoe. He did so not as a native, for whom such difficult journeys were commonplace, but as a visitor from another world, an alien creature who managed to adapt and survive and eventually to communicate what he had learned to those at home. Hearne was one of the first to demonstrate that to thrive in the North, Europeans would be wise to apprentice themselves to the native peoples who had lived there for centuries—a strategy that eluded many who followed.

In 1772, back at Prince of Wales Fort, Hearne turned his field notes into an official report. The highly regarded Andrew Graham, acting chief factor at York Fort, appreciated his accomplishment and wrote in support: "Mr. Samuel Hearne, a young gentleman of good education, being employed by the Hudson's Bay Company to examine the country to the NW of Churchill River, in order to find whether or not there were any passage by water from the Bay to the South Seas; after being absent three years returned, having travelled to Coppermine River . . . without crossing any river worth notice . . . This great undertaking has fully proven that no passage is to be expected by way of Hudson Bay."

A decade later, in 1782, tragedy struck both Hearne and Maton-abbee. With France and England at war, two French warships arrived in Hudson Bay and set about destroying Hudson's Bay Company posts. With Matonabbee and his warriors at work hundreds of kilo-metres to the west, the French razed Prince of Wales Fort. They took Hearne and his HBC men prisoner. Having become governor of the Fort, Hearne strove to minimize the impact on the native peoples who remained behind—and especially on his beloved native wife, Mary Norton.

With winter looming, and the French lacking experience in northern waters, Hearne struck a deal: he would guide the invaders through Hudson Strait if they would release him and his men to cross the Atlantic in a small sloop they were towing. Remarkably, with thirty-two men, Hearne made this happen. He succeeded in reaching Orkney and then Portsmouth.

Now he was a man on a mission. The following spring, having amassed materials to rebuild a trading post, he sailed from London on the first ship to Hudson Bay. He was bent on returning to Chur-chill and resuming life with Mary Norton. Soon after he arrived, however, he learned that, during his absence, the love of his life had starved to death. Then he received a second devastating blow: his best friend, too, was dead. As a "leading Indian," Matonabbee had flourished with the fur trade. When he arrived back at Prince of Wales Fort and saw the destruction, he believed it to be final. Seeing no way forwards, he hanged himself.

As for Hearne, he spiralled downwards but managed to survive. After five years, he made it back to England. He completed his classic work, which appeared in 1795, three years after he died, as *A Journey from Prince of Wales's Fort in Hudson's Bay to the Northern Ocean in the Years 1769, 1770, 1771, 1772*. The book showed that by reaching the Arctic coast, Hearne had fixed a first point along the southern channel of what would prove to be the only Northwest Passage navigable by ships of that century or the next.

Northwest View of the Prince of Wales Fort in Hudson Bay, *engraving from* Journey to the Northern Ocean *by Samuel Hearne, 1795. The explorer's original drawing, from 1777, gave rise to this engraving.*

Early in the twentieth century, the geologist and fur-trade scholar Joseph B. Tyrrell would introduce a new edition, noting that he considered the work invaluable "not so much because of its geographical information, but because it is an accurate, sympathetic, and patently truthful record of life among the Chipewyan Indians at that time. Their habits, customs and general mode of life, however disagreeable or repulsive, are recorded in detail, and the book will consequently always remain a classic in American ethnology."

As a gifted natural artist, Hearne also included sketches of Prince of Wales Fort, York Fort and Great Slave Lake, and of many aboriginal artifacts—images that, because they are unique and irreplaceable, continue to turn up in new books on northern history. Hearne did groundbreaking work as a naturalist, devoting more than fifty pages to describing the animals of the Subarctic. He produced the only written record of one of the most controversial moments in Canadian history: the massacre of innocents at Bloody Falls. And with his word-portrait of his best friend, he etched the peerless Matonabbee into the story of northern exploration.

5.

Mackenzie Establishes a Second Location

Like many of his fellow fur traders, rugged men who lived and worked in the North Country, Alexander Mackenzie was keenly interested in the search for the Northwest Passage. But in 1789, when he was preparing to paddle northwest out of Fort Chipewyan, a new fur-trading post at the mouth of the Athabasca River, the history of that search said nothing about Samuel Hearne, whose narrative had yet to be published. Mackenzie had heard rumours that, almost two decades before, while working for the Hudson's Bay Company, Hearne had "gone native" as he made his way to the mouth of the Coppermine River. He found no gold or copper—nothing of interest. But none of that concerned him.

For Mackenzie, the relevant exploration was that of Captain James Cook, who had sailed from England to seek not the eastern but the western entrance to the Northwest Passage. Someone at the British Admiralty sent him to do so after reading accounts of voyages supposedly undertaken in 1588 and 1640. In the first narrative, a Portuguese mariner named Lorenzo Ferrer Maldonado claimed he had sailed through North America from Davis Strait to the Pacific Ocean. In the second, a man calling himself Bartholomew de Fonte wrote that he had completed the voyage in the opposite direction. Then there was the Greek sailor who claimed that in 1592, using the name Juan de Fuca, he had sailed from the Pacific coast to the Atlantic Ocean and back again.

In 1778, after voyaging in the South Seas, James Cook gave the lie to these tales by charting the west coast of North America from northern Oregon to Alaska. Before heavy ice precluded further progress, he had sailed through Bering Strait to a latitude just above 70°, where on the northwest coast of Alaska he named Icy Cape. Earlier, north of 60°, Cook had explored an inlet with two branches, or arms, which effectively embrace present-day Anchorage. He and his men had determined that a river flowed into each arm of "Cook Inlet," as it came to be called. Today, we identify those rivers as the Susitna flowing from the north, and the Matanuska from the east.

And when, on June 3, 1789, Alexander Mackenzie paddled northwest out of Fort Chipewyan, he believed he was already on the latter river. If he could reach Cook Inlet by canoe, he could claim discovery of the Northwest Passage—not a waterway navigable by sailing ships, perhaps, but one accessible to brigades of large canoes. He would establish that a continental network of rivers and lakes extended westward from the east to the Pacific Ocean.

Such a discovery would transform the fur trade. Instead of transporting goods thousands of kilometres to and from Montreal, Mackenzie's business concern, the North West Company, would be able to trade directly with China and Russia, exploiting the Pacific inlet as a fur-trading base the same way its archrival, the Hudson's Bay Company, used Hudson Bay.

Now twenty-five, Mackenzie had been working in the Montreal-based fur trade for a decade. Five years before, he had taken "a small adventure of goods" west by river to Detroit. These goods he had traded so successfully that his employer had offered him a share in the firm's profits, on condition that he serve in a post still farther west at Grand Portage, sixty kilometres southwest of present-day Thunder Bay.

This portrait of Alexander Mackenzie was painted around 1800 by Thomas Lawrence.

The following year, as the company expanded to meet competition, Mackenzie had taken charge of the English River (Churchill) department, based in northern Saskatchewan at Lac Île-à-la-Crosse. In 1787, after his employer joined forces with the North West Company, Mackenzie had ventured still farther north and west to an old fur-trading post on Lake Athabasca.

At this cluster of rough log cabins in the wilderness, before assuming responsibility for the surrounding area, Mackenzie spent a winter as second-in-command to veteran fur trader Peter Pond, who was soon to retire. Pond believed that at Great Slave Lake, some distance to the north, he had identified the source of a river that flowed to the Pacific coast of the continent. It would culminate, he believed, in one of the two arms of an inlet charted, at latitude 60°, by Captain Cook.

In 1789, after helping to build the splendid Fort Chipewyan, Mackenzie set out to investigate the broad river that flowed northwest out of Great Slave Lake. The optimistic Pond had estimated that from this post, situated at a latitude above 58°, paddlers could reach the Pacific in six or seven days. Each degree of latitude represented about 110 kilometres. But the distance westward might be considerable, and Mackenzie suspected that the journey might take more than a few days. Still, on June 3, when he left Fort Chipewyan with four birch-bark canoes, he felt confident that, within a couple of weeks, he would reach the Pacific coast, and so transform the fur trade while making exploration history.

By this time, three decades after francophone Quebec had become a British colony, Scottish immigrants had gained control of the Montreal-based fur trade. They hired and authorized voyageurs to replace coureurs de bois, who had worked as independent merchants. The vast majority of voyageurs were French Canadians expert in long-distance canoe transportation, and crucial in the rugged northwest. While travelling, they would rise as early as two o'clock in the morning and set off without eating. At around eight, they would stop for breakfast. Then they would paddle, eating pemmican for lunch as they worked, until eight or ten o'clock at night. During a portage, voyageurs would carry two bundles of ninety pounds each, although certain legendary figures were said to have staggered half a mile lugging as many as seven—a total of 630 pounds.

To avoid such arduous trials, and though few of them could swim, voyageurs would often try to run dangerous rapids. The geographer David Thompson (1770–1857) would describe one such occasion, when voyageurs tackled the Dalles des Morts, or Death Rapids, on the Columbia River near present-day Revelstoke, British Columbia. "They had not gone far," he wrote, soon losing his way in a complex sentence, "when to avoid the ridge of waves, which they ought to have kept, they took the apparent smooth water, were drawn into a whirlpool, which wheeled them around into its Vortex, the Canoe with Men clinging to it, went down end foremost, and all were drowned." The incident is clear enough.

Now, in 1789, Alexander Mackenzie led a disparate party, but followed no unusual practice. From Fort Chipewyan he embarked with four French-Canadian voyageurs, two of their wives, a German who had been a soldier, a renowned Chipewyan guide known as the "English Chief," two more wives and two hunters. The women would handle cooking, moccasin sewing, fire building and campsite maintenance, while the men would paddle, hunt, fish and erect tents.

Despite bad weather, Mackenzie set a rapid pace. By rising before dawn and paddling until late afternoon, the travellers reached Great Slave Lake in a week. Here they encountered whirling ice floes, and for two weeks, socked in by rain and thick fog, they sheltered in an abandoned trading post. As the ice slowly cleared, they searched for the outlet of the great river, tormented by swarms of black flies and mosquitoes. Finally, after twenty days on the lake, they discovered the channel they sought. Travelling now with the current, they found paddling easier. Jubilant, they raised their rough sails.

But soon, with a mountain range looming to the west, Mackenzie grew concerned. The river changed direction. Instead of flowing west towards the coastal inlet, it veered north. Mackenzie and his men began coming upon villages of Dogrib people. Several times the explorer hired local guides, but none proved able to point the way westward. Invariably, they slipped away home.

After passing 61°, some distance north of the latitude of Cook Inlet, Mackenzie wrote in his journal that going farther seemed pointless, "as it is evident that these waters must empty themselves into the Northern Ocean." His fellow travellers urged him to turn back. Curious and obstinate, determined to learn the truth of this waterway, Mackenzie persevered. After a few more days, rolling hills gave way to flat land and the river split into channels.

At last, while encamped on a large island, and after seeing

whales, Mackenzie realized that a salt tide washed the shoreline. He had reached the Arctic coast of the continent. From Great Slave Lake, in fourteen days, he had travelled 1,650 kilometres at a rate of more than 110 kilometres per day. Among overland explorers, only Hearne had attained a similar latitude, when he had reached the mouth of the Coppermine River.

By paddling down this greater river—which now bears his name, but which he called River Disappointment—Alexander Mackenzie located a second point along the southern channel of what would prove to be the Northwest Passage. On July 14, 1789, at just above 69° north, he erected a wooden post to mark his achievement.

The return trip, because it was upriver, proved an endurance test. But on September 12, after 102 days on the water, the explorer reached Fort Chipewyan. He was exhausted, but in addition to having discovered the second longest river in North America after the Mississippi, Mackenzie had honed his skills as both traveller and leader.

Four years later, in July 1793, Mackenzie would become the first explorer to reach the Pacific Coast from the east. But the route he followed through the Rockies would prove so dangerous, and feature so many arduous portages, that nobody could ever mistake it for a northwest passage.

In 1801, when Alexander Mackenzie published the journals of his two voyages, he vindicated Samuel Hearne and put paid to any notion that there might be a continent-spanning waterway south of 69°. Any northwest passage would have to be discovered not in the latitudes of Hudson Bay, but in the Arctic waters north of continental North America. And that revelation would interest the British Admiralty.

Part Two

AN ARRIVAL OF STRANGERS

6.

An Inuit Artist Sails with John Ross

B y the early 1800s, British merchants had lost interest in searching for the Northwest Passage. Since the 1570s, they had sponsored expeditions by such adventurers as Martin Frobisher, John Davis, Henry Hudson and William Baffin. Fur-trading concerns had supported the overland searches of Samuel Hearne and Alexander Mackenzie. The Admiralty itself had underwritten the third voyage (1776–1778) of Captain James Cook, who sought the Passage from the Pacific and, in Bering Strait, encountered an impassable wall of ice which, he wrote, "seemed to be ten or twelve feet high at least."

Today, Cook's maps and logs speak to the issue of climate change. In 2016, after analyzing them, a University of Washington mathematician determined that, as a phenomenon, a lightning-fast shrinkage of Arctic pack ice began just three decades ago. Harry Stern, quoted in the *Seattle Times*, said that from Cook's time until the 1990s, voyagers "could count on hitting the ice somewhere around 70 degrees north in August. Now the ice edge is hundreds of miles farther north." In the United States, the National Oceanic and

Atmospheric Administration confirmed that, since the 1980s, the total volume of Arctic ice in summer has dropped a staggering 60 to 70 percent. Global warming is no hoax.

But pass on. The earliest searchers had demonstrated that, because of the harsh conditions, traversing any northwest passage would at best prove slow and dangerous. Even so, in 1745, the British government established a monetary award for completing the passage. It attracted little interest, and in 1775, the Board of Longitude increased its value. It offered a series of incremental rewards, starting with £5,000 to the first expedition to attain 110° west. The first to reach the Pacific from the Atlantic would receive £20,000.

Still, nobody expressed much interest. Even whalers, who fished annually off Greenland, considered the proposition a bad risk. The quest languished. But then, in 1815, Britain won the decisive Battle of Waterloo, ending a war against Napoleonic France that had been raging sporadically for a dozen years. The Royal Navy found itself with scores of idle ships and hundreds of unemployed officers collecting half-pay. At the British Admiralty, Second Secretary John Barrow, the senior civil servant in charge of the Navy, hit upon geographical exploration as the solution to the excess of both ships and men. Barrow sent an expedition to explore the Congo in West Africa and, when that ended in a yellow-fever catastrophe, turned his attention to the Arctic.

At this point, Great Britain boasted the most powerful navy in the world. But in recent years, the Russians had begun probing the Arctic for a navigable northeast passage. If they proved successful, what a blow to British pride and pre-eminence! What a threat to British trade! Barrow gained political approval to send two Arctic expeditions to seek a route to the Pacific: one to proceed via the North Pole (and the open sea that supposedly encircled it), and the other to sail via Baffin Bay and the Northwest Passage. Each expedition would comprise two ships.

Early in 1818, the Royal Navy began fitting out all four vessels at Deptford, fourteen kilometres south of London. The endeavour became a *cause célèbre*. In *Lady Franklin's Revenge*, I describe how a young London woman organized an outing to Deptford when final inspection was just one week away. On Easter Monday, late in March, twenty-six-year-old Jane Griffin—who would one day be styled "Jane, Lady Franklin"—arrived with a letter of introduction to Commander John Ross, who would lead the Northwest Passage expedition in HMS *Isabella*.

Now forty years old, Ross had joined the Royal Navy at age ten.

Passage Through the Ice, *engraving based on a sketch by John Ross, 1818. Here we see the challenges that mariners faced.*

Of the nine hundred commanders available to the Admiralty, he was one of only nine who, over the past four years, had remained continually employed. He was assured that leading this expedition would secure him a long-sought promotion to captain. The veteran Ross was on his way to becoming Royal Navy royalty, and young Jane Griffin was suitably excited. In her journal, she noted that while the *Isabella* and the *Alexander* would seek the Passage under Ross and Lieutenant William Edward Parry, the other two vessels, "the *Dorothea*, Captain Buchan, and the *Trent*, Lieutenant Franklin, are going directly to the Pole."

Miss Griffin poked around Ross's ships below decks and recorded that, although she was only five foot two, she could not stand upright. She saw deal chests filled with coloured beads for trading, as well as harpoons and saws for cutting ice. And she was much taken with a sealskin kayak that belonged to the "Eskimo" who would sail with Commander Ross as interpreter. She regretted having arrived too late to see this English-speaking Inuk, John Sakeouse, demonstrate the use of his kayak.

The kayak was not completely unknown to the British. As early as the 1680s, a well-read Orkney clergyman reported that islanders had spotted some Inuit from Greenland, whom they wrongly called "Finnmen." James Wallace wrote that the visitors paddled their craft around off one of Scotland's Orkney Islands (Eday), apparently fishing. They fled when Orcadians sought to approach. Had they crossed the Atlantic by kayak? Perhaps they had sailed aboard a British ship and set out after debarking.

More sightings of Inuit were reported in Orkney (1701) and Aberdeen (1728). But John Sakeouse (Hans Zachaeus) was the first Inuk to enter history by name. He was the first of two hunters to elbow their way into the written record in the first half of the nineteenth century. Born twenty-three years apart, one in southern Greenland, the other in Baffin Island, the two never met. But as young men, both made their way to Scotland. The second we shall meet later.

In 1816, John Sakeouse—as he eventually signed his name to a stipple print—was a resourceful young man, not yet twenty, who befriended some visiting sailors in southern Greenland. With their help, he stowed away (with his kayak) on the *Thomas and Anne*, a whaling ship. On being discovered, he convinced the captain, a man named Newton, to let him remain aboard and sail to Leith, the main port of Edinburgh.

Why did he leave home? Sakeouse would offer various explanations. Having been converted to Christianity by Danish missionaries, he said, he wanted to see more of the Christian world, and perhaps return one day to educate his people. Better: he had quarrelled with the mother of a young woman he wished to marry and needed to get away. Commander John Ross, with whom he later sailed, suggested that accident played a role: "Sakeouse related many adventures and narrow escapes he had experienced in his [kayak], in one of which he stated himself to have been carried to sea in a storm with five others, all of whom perished, and that he was miraculously saved by an English ship."

According to the *Penny Magazine of the Society for Useful Information*, the enterprising Sakeouse was born in 1797. He was "about five feet eight inches high, broad in the chest, and well set, with a very wide face, and a great quantity of coarse black straight hair.

John Sakeouse, Inuit whaler and artist, enjoyed demonstrating his prowess with a harpoon in the harbour at Leith. Scottish artist Alexander Nasmyth painted this portrait in 1814, when Sakeouse was twenty-two.

The expression of his face . . . was remarkably pleasing and good humoured."

During the voyage to Scotland on the *Thomas and Anne*, he improved his English and learned the ropes as a seaman. In Leith, he became a minor celebrity by demonstrating kayak tricks, among them an underwater roll that proved a crowd-pleaser. The next year, with Captain Newton, he went whaling. But on reaching Greenland, he learned that his beloved sister had died while he was away. Sakeouse insisted on going back to Scotland, and vowed to return home no more.

In Edinburgh, the well-known artist Alexander Nasmyth painted his portrait. Nasmyth discovered that the Inuk "had not only a taste for drawing, but considerable readiness of execution," and began giving him lessons. On learning that the British Admiralty would soon dispatch a northwest passage expedition under Commander John Ross, he drew their attention to the remarkable young Inuk. The Admiralty offered generous terms. Sakeouse readily accepted, though he stipulated that, as the *Penny Magazine* put it, "he was not to be left in his own country."

On April 18, 1818, when the 352-ton *Isabella* emerged from the River Thames, John Sakeouse was aboard, soon to play a crucial role as interpreter and recorder. By June 3, the *Isabella* and the 252-ton *Alexander* had reached the west coast of Greenland. John Ross and Edward Parry could see the central ice pack in Davis Strait, fifteen kilometres to the west, and hugged the open water along the coast as they proceeded north towards Baffin Bay. At Disko Island, near present-day Ilulissat, they found a British whaling fleet of thirty or forty ships, "giving to this frozen and desolate region," Ross wrote, "the appearance of a flourishing seaport." The whalers cheered as the naval vessels entered among them.

The Ilulissat Icefjord, an extension of the Greenland ice cap and today a UNESCO World Heritage site, spawns or "calves off" the largest icebergs in the world. "It is hardly possible to imagine anything more exquisite," Ross wrote. "By night as well as day they glitter with a vividness of colour beyond the power of art to represent." One calm night, Parry remarked on the serenity and grandeur of the scene: "The water was glassy smooth, and the ships glided among the numberless masses of ice." The hills of Disko Island reflected "the bright redness of the midnight sun."

While moored near an island among a number of whaling vessels, and spotting a village of perhaps fifty persons, Commander Ross sent Sakeouse ashore to inquire about doing some trading. The young Inuk returned with seven men and a number of birds. Ross offered them a musket in exchange for a sledge and dogs. The men accepted, went ashore, and promptly returned with a sledge, a team of dogs and five women, two of whom were said to be daughters of a "Danish president" by an Inuit woman.

Ross treated the visitors to coffee and biscuits in his cabin. After leaving the cabin, we learn in *The Last Voyage of Captain John Ross*, "they danced Scotch reels on the deck with the sailors, during which the mirth and joy of Sakeouse knew no bounds. In his own estimation he was an individual of no little consequence, and certainly an Esquimaux master of ceremonies on the deck of one of his majesty's ships, in the icy seas of Greenland, was an office somewhat new."

Ross observed that one of the daughters of the "Danish President, about eighteen years of age, and by far the best looking of the group, was the particular object of the attentions of Sakeouse." One of the ship's officers, seeing what was happening, gave the Inuk "a lady's shawl, ornamented with spangles as an offering for her acceptance." Sakeouse "presented it in a most respectful, and not ungraceful manner to the damsel, who bashfully took a pewter ring from her finger and gave it to him in return, rewarding him at the same time with an eloquent smile."

After the festivities, when the visitors left the ship in high spirits, promising to return with more useful goods, Sakeouse escorted them ashore. Next day, when he failed to return, a boat went to fetch him. The young Inuk had broken his collarbone while demonstrating how his gun worked. He had overloaded it to make an impression—"plenty of powder, plenty of kill"—and had failed to anticipate the greater recoil. Apparently, he took some time to heal.

In mid-June, Ross tried and failed to find a way west through the ice pack. Whalers told him that the ice would not begin breaking up for another month, and he resumed heading slowly north along the Greenland coast. For a while he kept company with three whaling ships. But by the end of July, amidst heavy gales and enormous icebergs, the naval vessels were sailing alone. In one storm, the two ships were driven together and nearly crushed. Those sailors who had previously served on whaling ships in the "Greenland service" exclaimed that they owed their lives to the reinforcements done at Deptford, because "a common whaler must have been crushed to atoms." In 1819, fourteen whaling ships would be smashed here, and in 1830, nineteen.

First Communication with the Natives of Prince Regent's Bay, *as drawn by John Sakeouse, 1819. The British naval officers have come onto the ice in their uniforms and the artist entertains the local Inuit by showing them a mirror.*

But now the weather calmed. On August 9, while the two ships sailed north through Melville Bay, someone spotted a small group of men gesticulating from the ice between the ship and the shore. John Ross sent a party to make contact, but the men fled on their dogsleds, disappearing among the hummocks. Ross did not give up. In addition to two years' allowance of food and an array of scientific instruments, he had brought a great many items for trade. These included 2,000 needles, 200 mirrors, 30 pairs of scissors, 150 pounds of soap, 40 umbrellas and 129 gallons of gin.

He placed a cache of goods on shore. This failed to attract visitors, but the following day, the Inuit came charging across the ice, driving eight dogsleds. One mile from the ships, they halted and stood waiting. As a boy, John Sakeouse had heard that northern Greenland was "inhabited by an exceedingly ferocious race of giants, who were great cannibals." Even so, unarmed, alone, he went out to meet the northerners carrying a white flag. He halted on one side of a great crack or lead in the ice.

After some initial difficulty, Sakeouse found a dialect, Humooke, in which he could communicate with the strangers. They had never before seen a sailing ship or, even from a distance, a white man. Sakeouse tossed the men a string of beads and a checkered shirt. The boldest among them drew a rough-looking iron knife from his boot and told Sakeouse, "Go away, I can kill you." The visitor threw the man a well-cut British knife: "Take that." The men pointed to his wool shirt and asked about it. Sakeouse responded that it was made from the hair of an animal they had never seen.

Now the questions came thick and fast. Pointing to the ships, which they took to be alive, they asked if they came from the sun or the moon. Sakeouse said they were floating houses made of wood, but the men said, "No, they are alive. We have seen them move their wings." Sakeouse said he was a man like them, with a mother and a father, and indicated that he came from a distant country far to the south. The northerners said, "That cannot be, there is nothing but ice there."

John Ross watched all this through his telescope. He sent out two men with a plank to stretch across the open water separating Sakeouse and the men. Alarmed, they asked that the Inuk should come over alone. They feared that he might be a supernatural creature who could kill them with a touch. Sakeouse insisted that he was a man like them. The bravest touched his hand, and then let out a whoop of joy.

With friendliness established, John Ross gathered more presents and, with Edward Parry, set out across the ice. They emerged in their naval uniforms, complete with cocked hats and tailcoats, and together with Sakeouse, they distributed gifts—beads, mirrors and knives—to a welcoming party that had now grown to eight local men and fifty howling dogs. Soon enough, all the ships' officers had come ashore, while the crews of both ships stood laughing and shouting encouragement from the bow of the nearest ship, the *Alexander*.

"The impression made by this scene upon [Sakeouse] was so strong," according to the *Penny Magazine*, "that he afterwards executed a drawing of it from memory"—his first historical composition. That drawing, illustrating the first meeting of native northern Greenlanders and British sailors, turned up in John Ross's book about his voyage. The Beinecke Library declared it "certainly the earliest representational work by a Native American artist to be so reproduced."

Eventually, Sakeouse convinced the northerners to board the *Alexander* by climbing a rope ladder. Over the next few days, he and his fellows entertained them, and learned that they had no collective memory of where they came from, and no knowledge even of southern Greenlanders. One of them tried to make off with Commander Ross's best telescope, a case of razors, and a pair of scissors, but he was spotted and readily returned the articles.

The Greenlanders demonstrated their skill with dogs and sledges, and showed how they hunted foxes using spears they made from narwhal tusks. Seeing the hills and mountains rolling away into the distance, and realizing that these isolated northerners lived in a world of their own, John Ross called them "Arctic Highlanders"—a poetic formulation that would elicit unfair ridicule back in London.

Ross was surprised to learn from Sakeouse that these Inuit had made their own iron knives. With the help of the Inuk, he determined that they chipped the iron off a massive ball that lay on the ground a few days' journey away. Ross guessed, correctly, that this was a meteorite. Decades later, with the help of local guides, American explorer Robert E. Peary would locate this "Cape York meteorite." In 1894, he would contrive to carry it off and sell it to the American Museum of Natural History in New York City.

John Ross didn't realize it, and would have scoffed at the idea, but his groundbreaking meeting with the polar Inuit—an encounter made possible by John Sakeouse—would prove to be the highlight of his voyage.

In August 1818, he resumed sailing. He followed the same counter-clockwise route that Robert Bylot and William Baffin had pioneered two centuries before. The accuracy of the Bylot-Baffin map of the west coast of Greenland had surprised him. And now he emulated them in making two navigational errors. Near the northwest corner of Greenland, having attained a latitude just above 77°, Ross judged the ice-choked Smith Sound to be a bay. Then, sailing south past Ellesmere Island, he decided the same of Jones Sound.

These errors he could have survived. But the next one would culminate in the destruction of his naval career.

On September 1, 1818, after sailing some distance into Lancaster Sound, John Ross judged it to lead nowhere. According to his journal, when a morning fog lifted, he saw "a high ridge of mountains, extending directly across the bottom of the inlet." His quest for a passage seemed hopeless, but he "was determined completely to explore it, as the wind was favourable; and, therefore, continued all sail."

The wind abated and, with the *Alexander*, a poor sailing vessel, several kilometres behind him, he paused and checked the depth:

In 1818, after entering Lancaster Sound, Commander John Ross was fooled by a vivid mirage of a mountain range, and so turned around and sailed for home. This mistake cost him his naval career.

674 fathoms (1,213 metres). His orders had stipulated that he should follow any current, and he wrote: "There was, however, no current." Later, Edward Parry would dispute this, and insist that, in the trailing *Alexander*, he had registered a noticeable current. Ross noted that the weather was variable. One of his men went up to the crow's-nest and reported that "he had seen the land across the bay, except for a very short space."

Ross added that, although everyone had by now given up hope of finding a north-west passage, and the weather remained foggy, he "determined to stand higher up," and possibly locate a harbour in which to make magnetical observations. At three in the afternoon, the officer of the watch told him that the fog was lifting. He immediately went on deck, "and soon after it completely cleared for about ten minutes, and I distinctly saw the land, round the bottom of the bay, forming a connected chain of mountains with those which extended along the north and south sides."

Ross judged this mountain range to be roughly eight leagues (thirty-eight kilometres) away. He also saw "a continuity of ice, at the distance of seven miles [eleven kilometres], extending from one side of the bay to the other." At quarter past three, with the fog descending again, "and being now perfectly satisfied that there was no passage in this direction, nor any harbour into which I could enter," Ross turned around to rejoin the *Alexander*.

But first, he named the features he had discovered. The mountain range he called the Croker Mountains, after the irascible first secretary of the Admiralty, John Wilson Croker; and the bay before them became Barrow Bay, after the second secretary. And with that, to the dismay, bafflement and outrage of most of his officers, and certainly of Edward Parry, he led the expedition home.

The Croker Mountains do not exist. John Ross had seen a Fata Morgana, a complex, vivid mirage caused by a temperature inversion. This phenomenon is relatively common in the Arctic, but nobody in Victorian England had ever heard of a Fata Morgana. And failing to recognize this one for what it was, an "ice-blink," cost the veteran sailor his naval career.

None of his officers on either ship had seen the mountain range. Those on the distantly trailing *Alexander* were astonished when Ross signalled that they were to turn around and sail for home. The science-minded Parry had discerned a powerful current that allowed of only one explanation. He was certain, and soon convinced others, that the expedition had discovered the entrance to the Northwest Passage. He and his fellow officers began voicing their distress even before they arrived back in London on November 16, 1818. From Shetland, in the northern reaches of Scotland, Parry sent a letter to his family: "That we have not sailed through the North-West Passage, our return in so short a period is, of course, a sufficient indication. But I know it is there, and not very hard to find. This opinion of mine, which is not lightly formed, must, on no account, be uttered out of our family; and I am sure it will not, when I assure you that every future prospect of mine depends on it being kept a secret."

The twenty-seven-year-old Parry wondered if he should dare to contradict one of the most senior officers in the Royal Navy. But soon after arriving in London, summoned to speak with the First Lord of the Admiralty—soon after he had chatted with John Barrow—Parry did precisely that. Afterwards, to his family, unable to contain himself, he wrote: "You must know that, on our late voyage, we entered a magnificent strait, from thirty to thirty-six miles wide, upon the west coast of Baffin's Bay, and—*came out again*, nobody knows why! You know I was not sanguine, formerly, as to the existence of a north-west passage, or as to the practicability of it, if it did exist. But our voyage to this Lancaster Sound . . . has left quite a different impression, for it has not only give us reason to believe that it is a broad passage into some sea to the westward . . . but, what is more important still, that it is, at certain seasons, practicable; for when we were there, there was not a bit of ice to be seen."

Parry, second-in-command of the expedition, was far from alone in taking this view. He had the support of Edward Sabine, a captain in the Royal Artillery and the expedition's appointed astronomer, and even of James Clark Ross, the eighteen-year-old nephew of John Ross, who had sailed as a midshipman on the *Isabella*. In 1819, after John Ross published his journal as *A Voyage of Discovery*, John Barrow wrote a blistering, fifty-page critique in the *Quarterly Review*, denouncing Ross for, among other things, his lack of perseverance: "A voyage of discovery implies danger; but a mere voyage like this, round the shores of Baffin's Bay, in the summer months, may be considered as a voyage of pleasure."

Drawing on Parry's private journal, Barrow lambasted Ross's decision to turn back in Lancaster Sound "at the very moment which afforded the brightest prospect of success." Sabine weighed in with further criticism, accusing Ross of plagiarism and misrepresentation. In December 1818, before this controversy reached a crescendo, Ross had received the promised promotion from commander to captain. But Barrow ensured that, for the Royal Navy, he would never sail again.

The British Admiralty recognized that on his first voyage, John Sakeouse had made a singular contribution. The governing board proposed to send the Inuk on another Arctic expedition under Lieutenant Edward Parry. In London, while sorting out details, the *Penny Magazine* tells us that Sakeouse took "great delight in relating his adventures with the 'Northmen.'" Always able to laugh at himself, he alluded "with great good humour and somewhat touchingly . . . to his own ignorance when first he landed in this country. He then imagined the first cow he saw to be a wild and dangerous animal, and hastily retreated to the boat for the harpoon, that he might defend himself and his companions from this ferocious-looking beast."

Sakeouse became so popular in London drawing rooms that his friends feared "either that the poor fellow's head would be turned, or that he would get into bad company and acquire dissipated habits." He soon tired of the big city, however, and returned to Edinburgh to live among his old friends.

The Admiralty Board, not known for free spending, sent money north, stipulating that Sakeouse "be educated in as liberal a manner as possible." The young man welcomed this initiative, and applied himself to his courses "with astonishing ardour and perseverance." The artist Alexander Nasmyth resumed teaching him art, and introduced Sakeouse to his own family. Another man traded English lessons for instruction in Inuktitut. Sakeouse enjoyed meeting people, and was so entertaining that he spent his evenings "cheerfully and profitably."

One evening, however, when he was "attacked in a most ungenerous and cowardly way in the streets, he resented the indignities put upon him in a very summary manner, by fairly knocking several of the party down . . . It is due to poor John to state that upon this occasion he behaved for a long time with great forbearance. But upon being struck, he was roused to exert his strength, which was prodigious."

In January 1819, Sakeouse was delighted to learn that the Admiralty wished him to accompany Edward Parry on another two-ship expedition to the Arctic. He eagerly anticipated sailing into Lancaster Sound when, without warning, according to the *Penny Magazine*, he "was seized with an inflammatory complaint." The finest doctors in Edinburgh attended him and, after a few days, he seemed to recover. But as "he began to gain strength, he by no means liked the discipline to which he was subjected, and the prescribed regimen still more displeased him." Sakeouse suffered a relapse, and on Sunday evening, February 14, 1819, at the age of twenty-one or twenty-two, he died.

Many of Edinburgh's leading lights attended his funeral, and several luminaries journeyed north from London. People remembered Sakeouse as gentle, modest and obliging, and noted that he appreciated any kindness extended to him. "In a snowy day, last winter," according to *Blackwood's Magazine*, "he met two children at some distance from Leith, and observing them to be suffering from the cold, he took off his jacket, and having carefully wrapped them in it, brought them safely home. He would take no reward, and seemed to be quite unconscious that he had done anything remarkable." In May 1819, when Edward Parry sailed again for the Arctic, he bitterly regretted the absence of John Sakeouse.

7.

Edward Parry Identifies a Northern Channel

Because he did not believe in the existence of the Croker Mountains, John Barrow, the Admiralty mastermind, decided to double-down—to dispatch not one but two expeditions to investigate the Northwest Passage. Both would become legendary, though for dramatically different reasons. The lesser, an overland expedition, would be led by John Franklin (see the next chapter).

William Edward Parry would lead the more important. Recently turned twenty-eight, and newly appointed to the rank of lieutenant commander, Parry received orders to sail directly to Lancaster Sound, in which John Ross had apparently sighted the disputed mountains. Early in May of 1819, less than six months after he returned from that voyage, Parry set out from London with two former bomb-ships, the 352-ton *Hecla* and the 180-ton *Griper*. They carried complements, respectively, of fifty-seven and thirty-seven men.

At Davis Strait, instead of taking the whaling route northward along the west coast of Greenland before swinging west, as John Ross had done, Parry challenged the Middle Ice—a generally impassable array of massive icebergs and lethal bergy bits between Greenland and Baffin Island. Whalers avoided it. Parry's risky manoeuvre could save time, but meant butting through the ice. This time out he was lucky. By the end of July, having survived several close calls, he reached the entrance to Lancaster Sound. Had he been correct in repudiating Ross? An "oppressive anxiety . . . was visible in every countenance," he wrote later, "while, as the breeze increased to a fresh gale, we ran quickly to the westward."

At 6:00 p.m. on August 2, 1819, while noting a long swell "rolling in from the southward and eastward," Parry wrote, "land was reported to be seen ahead. The vexation and anxiety produced on every countenance by such a report was but too visible." On drawing nearer, however, this "was found to be only an island, of no very large extent, and that, on each side of it, the horizon still appeared clear for several points of the compass."

Directly ahead, as far as the eye could see, lay an open channel 130 kilometres wide. The Croker Mountains did not exist. Vindicated, jubilant and relishing the cheers of his companions, Edward Parry sailed onwards. On August 6, he came upon a broad channel, at least

In 1819, William Edward Parry led one of the most successful of all Arctic voyages.

fifty kilometres wide, that opened to the south. Thinking this might lead to a coastal waterway, Parry sailed into Prince Regent Inlet, as he named it, for about two hundred kilometres. But then, encountering ice, he turned around and, back at Lancaster Sound, resumed sailing westward through the broad channel that, from this inlet onwards, he called Barrow Strait.

On September 4, after sailing through heavy weather, and also past a notable waterway leading north, "Wellington Channel," Parry reached 110° west longitude. After Sunday prayers, he told his men that, having achieved the first objective set by the Board of Longitude, they had won £5,000 (£1,000 for him as captain and the rest

Crewmen work HMS Hecla *and* Griper *into Winter Harbour in 1819. This engraving is based on a sketch by Parry's Lieutenant Frederick William Beechey, who visited Beechey Island during this voyage and named it after his father, artist William Beechey.*

to be distributed among his men). The next day, at Melville Island, the two ships dropped anchor for the first time. The men raised the Union Jack. Over the next several days, they spent time on shore, found coal for burning, and hunted and bagged a great many succulent ptarmigan.

With temperatures falling and the days growing shorter, Parry beat farther west. On September 17, at nearly 113°, he met impenetrable ice at what would later be named McClure Strait. He retreated to a cove he had spotted on Melville Island. As ice formed around the two ships, Parry managed to warp them, or haul them by using a line attached to a fixed anchor, into a safe spot at a place he called Winter Harbour. He wrote of feeling exhilarated, and why not? His voyage was already an unprecedented success. He had charted more than 1,600 kilometres of coastline and discovered a waterway that, measured from Greenland, extended roughly halfway to the Icy Cape that, four decades before, Captain James Cook had reached from the west.

Now came a second great challenge: wintering in the High Arctic. For this, Parry had prepared. As cold and twenty-four-hour darkness gripped the expedition, he engaged his men with literacy classes and theatrical entertainments. Geophysicist Edward Sabine, the thirty-one-year-old Royal Artillery captain, set up a magnetic observatory 650 metres from the ships—far enough that the iron in the vessels would not interfere with his readings.

Sabine had sailed on the Croker Mountain expedition with Ross, and later recalled his "mortification at having come away from a place which I considered as the most interesting in the world for magnetic observations, and where my expectations had been raised to the highest pitch, without having had an opportunity of making them." Now, when he wasn't taking readings, Sabine edited a newspaper filled with jokes and shipboard shenanigans.

Midshipman James Clark Ross, still just nineteen, emerged as the most popular actor in the Royal Arctic Theatre, and proved sporting enough to take on many female roles. Early in June, Edward Parry took a dozen men and spent two weeks hauling a handcart filled with supplies along the coast of Melville Island. Then came a six-week struggle to free the ships from the surrounding ice.

Finally, on August 1, the vessels escaped into open water. Parry again steered west. At the southwestern tip of Melville Island, just beyond 113°, he sailed up near a wall of multi-year ice that stood thirteen to sixteen metres (fifty feet) high. Recognizing an impenetrable barrier when he saw one, Parry turned around and sailed for home.

Early in November, having completed one of the most successful Arctic sailing expeditions of all time, Edward Parry arrived in London to a hero's welcome. Overnight, he became the most celebrated man in England. He was promoted to commander and, in his hometown of Bath, he received the keys to the city. In his journal, he wrote that he was confident that the western outlet of the Passage would be found at Bering Strait.

But that wall of ice at 113° had made an impression. Parry doubted now that anyone would be able to reach Bering Strait through Lancaster Sound. Wondering about the thoroughness and efficiency of earlier explorers, he turned his attention to Hudson Bay. Perhaps a channel swung north before it reached those areas traversed by Hearne and Mackenzie? He identified Cumberland Sound, Sir Thomas Rowe's Welcome and Repulse Bay as "the points most worthy of attention." And he added that "one, or perhaps each of them, may afford a practicable passage into the Polar Sea."

Parry wanted to lead an expedition into those reaches, where "there certainly does seem more than an equal chance of finding the desired passage." But he also realized, as he told his family, that "the success we met with is to be attributed under Providence to the concurrence of many very favorable circumstances." In his journal he went further still, tempering his earlier optimism and cautioning against "entertaining too sanguine a hope of finding such a [northwest] passage, the existence of which is still nearly as uncertain as it was two hundred years ago, and which possibly may not exist at all."

8.

The Yellowknife Rescue John Franklin

The Inuit hamlet of Kugluktuk, formerly known as Coppermine, is located at the mouth of the Coppermine River, where it empties into the Arctic Ocean. From a ridge at the edge of town, you can gaze across the river and see the bluff where, on July 17, 1771, at latitude 67°8′25″ north, Samuel Hearne stood looking out when he became the first explorer to reach this northern coast of North America. Fifty years later almost to the day, on July 18, 1821, having followed Hearne's route to this location, John Franklin of the Royal Navy established a campsite at that vantage point.

A few kilometres upriver, he had taken unhappy leave of Akaitcho, an eminent Yellowknife-Dene who had warned him against continuing his journey this late in the year. A fearsome leader of about 190 people, and a man who had lived all of his thirty-five years in this part of the world, Akaitcho told Franklin that if he now set out eastward along the coast, he would never return alive. The naval officer proved impervious to advice. He said goodbye to Akaitcho and his hunters and proceeded to this location with twenty men. He would follow his Royal Navy orders to the letter.

Lieutenant John Franklin had left England on May 23, 1819,

eleven days after Edward Parry embarked on his epochal voyage. He was ordered to explore the Arctic coast of North America from the mouth of the Coppermine eastward to Hudson Bay. The hope was that, in tandem with Parry's voyage, this two-pronged exploration might locate the Northwest Passage. In *Sir John Franklin's Journals and Correspondence: The First Arctic Land Expedition,* editor Richard C. Davis notes that a growing interest in geomagnetism and the shifting magnetic poles provided a second motivation.

From this campsite at the mouth of the Coppermine River, ignoring warnings from Yellowknife guides who knew the area, John Franklin set out eastward along the Arctic coast. George Back, one of two artists on the expedition, painted this view.

The Admiralty's John Barrow, increasingly aware of the unreliability of compass readings near the north magnetic pole, surmised that Samuel Hearne might have been wrong about the latitude he had reached. To ascertain the position and direction of the coastline eastward from that location, he wanted "an officer well skilled in astronomical and geographical science, and in the use of instruments."

Franklin had shown some aptitude. Officially appointed in April, he departed one month later with five fellow Royal Navy men. In a biography of George Back, one of two junior officers (midshipmen) who joined the expedition, Peter Steele writes that the deeply religious Franklin "was plump, unfit and unused to hard exercise, with no experience of travelling on foot, or running rivers in canoes, or hunting for food—as neither did any of his chosen officers." No competent contemporary traveller, he adds, "would contemplate allowing less than a year to embark on such a major journey, even over already known and mapped country."

Together with some Selkirk settlers bound for Red River Settlement, Franklin sailed on a Hudson's Bay Company ship, the *Prince of Wales*, with instructions to make his way from Coppermine to Hudson Bay while keeping detailed meteorological and magnetic records. The Admiralty, with no experience mounting overland expeditions, and no appreciation of the challenges involved, proposed to draw logistical support from the two fur-trading companies active in Rupert's Land.

In London, representatives of the HBC and the North West Company agreed to assist Franklin in every way possible. But in the North Country, their rivalry was spiralling into a murderous crescendo. Each company accused the other of ambushing and killing agents. This poisonous situation would make cooperation difficult at best. And on August 30, 1819, when Franklin arrived at York

This is probably the earliest likeness of John Franklin. It is based on a painting by William Derby, born the same year as Franklin (1786), and illustrates an article by L. T. Burwash in the Canadian Geographical Journal *of November 1930.*

Factory, headquarters of the HBC, he discovered that three North West Company partners were being detained there—hardly a good omen.

Franklin spent twenty-three months making his way 4,090 kilometres northwest from York Factory on Hudson Bay to the mouth of the Coppermine at the edge of the Arctic Ocean. He faced one obstacle after another. Initially, the HBC could spare only one traditional York boat and a single man, so he had to leave much of his gear for later forwarding. The explorer Alexander Mackenzie had responded to a pre-departure request for information by observing that Franklin should not expect, in his first season, to get beyond Île-à-la-Crosse—wise words.

A newcomer to Red River Settlement, on the other hand, had written recommending bacon as a primary meat source. Words not so wise. As yet unfamiliar with pemmican, the light-weight, dried-meat staple of the voyageur diet, much less with hunting buffalo and caribou, Franklin had brought seven hundred pounds of salted pig, which on arrival was already mouldy and inedible.

The hefty lieutenant did not take naturally to rough-country trekking. On the Hayes River at Robinson Falls, according to George

Back, Franklin was walking along a rocky bluff when he slipped on some moss "and notwithstanding his attempts to stop himself, went into the stream." He landed in deep water ninety metres downstream, "and after many fruitless trials to get a landing, he was fortunately saved by one of the boats, which by dint of chance was near the spot."

With the occasional help of HBC men travelling in the same direction, Franklin and his men transported a huge weight of supplies and instruments along rough trails and over portages. They travelled 1,130 kilometres up the Nelson and Saskatchewan Rivers to Cumberland House, arriving late in October. Franklin sent one able seaman home because, assigned to carry supplies with the voyageurs and four tough Orcadian Scots, he had been unable to maintain the pace.

Franklin stayed a couple of months at Cumberland House, some 685 kilometres short of Île-à-la-Crosse. Then, starting in mid-January 1820, with George Back, a single seaman (John Hepburn) and some Indian guides, Franklin spent another two months trekking north on snowshoes. He made his way to Fort Chipewyan on Lake Athabasca, with a view to organizing the next leg of the trip. He arrived on March 26, having covered 1,380 kilometres in sixty-seven days.

This travel rate, about twenty-one kilometres per day, would have drawn derisive laughter from expert snowshoers, who regularly travelled at three times that speed. George Back, age twenty-two, wrote in a letter to his brother that the journey highlighted "a wide difference between Franklin and me . . . he had never been accustomed to any vigorous exertion; besides, his frame is bulky without activity."

Even so, George Simpson, now emerging as a fur-trade impresario, exaggerated when he disparaged Franklin: "He must have three meals per diem. Tea is indispensable, and with the utmost exertion, he cannot walk above *Eight* miles in one day." By the time Simpson wrote that, the two men had exchanged acerbic letters, with the HBC governor challenging Franklin's Royal Navy assumption that the fur trade existed primarily to serve his expedition.

After Franklin left Cumberland House, two naval men remained there to transport anticipated supplies. But shortages throughout the North Country meant they arrived at Fort Chipewyan with ten bags of rotting pemmican. The party spent eleven days canoeing north to Fort Providence on Great Slave Lake.

Akaitcho grew impatient with the expedition's "slow mode of travelling." Artist Robert Hood, rival to George Back in many ways, drew this likeness of the Yellowknife leader.

Here Franklin met Willard Ferdinand Wentzel. This North West Company veteran had been hired to recruit guides, hunters and interpreters from among the Yellowknife or "Copper Indians," and to accompany the expedition to the coast. Here, too, on July 30, 1820, Franklin met Akaitcho, from whom, the following July, he would part angrily near the mouth of the Coppermine. Akaitcho was known as a man "of great penetration and shrewdness," Franklin wrote

now, and his older brother, Keskarrah, had travelled with Matonabbee. Akaitcho's immediate followers included forty warriors (men
and boys) known for their ferocity. For the past decade, while working as hunters out of Fort Providence, Akaitcho and his men had
ravaged nearby tribes of Dogrib and Hare Indians, stealing furs and
women with impunity.

At their first meeting in the wilderness, to assert British superiority, Franklin and his officers donned full-dress uniforms, complete
with medals, and placed a silk Union Jack atop their tent. Akaitcho was not impressed. Accompanied by two lieutenants, the Yellowknife leader arrived wearing a blanket over a white cloak. He
smoked a peace pipe, downed some spirits and informed the visitors
that they would not be travelling much farther this season.

Franklin said that he hoped to reach the Arctic coast, and that he
was bent on discovering a northwest passage that would accommodate sailing ships. He promised that if Akaitcho and the Yellowknife
would accompany his expedition as guides and hunters, he would
give them cloth, ammunition, tobacco and iron tools, and also settle
their outstanding debts with the North West Company. Akaitcho
agreed, though he warned that, because of the history of hostilities,
he would not enter Inuit-controlled territory.

After setting out from Fort Providence, Akaitcho reiterated that
the expedition could not even try to approach the Arctic coast this
season. He had not realized, he explained, that Franklin and his men
would adopt such a "slow mode of travelling."

The native leader and his men pressed on ahead, and waited for
Franklin 320 kilometres farther north, at Winter Lake. While they
were catching up, according to Back, "a mutinous spirit displayed
itself amongst the men. They refused to carry the goods any farther, alleging a scarcity of provisions as the reason for their conduct."

In truth, they weren't eating nearly enough. Franklin responded by observing they were "too far removed from justice to treat them as they merited. But if such a thing occurred again, he would not hesitate to make an example of the first person who should come forward by 'blowing out his brains.'"

This speech had the desired effect, though the overworked voyageurs would later reiterate their distress with increasing urgency. At Winter Lake, roughly halfway to the coast from present-day Yellowknife, Franklin's men built Fort Enterprise. The expedition now comprised six Europeans, including Wentzel, and also two Métis interpreters and seventeen voyageurs, plus three wives and three children.

The four Orcadian Scots, who had studied the fine print before signing on in Stromness, had exercised an option clause at Fort Chipewyan, and turned around and headed for home. Franklin noted that they had "minutely scanned our intentions, weighed every circumstance, looked narrowly into the plan of our route, and still more circumspectly to the prospect of return."

At Fort Enterprise, Akaitcho again warned Franklin against descending the Coppermine with winter approaching: "I will go in spring, but not now, for it is certain destruction. But if you are determined to go and die, some of my young men shall also go [to the coast] because it shall not be said that you were abandoned by your hunters." As for proceeding along the coast for any distance, he declared that madness. Finally, Akaitcho convinced Franklin to settle for a couple of scouting forays to the headwaters of the Coppermine River—difficult sorties that vindicated his opinion.

Back at Enterprise, where Wentzel had supervised the building of three log houses, the two midshipmen, George Back and Robert Hood, got into a jealous competition over a young Yellowknife woman they called Greenstockings. John Hepburn prevented a duel by surreptitiously removing ammunition from their guns. Franklin decided this was a good time to separate the two young men. With game proving scarce, and the party running low on ammunition, he sent the rugged George Back to Fort Chipewyan for supplies, a snowshoe journey of 885 kilometres.

Along the way, the plain-speaking Back berated fur-trade managers to see that expedition goods sent from York Factory were brought forward. He, too, traded sharp letters with George Simpson, who noted in his journal that Back had visited him at Fort Wedderburn, not far from Fort Chipewyan. "From his remarks I infer," Simpson wrote, "there is little probability of the objects of the expedition being accomplished . . . It appears to me that the mission was projected and entered into without mature consideration and the necessary previous arrangements totally neglected."

Early in the winter of 1821, two Inuit interpreters arrived at Fort Enterprise from York Factory: Tattannoeuck and Hoeootoerock. Among the English, they were known respectively as Augustus and Junius. Tattannoeuck would one day play a crucial role in keeping Franklin alive. Born in the late 1700s, and raised in a settlement over three hundred kilometres north of Fort Churchill, he had by now worked as a Hudson's Bay Company interpreter for four years. In 1820, having married and begun a family, he had signed on to travel with this overland expedition. Tattannoeuck was a proud man, according to editor C. Stuart Houston, "who asked from the voyageurs the same deference and respect that they showed the officers."

Pierre St. Germain, the "mixed-blood" hunter and interpreter who had fetched the two Inuit, interviewed some of Akaitcho's followers and learned of the dangers the expedition would face at the coast. Franklin got wind of this and threatened to take St. Germain to England and put him on trial. The voyageur replied, all too presciently, that he didn't care where he lost his life, "whether in England or accompanying you to the sea, for the whole party will perish."

On June 14, 1821, after an endless winter, the expedition—together with a number of Yellowknife hunters—set out for the headwaters of the Coppermine River. The men hauled sledges over rough and melting ice until early July. Then they took to the Yellowknife River, though shallows and rapids necessitated frequent portages. By July 12, with the hunters having only sporadic luck, the expedition retained enough food for fourteen days at what Franklin would describe as "the ordinary allowance of three pounds of meat to each man per day." The fur-trade standard, as noted elsewhere by John Richardson, Franklin's second-in-command, was in fact eight pounds of fresh meat per day. Not surprisingly, the voyageurs complained of hunger and exhaustion.

As the large party made its way down the Coppermine, Franklin sent Tattannoeuck ahead. The Inuk knew full well that at Bloody Falls, fifty years before, explorer Samuel Hearne had seen a great number of Chipewyan-Dene massacre two dozen Inuit. Accompanied by Hoeootoerock, he approached those rapids with caution. The two newcomers began making friends with the people they met. But when the locals saw Franklin approaching with a great many Yellowknife, they feared another massacre and melted into the surrounding countryside, never to be seen again.

One old man, Terreganoeuck, had been unable to flee. He assured Franklin through Tattannoeuck that he would find a few Inuit to the east—a suggestion that discounted any advance warnings from those who had fled, and which probably encouraged Franklin to forge ahead when he had no business doing so.

The expedition spent a few days camped at Bloody Falls, where a scattering of whitened skulls testified to the truth of Samuel Hearne's journal. As John Richardson put it, "The ground is still strewed with human skulls and as it is overgrown with rank grass, appears to be avoided as a place of encampment." George Back wrote: "The havoc that was there made was but too clearly verified—from the fractured skulls—and whitened bones of those poor sufferers—which yet remained visible." He later produced a painting that makes plain what he witnessed.

At the mouth of the Coppermine River, on July 18, 1821, Franklin established a camp on the eastern bluff overlooking the river. Coronation Gulf lay to the north, sprinkled with round islands, just as Samuel Hearne had reported. Like that earlier traveller, John Richardson noted the presence of many seals, and added: "The islands are high and numerous and shut the horizon in, on many points of the compass." Franklin took a series of observations and corrected Hearne's latitude. That first explorer had placed this location too far north.

For days, Akaitcho had been warning Franklin that the expedition did not have enough food to proceed. Animals were scarce, winter was approaching and his hunters would go no farther. Some of his men had already defected. To proceed along the coast would mean risking death. In this, not his first warning, but his first concerted effort to save the expedition, he urged Franklin to retreat to Fort Enterprise.

Now, despite these warnings from Akaitcho and his men, and also from his most experienced voyageurs, Pierre St. Germain and Jean

Baptiste Adam, John Franklin made a decision that would cost the lives of more than half his men. Dismissing all protests and objections, he insisted on adhering precisely to his original instructions as written in England. Eleven of the twenty men he led eastward would perish. But here is the most revealing statistic: four of the five Royal Navy men would survive, as opposed to only five of the fifteen voyageurs and interpreters.

Again: of the twenty men who followed Franklin beyond the mouth of the Coppermine, ten voyageurs and one Englishman would die. The British public, on reading about this discrepancy in the death rate, would hail it as a demonstration that Royal Navy men were tough, tenacious and resourceful. Later, Canadian analysts would advance an alternative interpretation, suggesting that Franklin coddled his fellow Britishers, allowing them to conserve their energies, while driving the voyageurs to do all the heavy, debilitating work.

Now, in 1821, John Franklin dismissed Akaitcho's concerns as groundless. He did not care what the fellow said. A British naval officer, he had his orders and he would follow them. His career depended on it. In his view, the voyageurs lacked British grit, courage and Christian faith. Surely the expedition would encounter Inuit hunters eager to assist. Franklin was a British naval officer. In a pinch, the Lord would provide.

The hubris of John Franklin was more cultural than personal. According to C. Stuart Houston, "Back's journal allows us to make a better assessment of the rigidity and stubbornness of Franklin, a product of the old British 'do or die' school who drove his men far too hard." Fellow Canadian scholar Richard C. Davis, editor of Franklin's journal, suggests that the lieutenant suffered from "a well-intentioned narrowness of vision that was systemic to his dominant culture, and that crippled Franklin when he found his culture dependent on others."

The ethnocentric arrogance of imperial Britain, Davis writes, "made it virtually impossible for Franklin to respect the traditionally-evolved wisdom of Yellowknife Indians and Canadian voyageurs, even though their assistance was crucial to the success of the expedition." What today we regard as insensitive, arrogant and overbearing "was viewed as the epitome of civilized enlightenment by all those who basked in its nineteenth-century glow."

The looming debacle derived partly from the Admiralty's lack of preparedness (how difficult could an overland expedition be?) and partly from supply shortages linked to the spiralling fur-trade rivalry. But as Davis notes, the expedition "could have reached a far happier conclusion had Franklin been less a man of his times."

The naval man told Akaitcho that nothing would stop him from making his way east along the coast. He would travel to Repulse Bay, or perhaps even to Hudson Bay. The Yellowknife leader said he doubted he would see Franklin again. But he agreed to cache some supplies at Fort Enterprise, just in case. Wentzel, the veteran fur trader, having fulfilled his contract, knew better than to linger. He returned south with the last few Yellowknife hunters. And, to reduce the size of the expedition, Franklin released four voyageurs to go with him.

The Métis interpreters, Pierre St. Germain and Jean Baptiste Adam, wanted to leave as well. They were rightly worried about starving to death, since the party had food enough for perhaps three weeks and only a thousand balls of ammunition. St. Germain noted that, with the departure of the Yellowknife, their interpretive services would no longer be required. But Franklin refused to release the two. Of those nineteen men who would remain with him, these were the two best hunters. They had signed a contract. He set a watch on them, so that, when the last Yellowknife departed, they did not slip away.

Nor did the other voyageurs wish to continue. During the portages from Fort Enterprise, they had frequently carried packs weighing 180 pounds through melting lake water, which had caused their feet and legs to swell. The Royal Navy officers, meanwhile, as Franklin would later observe, had carried "such a portion of their own things as their strength would permit."

As a group, the voyageurs again complained of hunger, swollen limbs and exhaustion. They warned that the two large birch-bark canoes they had hauled to this Arctic coast were designed for river travel, not for the rough waters and ice floes they would encounter along the coast. "They were terrified," Franklin later wrote, "at the idea of a voyage through an icy sea in bark canoes." Their fears would prove well-founded.

On July 21, 1821, three days after reaching the mouth of the Coppermine, Franklin set out eastward with nineteen men in two birch-bark canoes. Poling around ice floes and huddling on shore through gale-force winds, he and his men fought their way along the northern coast of the continent for 885 kilometres. They mapped Coronation Gulf, Bathurst Inlet and Kent Peninsula. Franklin wondered what lay farther east.

But on August 15, after weeks of slogging, with the canoes battered and broken, supplies running dangerously low and additional Inuit hunters notable only for their absence, he realized he could go no farther. George Back enumerated six reasons for turning around: "The want of food—the badness of the canoes—the advanced state of the season—the impossibility of succeeding [in reaching] Hudson Bay—the long journey we must go through the barren lands and . . . the dissatisfaction of the men."

On Kent Peninsula, Franklin planted the Union Jack on a hill. He named the location Point Turnagain. Then, having delayed for five days after supposedly making his decision, hoping always for the divinely inspired arrival of Inuit hunters, he gave the order to retreat to Fort Enterprise. Instead of tracing the coastline of Bathurst Inlet, as they had done during their advance, the men sought to save time by cutting straight across open water. The rough seas almost swamped the canoes. On reaching the far shore, instead of paddling west to the mouth of the Coppermine, Franklin and his men started tracking up the Hood River, which looked to be a shortcut. It was not.

While the voyageurs stumbled on, lugging ninety pounds each, including ammunition, hatchets, ice chisels, astronomical instruments, kettles, canoes and Bibles, the officers carried little. By September 4, the men had consumed the last of the pemmican. They were still more than six hundred kilometres from Fort Enterprise. They shot and shared the occasional partridge, and also a few muskox. They scoured the carcasses of caribou killed by wolves. And they choked down bitter lichen they cut from rocks, *tripe de roche*, which gave them diarrhea. Now winter weather arrived, as promised, bringing blizzards that forced the men to shelter in their tents.

"There was no *tripe de roche*," Franklin would write, "so we drank swamp tea and ate some of our shoes for supper." These shoes were leather moccasins from which the men could suck sustenance. They were starving. At one point, after standing up suddenly, Franklin fainted. One of the voyageurs, the interpreter Pierre St. Germain, gave each of the naval officers a small piece of meat he had saved from his allowance. This act "of self-denial and kindness," Franklin wrote later, "being totally unexpected in a Canadian *voyageur*, filled our eyes with tears." Unfortunately, in his narrative, judging from the more trustworthy journal of John Richardson, Franklin attributed the gesture to the wrong man.

Travelling grew more dangerous. While scrambling upwards on slippery rocks, the heavily loaded men fell often. They were suffering from both exhaustion and hypothermia, and George Back noted that "we became so stupid that we stumbled at almost every step." Then a canoe overturned and dumped Franklin into fast-rushing water. He lost a box containing his journals and meteorological observations, leaving him dependent on the writings of Richardson and Back, which he would commandeer for his final report.

Not surprisingly, the voyageurs began again to rebel. According to Back, who was the only Englishman able to speak French, "the Canadians talked seriously of starvation and became proportionally dispirited—and not without cause, for we had neither seen tracks of deer nor marks of Indians during the day." In their weakened state, the men could no longer carry the heavy loads. They jettisoned the fishing nets. They refused to share partridges they had secretly shot. Then, in an act of folly, one of them dropped the sole remaining canoe and saw it smash onto the rocks.

Franklin declared it beyond his power to describe the anguish he felt on hearing this news. The Hood River led to the Coppermine, which had to be crossed. John Richardson volunteered to swim to the other side with a line, but the water was so cold that his arms turned to lead and the voyageurs had to haul him back to shore. Finally, despite a scarcity of materials, St. Germain managed to improvise a makeshift raft that enabled the men to paddle across one by one. This operation, at a spot Franklin named Obstruction Rapids, wasted eight days.

Richardson had cut his foot and walked with a limp. The hefty Franklin had been reduced "almost to skin and bones." And midshipman Robert Hood, the frailest of the navy men, was reduced to crawling through snowdrifts on his hands and knees. Things had been terrible for some time. Now they grew desperate. Hoeooto-erock disappeared while hunting, and Tattannoeuck searched but failed to find him. Franklin sent George Back and four voyageurs to

During the desperate return flight to Fort Enterprise, Hoeootoerock (Junius) went hunting and never came back. Portrait by Robert Hood.

dash forward for help. Perhaps at Fort Enterprise they would find food, and someone could return with some of it.

Robert Hood could go no farther. He pleaded to be left alone. Richardson and Hepburn insisted on staying to care for him. Franklin left the two Scots with Hood and pushed on with nine voyageurs. But the next day, four of these, including a muscular Iroquois named Michel, pleaded that they could not continue. Franklin allowed them to return to the three British sailors. He pushed on with five voyageurs through heavy winds and drifting snow. When at last, having slogged more than sixty kilometres in five days, he and his men stumbled into Fort Enterprise, they found it empty. Where were the promised supplies? "It would be impossible to describe our sensations after entering this miserable abode," Franklin wrote later, "and discovering how we had been neglected. The whole party shed tears."

George Back had left a note. With his four men, he had gone

to seek help from Akaitcho, who had said he would winter in one of his camps south of Fort Enterprise. Franklin and his comrades, who soon determined they were too weak to go anywhere, huddled together for warmth as the temperature fell to almost thirty degrees below zero Celsius. They used chairs and floorboards to build a feeble fire. They pulled down deerskin curtains and chewed them for sustenance. They were starving to death and knew it.

Incredibly, after suffering through eighteen days, they heard footsteps and voices. Akaitcho? Had rescue arrived? No. John Richardson and John Hepburn stumbled into the room. They were the only two survivors from the invalid camp. And they had a terrible story to tell. Michel, the Iroquois voyageur, had reached them alone. He said that his companions had starved to death en route. To Hood, Richardson and Hepburn, he distributed meat, saying he had shot a hare and a partridge. "How I shall love this man," Hepburn had said, wolfing down the strange-tasting meat, "if I find that he does not tell lies like the others."

Michel began behaving strangely. To go hunting, in addition to his usual knife, he carried a hatchet—as if, Richardson thought, he meant to hack away at "something he knew to be frozen." The hunter produced slices of meat that came, he said, from a wolf he had killed with a caribou horn. Richardson began to suspect that Michel was butchering one or more of his dead companions. Half to himself, Michel muttered about how white men had murdered and eaten three of his relatives. Always one of the strongest voyageurs, he seemed now to grow stronger. When Richardson urged him to hunt, he answered: "It is no use hunting, there are no animals. You had better kill me and eat me."

Next morning, Richardson and Hepburn went looking for kindling. From the tent, they heard voices: Michel arguing with Robert Hood. Then came a shot. Rushing back to camp, they found Hood slumped over dead, with a book at his feet: *Bickersteth's Scripture Help*. He had accidentally shot himself, Michel said, while cleaning a gun. But when Richardson, a doctor, examined the body, he "discovered that the shot had entered the back part of the head, and passed out at the forehead, and that the muzzle of the gun had been applied so close as to set fire to the night-cap behind."

Richardson accused the voyageur of killing Hood. Michel adamantly denied it. But then he stayed close to camp, never allowing the two Scots to be alone for a moment. Richardson conducted a brief funeral service, and on October 23, the party set out for Fort Enterprise. When Michel left a campsite, ostensibly to collect *tripe de roche*, but probably to prime his rifle, the two Scots conferred. In a direct confrontation, they would be no match for Michel, who carried a rifle, two pistols, a bayonet and a knife. Hepburn volunteered to do the necessary. Richardson said no, he would take responsibility. He ducked down into some bushes. When Michel came back, carrying no *tripe de roche* but just a loaded gun, Richardson stepped out and shot him through the head.

The two Scots stumbled on to Fort Enterprise, where on October 29 they joined their fellows in starvation and prayer. Richardson wrote that language could not "convey a just idea of the wretchedness of the abode." The house had been torn apart for firewood, and the windows stood open to the cold except for a few loose boards. Only one man was still able to fetch firewood. Another lay immobile on the floor. "The hollow and sepulchral sound of their voices," Richardson wrote, "produced nearly as great horror in us as our emaciated appearance did on them, and I could not help requesting them more than once to assume a more cheerful tone."

Soon after he and Hepburn arrived, two voyageurs died of starvation. The survivors had barely enough strength to drag their bodies to the far side of the room. When one man fell to sobbing uncontrollably, Franklin read to him from the Bible. Then he became too weak to hold the Bible upright, and he and Richardson, reciting from memory, repeated verses from Psalm 23: "The Lord is my shepherd; I shall not want. He maketh me to lie down in green pastures . . ."

Later, Franklin wrote that he noticed a weakening not just in the men's bodies but in their mental faculties. "Each of us thought the other weaker in intellect than himself, and more in need of advice and assistance. So trifling a circumstance as a change of place, recommended by one as being warmer and more comfortable, and refused by the other from a dread of motion, frequently called forth fretful expressions . . ."

Franklin had reached Fort Enterprise on October 11. By November, he and his fellows were surviving on a refuse heap of sleeping robes and bones that had been left behind as garbage. But then, on November 7, three Yellowknife Indians arrived, bringing deer meat and tongues. They had travelled ninety kilometres in two and a half days. George Back, desperately searching here and there, had finally located the winter camp. Akaitcho had sent two of his best hunters with supplies. Now, these two tough Yellowknife men were shocked by what they saw at Fort Enterprise. According to Richardson, they "wept on beholding the deplorable condition to which we had been reduced."

The Yellowknife set about nursing Franklin and his fellows back to life. Richardson wrote, "The ease with which these two kind creatures separated the logs of the store-house, carried them in, and made a fire, was a matter of the utmost astonishment to us . . . We could scarcely by any effort of reasoning, efface from our minds the idea that they possessed a supernatural degree of strength."

When the survivors were well enough, they set out slowly on

snowshoes for Akaitcho's camp. "Our feelings on quitting the fort," Franklin wrote, "may be more easily conceived than described." Of the twenty men who had set out along the coast, nine survived, including Franklin. Now, encountering deep snow, the Yellowknife hunters lent their snowshoes to the invalids. Richardson wrote of being treated with the "utmost tenderness," and added that the Yellowknife "prepared our encampment, cooked for us and fed us as if we had been children; evincing humanity that would have done honour to the most civilized nation."

At the winter campsite of the Yellowknife, the fearsome Akaitcho insisted on preparing a meal for the survivors with his own hands—a remarkable gesture for a warrior leader. He had not been able to cache food at Fort Enterprise because his own people were going hungry. Three of his best hunters, close relatives, had drowned when their canoe capsized in Marten Lake. Their families, grief-stricken, had thrown away their clothes and destroyed their guns. As a result, the remaining men had killed fewer animals than might have been expected. This had worsened the prevailing shortage.

Even so, when Akaitcho learned that Franklin would be unable to repay him all that had been promised, he took it with good grace. In an oft-quoted paraphrase, he added: "The world goes badly. All are poor. You are poor. The traders appear to be poor. I and my party are likewise, and since the goods have not come in we cannot have them. I do not regret having supplied you with provisions, for a Yellowknife can never permit white men to suffer from want in his lands without flying to their aid."

Akaitcho accompanied the expedition southward, teaching the party, and notably the fair-skinned Franklin, how to treat frostbite by rubbing any telltale white patches that appeared on their faces. At parting from the Yellowknife, Richardson wrote, "We felt a deep sense of humiliation at being compelled to quit men capable of such liberal sentiments and humane feelings in the beggarly manner in which we did."

By the time Franklin reached England in October of 1822, the British public had already got wind of his Arctic ordeal. The Admiralty promoted him to post captain. Celebrated as "the man who ate his boots," he became a fellow of the prestigious Royal Society. When he published his *Narrative of a Journey to the Polar Sea*, drawing heavily on the journals of John Richardson, discerning readers labelled it ponderous—though it became an immediate bestseller.

Of the eleven men who had died, only one was British. Ten were "mixed-blood" Indians or French-Canadian voyageurs. Franklin's countrymen viewed this as confirming their own moral and constitutional superiority—their ability to meet and overcome adversity. Franklin himself became a symbol of the cultural supremacy of the British Empire.

Far from London, experienced observers saw things differently. They began developing a counter-narrative. The voyageurs died in such numbers because they were worn down by the unequal division of labour. They were the ones who hauled and repaired the canoes. They were the ones who did the hunting, the ones who trekked great distances while carrying packs weighing anywhere from 90 to 180 pounds. They did these things without enough food. No surprise, they grew weak. No wonder they died.

9.

Tattannoeuck Prevents a Second Debacle

H aving narrowly survived his first overland expedition thanks to Akaitcho, John Franklin returned from his second thanks only to a forgotten Inuk from the northern reaches of Hudson Bay. On that first expedition, as we have seen, Franklin lost more than half his men to exposure or starvation. During the desperate return to Fort Enterprise, Tattannoeuck had pushed on ahead of the struggling party, searching still for his friend Hoeootoerock, but got lost. When finally he stumbled into Fort Enterprise, Franklin was thrilled, and noted that "his having found his way through a . . . country he had never been in before, must be considered a remarkable proof of sagacity."

Afterwards, Tattannoeuck returned to Fort Churchill, worked again for the HBC and then for a missionary, John West, who converted him to Christianity. In the *Canadian Dictionary of Biography*, Susan Rowley neatly summarizes this period. In the spring of 1824, this time with another friend, Ouligbuck, Tattannoeuck agreed to join Franklin on a second expedition.

Back in England, buoyed by the fact that his countrymen judged his first misadventure a signal success, John Franklin set about preparing a second overland sortie. And here he gave the lie to those who say British naval officers were incapable of learning from experience. Soon after he arrived home, acting with his second, John Richardson, Franklin set to work planning.

First time in the field, as Canadian scholar Richard Davis has noted, Franklin relied for success on a diversity of peoples: the native peoples of Yellowknife, French-Canadian and Métis voyageurs, Scottish fur traders, Inuit interpreters. None of these were accustomed to naval hierarchy, and to blindly following orders. Second time out, he intended to rely mainly on men who would never question his directives. And he would have these Royal Navy seamen sent out early.

Franklin proposed to complete the mapping of the North American coastline to the west of the Coppermine River. He and John Richardson would cross the continent and then descend the Mackenzie River to the coast. From there, Richardson would travel east to the Coppermine, while he himself would explore westward to Icy Cape, which Captain James Cook had reached from the Pacific in 1778.

This expedition would constitute a rebuttal to Russia's expansionary claims in the Arctic. In his detailed proposal to the Admiralty, Franklin also outlined scientific objectives. Having kept abreast of research by Michael Faraday and others, he proposed to take magnetic observations to locate the north magnetic pole and help determine whether the aurora borealis was an electromagnetic phenomenon.

The Admiralty approved. On February 16, 1825, accompanied by Richardson, John Franklin sailed out of Liverpool for New York City. From there, the two men travelled north by coach through Albany and Rochester, then crossed the Niagara River to Queenston

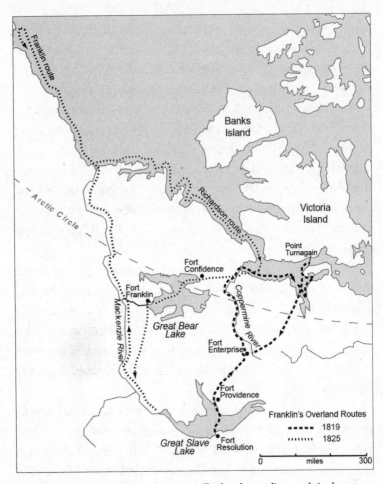

Franklin's overland expeditions are usually dated according to their departures from England in 1819 and 1825.

Heights. Franklin admired the lofty monument to Sir Isaac Brock, who had died there in 1812, and who, like himself, had been present in 1801 at the Battle of Copenhagen.

Franklin sailed by schooner to York, which would eventually become the metropolis of Toronto, but was then a town of 1,600 that failed to engage him. The designated voyageurs had yet to arrive from Montreal and, after waiting a few days, Franklin proceeded north 150 kilometres to Penetanguishene on Georgian Bay, a naval base built to protect British interests on the Great Lakes. Here, experts had readied two of the largest canoes used in the fur trade—"Montreal canoes" or *canots de maître*. These were roughly eleven metres long and almost two metres wide, and could carry three tons of cargo (sixty-five of the usual ninety-pound packs).

The voyageurs from Montreal caught up with Franklin on April 22, 1825. They gave him a letter that said his talented young wife, born Eleanor Porden, had died of tuberculosis mere days after he sailed out of Liverpool. "Though I was in some measure prepared for this melancholy event," he wrote later, he had "fondly cherished the hope that her life might have been spared till my return." Grief "rendered me little fit to proceed" with organizing the next day's departure. Not wanting to slow the expedition, Franklin left final preparations to Back and Richardson.

Next day, the expedition set out westward. At this point, it comprised thirty-three men: four British officers, four marines, a naturalist and two dozen voyageurs. The party reached Fort William on May 10, and there traded the two big canoes for four smaller (twenty-five-foot) *canots du nord*. Leaving George Back to bring forward three heavy-laden craft, Franklin and Richardson went ahead with a light load. They followed the old fur-trade route through Lake Winnipeg, then up the Saskatchewan River to Cumberland House.

Arriving in mid-June, they learned that an advance party sent out the previous year through Hudson Bay had wintered here and left thirteen days before. It included boatmen and carpenters with three sturdy boats, as well as two Inuit interpreters from Fort Churchill, Tattannoeuck and Ouligbuck. Franklin and Richardson ascended the Churchill or English River and overtook that slow-moving brigade on June 29. After traversing the nineteen-kilometre Methye Portage, the two officers pushed northward to Fort Chipewyan on Lake Athabasca.

Here, Franklin sent Richardson ahead to Great Slave Lake, in present-day Northwest Territories. On July 23, George Back arrived with the three canoes. With most of the continent crossed, and the heavy lifting done for now, Franklin discharged a number of men. He joined Richardson at Fort Resolution, where he met two guides from his previous expedition, Keskarrah and Humpy, brothers to Akaitcho. They confirmed that many of the Yellowknife hunters who had saved his life during his first expedition had since been killed by a group of Dogrib people.

The expedition proceeded 550 kilometres farther north down the Mackenzie River to Fort Simpson. Here Franklin met up with two voyageur-guides sent by Peter Warren Dease, a Hudson's Bay Company officer appointed to assist him. On August 5, the party continued still farther north to Fort Norman, and there split into three groups. George Back went up the Great Bear River to where Dease was building Fort Franklin. Richardson followed, but travelled beyond that site to scout Great Bear Lake for a route of eventual return from the Coppermine River.

Franklin continued north down the Mackenzie. He brought Tattannoeuck, whom he called "Augustus," because he spoke better English than Ouligbuck. During this initial sortie down the Mackenzie, the expedition surprised a group of Dene, who immediately sprang to arms. Tattannoeuck calmed them and, according to Franklin, quickly became "the centre of attraction." The Dene had recently made peace with local Inuit, and were excited to meet an Inuk from the faraway shores of Hudson Bay. Franklin and junior officer Edward Kendall donned their uniforms and distributed small gifts, but Tattannoeuck remained the star attraction.

"They all caressed and played around him with the greatest possible delight," Franklin wrote, "and repeatedly expressed their joy at seeing him. My former high opinion of Augustus was even increased by the great propriety and modesty he evinced under these bursts of applause and favour. He treated them all with kindness and affability at the same time that he continued to perform his office of cooking, which he had undertaken to do for Mr. Kendall and myself on the journey. And when he sat down to breakfast, he gave to each of them a portion of his fare."

Franklin reiterated: "We could not help admiring the demeanour of our excellent little companion under such unusual and extravagant marks of attention. He received every burst of applause . . . with modesty and affability, but would not allow them [the Dene] to interrupt him in the preparation of our breakfast, a task he always delighted to perform."

Continuing north, the men saw many signs of Inuit habitation, but no people. On August 17, having emerged from the Mackenzie River delta into the salt waters of what is now the Beaufort Sea, Franklin named Garry Island, built a small cairn and left an account of his expedition so far. He also planted a silk Union Jack that had been embroidered by his late wife. Later he wrote, "I will not attempt to describe my emotions as it expanded to the breeze. However natural and, for the moment, irresistible, I felt that it was my duty to suppress them, and that I had no right by an indulgence of my own sorrow to cloud the animated countenances of my companions."

Franklin turned then and headed back up the Mackenzie, with the men "tracking" or towing the boats against the current. The party reached their winter quarters on the evening of September 5. During the past couple of months, the veteran fur trader Peter Warren Dease had supervised construction of Fort Franklin, which comprised several buildings at an old fur-trading site on Great Bear Lake.

In his famous *Character Book*, governor George Simpson had assessed Dease in 1832: "Very steady in business, an excellent Indian Trader, speaks several of the Languages well and is a man of very correct conduct and character. Strong, vigorous and capable of going through a great deal of Severe Service but rather indolent, wanting in ambition to distinguish himself in any measure out of the usual course . . . His judgement is sound, his manners are more pleasing and easy than those of many of his colleagues, and altho' not calculated to make a shining figure, may be considered a very respectable member of the concern."

Approximately fifty people settled in for the winter, among them Dease, four naval officers, nineteen British sailors, nine voyageurs, the two Inuit, yet another interpreter, four hunters, ten women and a few children. Over the next few months, the officers taught classes and took meteorological and magnetic readings. The carpenters built a fourth boat, and the men hunted and fished and hauled firewood. Many of the sailors were Highland Scots, and one of them, a bagpiper named George Wilson, found his talents much in demand. The men also played ball hockey, danced and enjoyed occasional puppet shows mounted by George Back.

By June 22, after much preparation, all the men were out on the water except Dease, who happily stayed behind to maintain Fort Franklin. The men proceeded down the Mackenzie River to the coast, where on July 4, 1826, at Point Separation, Franklin divided the expedition. With the interpreter Ouligbuck and nine other men, Richardson and Kendall went east in two boats, the *Dolphin* and the *Union*. They had twenty-six bags of pemmican and enough food to last eighty days. They would proceed to the mouth of the Coppermine River, and return to Fort Franklin by ascending that waterway.

Franklin and George Back, with fourteen men, including Tattannoeuck, would follow the Arctic coast westward. They hoped to reach Icy Cape, pinpointed by James Cook, and there possibly meet a naval vessel coming from the Pacific under Frederick Beechey. If they succeeded, they would sail home on that ship. If not, they would reverse their outwards journey. For three days, Franklin and his men probed the island maze, seeking a westward channel.

Then, at the mouth of the Mackenzie River, came the great crisis of the expedition. July 7, 1826. Early afternoon. With fifteen men and two sturdy boats, the *Lion* and the *Reliance*, Franklin hit upon a westward channel. He was preparing to set out along the coast when one of his men spotted a "crowd of Esquimaux tents" on an island four kilometres distant. The sailors took out an assortment of gifts and covered everything else.

They proceeded slowly under sail. About two kilometres out, shallow waters forced a halt. The visitors beckoned to the Inuit to approach. Three canoes set out from the island, followed by seven more, and then an additional brigade of ten. Then came another brigade, and another, and Franklin found himself surrounded by 250 Siglit Inuit in seventy-eight canoes.

The older men in the first canoe, clearly the leaders, kept their distance until Tattannoeuck managed to assure them, as Franklin wrote, "of our friendly intention." He explained that the visitors were "seeking a channel for ships"—the Northwest Passage—that would benefit the local people.

The Siglit Inuit, who would later be superseded in this area by Inuvialuit, expressed delight. In the shallow water, and with the tide at a low ebb, they crowded around. Franklin ordered the two boats seaward to escape the crush, but both ran aground in midstream. Several Inuit tried to help, but "we unluckily overturned one of the canoes with our oars."

This was obviously a kayak, because the Inuk was "confined in his seat, and his head under water." Franklin granted permission to haul him aboard. To warm the man, Tattannoeuck wrapped him in his own greatcoat. The welcome prompted other Inuit to try to come aboard. Two of the leaders communicated that if they were permitted to do so, they would keep the others away. Franklin allowed this.

George Back, his second-in-command, managed to get the second boat, the *Reliance*, afloat. He waited nearby. But now a number of Inuit were walking "in the water not up to their knees . . . and striving to get into the boats." They proceeded to drag the two boats ashore, still smiling and expressing friendly intentions by tossing their knives and arrows into the *Reliance*. As soon as that first boat reached shore, however, forty men crowded around with knives in their hands. They began plundering the *Reliance*, and though badly outnumbered, Back and his men fought them for every article.

Meanwhile, as other Inuit dragged the *Lion* ashore, the two chiefs in the boat caught hold of Franklin's wrists, one to each side, "and made me sit between them." Three times Franklin struggled free, but "they were so strong as to reseat me and had I judged it proper to have fired I certainly could not have done it."

Tattannoeuck "was most active on this trying occasion," Franklin wrote. He jumped into the water "and rushing among [the Inuit] on the shore, endeavoured to stop their proceedings, till he was quite hoarse with speaking." George Back got the *Reliance* afloat and ordered his crew "to present their guns." This "so alarmed the Esquimaux that they ran off in an instant behind the canoes."

Franklin then got the *Lion* afloat. The two boats reached deeper water, but soon ran aground again. A party of eight men approached and invited Tattannoeuck to speak with them. At first, Franklin refused to hear of this. But the interpreter "repeatedly urged that he might be permitted, as he also was desirous of reproving them for their conduct." Franklin relented.

But for the courage of Tattannoeuck (Augustus), Franklin's second overland expedition would almost certainly have ended in disaster. Robert Hood drew this portrait at Fort Enterprise.

Tattannoeuck "intrepidly went and a complete explanation took place." He pointed out, Franklin writes, "that it was entirely forbearance on our part that many of them had not been certainly killed, as we were provided with the means of firing at a long distance. He told them that we were come here entirely for their benefit." He said that he himself, well clothed and comfortable, was proof "of the advantages to be derived from an intercourse with the whites." Tattannoeuck went on in this vein with more than forty people around him, Franklin wrote, "and all of them with knives, and he quite unarmed. A greater instance of courage has not been I think recorded."

The Siglit said they were sorry, that they had never before seen white men, and that everything looked so new and desirable "that they could not resist the temptation." They promised that they would never repeat this reception. When Tattannoeuck relayed this information, Franklin asked him to test their sincerity by demanding the restoration of a kettle and a tent. This he did and soon got them back.

Tattannoeuck remained on shore with the Siglit Inuit and sang with them, delighting them "as they found the words he used to be exactly those used by themselves on occasions of a friendly interview." The tide began to rise at midnight, with the sun still visible in the sky. Around 1:30 a.m., Franklin and his men were able to set off rowing.

Without Tattannoeuck, these events at "Pillage Point"—the worst crisis of Franklin's second expedition—would certainly have ended differently. Franklin and his men might well have shot dead a couple of dozen Inuit before they themselves were overpowered and killed. Imagine the repercussions, the way Britain would have reacted, and give thanks for Tattannoeuck.

Franklin and his men proceeded westward. Over the next few weeks, battling gales, fog, blizzards and lingering ice, they made slow progress. The expedition met several groups of friendly Inuit, some of whom expressed surprise that they had brought no sleds or dogs so they could travel over the ice. On July 31, the expedition reached "Demarcation Point," which then marked the boundary between Russian and British territories, and today indicates the border between Alaska and Yukon.

The first two weeks of August brought more ice, fog and stiff breezes. With rare exceptions, the men could travel westward only ten or eleven kilometres a day. Finally, on August 16, at a place he called Return Reef, Franklin acknowledged that he would not be able to reach Icy Cape. He was just shy of 149° west longitude. From the mouth of the Mackenzie, he had travelled little more than halfway to Icy Cape. Later he would learn that a boat sent from

Beechey's ship had reached within 260 kilometres of Return Reef.

A brief sunny spell allowed Franklin to extend his survey twenty-four kilometres more to Beechey Point, but on August 18, he started back towards the Mackenzie. During the ensuing journey, more than once, friendly Inuit told Tattannoeuck that some of the hunters who had assaulted the expedition at Pillage Point intended to attack again, and this time to take what they wanted. They would do so under the guise of seeking to return stolen kettles. Franklin and his men kept a close watch, but did not again encounter the aggressive Siglit.

On September 21, after a tough slog up the Mackenzie, the expedition reached Fort Franklin. The party had added 630 kilometres to the coastal map. John Richardson had already returned and, as a naturalist, departed to do more scientific research. His eastern detachment, having travelled 2,750 kilometres in seventy-one days, had mapped 1,390 kilometres along the coast between the Mackenzie and the Coppermine. With their Mackenzie River journeying, Franklin and his men had travelled farther, a total of 3,295 kilometres. But they had charted less. The expedition as a whole had mapped 2,018 kilometres of coastline.

Canadian scholar Richard Davis writes that "Franklin's contribution as leader of the main expedition . . . should not be eclipsed by Richardson's greater success." That accords with hierarchical Royal Navy conventions, certainly, which bestow all accomplishments on the nominal leader of any enterprise. But with Richardson (and Ouligbuck) having charted almost 70 percent of the total, some readers may wonder why Franklin should get all the credit.

John Franklin left winter quarters in late February 1827. He travelled mostly overland to Great Slave Lake and then to Fort Chipewyan, on Lake Athabasca, where he watched the arrival of spring. On May 26, the annual fur-trade brigade departed for York

Factory. A few days later, Franklin set out for Cumberland House, where, for the first time in eleven months, he met up with Richardson.

The two men agreed that they had virtually completed the discovery of the Northwest Passage—although how, exactly, is hard to say. The southern channel they had begun mapping lacked a south-north link to Barrow Strait and Lancaster Sound. Yet, writing to his wife, Richardson articulated the first of several specious claims he would advance: "The search has extended over three centuries, but now that it may be considered as accomplished, the discovery will, I suppose, be committed, like Juliet, to the tomb of all the Capulets, unless something more powerful than steam can render it available for the purpose of mercantile gain."

At Norway House, Franklin and Richardson said goodbye to Tattannoeuck, who reportedly grew teary-eyed at the separation. He swore that the two naval officers could count on him, should they ever need him again. The two naval officers carried on to Lachine, near Montreal, and settled accounts with the Hudson's Bay Company. They proceeded south to New York City and, on September 1, 1827, sailed for home in a packet ship.

Tattannoeuck made his way from Norway House to Fort Churchill, where he spent three years working as a hunter and interpreter. He then did the same at Fort Chimo, in what is now northern Quebec. In 1833, he heard that George Back was organizing an expedition to search for John and James Clark Ross, who had disappeared into Prince Regent Inlet on a private expedition. Having enjoyed working with Back during the two Franklin expeditions, Tattannoeuck hurried to Fort Churchill, bought supplies—a pound of gunpowder, two pounds of ball shot, one-half pound of tobacco—and set out on foot to join the naval officer at Fort Resolution.

After travelling for weeks, he reached that location and learned that Back had moved 320 kilometres northeast to Fort Reliance. Tattannoeuck set out to join him there but got lost when a storm came on. He tried to retrace his steps but died at Rivière-à-Jean, just 32 kilometres from Fort Resolution. On hearing what had happened, a saddened George Back wrote: "Such was the miserable end of poor Augustus!—a faithful, disinterested, kind-hearted creature, who had won the regard not of myself only, but I may add of Sir John Franklin and Dr. Richardson also, by qualities, which, wherever found, in the lowest as in the highest forms of social life, are the ornament and charm of humanity."

To that, a contemporary reader might add that George Back was forgetting the best reason of all to remember Tattannoeuck. At the mouth of the Mackenzie River, in July 1826, that brave and modest Inuk saved John Franklin and his second overland expedition from almost certain destruction. Tattannoeuck saved the life of Franklin, which meant that, two decades later, that naval officer was still alive when the British Admiralty began casting about for someone to lead yet another expedition to solve the riddle of the Northwest Passage.

Part Three

MYSTERIES AND COMPLICATIONS

10.

James Clark Ross Locates Magnetic North

The nineteenth-century search for the Northwest Passage was linked to the drive to solve the mystery of the shifting north magnetic pole. The two quests, geographical and scientific, had been intertwined since the 1300s, when science-minded "philosophers" began wrestling with geomagnetism. They were responding to European mariners who claimed that, when they sailed far to the north, their compasses ceased to be reliable.

By the 1500s, with the growth of international trade dependent on ships, this problem grew more urgent. Leading thinkers suggested that compass needles might be attracted by Polaris, the pole star, or perhaps by a magnetic mountain or island situated near the North Pole. But given the fixed position of such natural attractors, why would compasses behave so erratically? Perhaps the instruments themselves were faulty?

In 1538, to test this theory, the chief pilot of the Portuguese navy sailed out of Lisbon on a three-year voyage to the East Indies. João de Castro carried the most advanced magnetic compass yet made, a splendid "shadow instrument" that measured magnetic direction and solar altitude. De Castro made forty-three careful observations, and his wildly fluctuating readings made no sense whatsoever.

Bizarre theories about the shifting north magnetic pole persisted through the nineteenth century. They were reflected in this fanciful depiction of the 1831 celebration that ensued when James Clark Ross became the first to locate the pole.

A few years after de Castro returned with his bewildering results, the royal cosmographer of Seville, Pedro de Medina, published a widely translated manual insisting that compass variation was the result of inconsistent materials and human error. From his armchair in southern Spain, he declared, reassuringly, that well-made compasses would always point to the geographical North Pole. The manufacturers were at fault.

Those who built the instruments thought otherwise. Robert Norman, a leading British compass maker, began experimenting. He mounted compass needles on a vertical pivot and so discovered "magnetic dip" or inclination: the needles always dipped below the horizon line. The north-south or bipolar nature of any magnet had been established three centuries before. Now, Norman concluded that the north end of a magnet was pulled downwards by a "point respective" inside the Earth. In 1581, he published this argument in an influential pamphlet called *The Newe Attractive*. Moving beyond theorizing, it sought to provide mariners with practical solutions to navigational challenges. In this, however, it proved useless.

Mariners continued blaming their compasses until the early 1600s, when Englishman William Gilbert, physician to Queen Elizabeth I, revolutionized thinking on the subject. Born in Colchester, England, in 1544, Gilbert was the son of a prosperous "borough recorder" or magistrate. He attended St. John's College, Cambridge, and graduated as a doctor at age twenty-five. Then he travelled on the continent and practised medicine in London, becoming a fellow of the College of Physicians in 1573, and president of that institution in 1600.

While ascending to professional eminence, Gilbert devoted his attention to exploring the mysteries of Earth's magnetism. Writing in Latin, he defined the north magnetic pole as the point where a compass needle points vertically downwards—a definition that still stands. And in 1600, he published *De Magnete*, usually referred to in English as *On the Magnet*. This pioneering work relied on physical experiments to make its case. It surfaced at the tail end of the Renaissance, when universities were still teaching that the heavens revolved around the Earth and the natural magnet, or "loadstone," could attract or move iron because it had a soul.

De Magnete was revolutionary in both argument and method. By relying mainly on experimentation—on trial, error and discussion—Gilbert pioneered what would become known as the scientific method. He built a "terrella," a model Earth with a magnet inside. He used this to test compass needles and demonstrate, by analogy, the workings of planetary magnetism. By carving out miniature "oceans" and adding tiny "mountains," he showed how raised or lowered land masses can cause compass variations. He also designed a "dip circle" to measure magnetic inclination. He hoped that navigators might be able to use this instrument to determine latitude, a practice that would show "how far from unproductive magnetic philosophy is."

Gilbert argued, and demonstrated with his terrella, that compass needles point north because the Earth is itself a spherical loadstone—a giant magnet. By moving beyond opinion and argument into experimentation, he pointed the way forward for science. Two centuries would elapse before anyone would again make such a profound contribution to "terrestrial magnetism," integrating all that had been learned during the intervening decades and laying the foundations of another advance. That figure, the man who inspired the international enterprise called the Magnetic Crusade, would strongly influence such Arctic explorers as James Clark Ross, John Franklin, Elisha Kent Kane and Roald Amundsen. His name was Alexander von Humboldt.

Like Einstein in a later century, Humboldt was a scientific colossus who dominated an era. In addition to other accomplishments, his probing of "terrestrial magnetism" laid the foundations of twenty-first-century geomagnetism and geophysics. He pointed the way to contemporary understanding of Earth's shifting magnetic poles. And he did so by insisting on the importance of measurement and observation.

Humboldt led by example. In 1800, while travelling rough in South America, he took 124 sets of magnetic observations through 115° of longitude and 64° of latitude. He located the magnetic equator and determined that Earth's magnetic intensity varies with distance from that equator—a discovery that would enable mathematicians to develop a formula describing the planet's magnetic field.

Back in Berlin, he set up a magnetic laboratory in a small wooden outbuilding. Over a period of thirteen months, he took more than six thousand daily observations. Once, with a single assistant, he went seven straight days and nights, reading magnetic variations every half hour—a marathon that, he admitted, left him "somewhat exhausted."

Humboldt convinced Carl Friedrich Gauss, the "mathematical genius of the age," to tackle a challenge that had stumped everyone else: how to make sense of magnetic observations. Gauss showed him how to make crucial calculations. Yet even that peerless mathematician confirmed what Humboldt already suspected. Magnetic science needed more experimental data. To solve the mystery of Earth's magnetism, and of the shifting magnetic poles, scientists required a global network of magnetic observatories.

Generations of polar explorers would participate in gathering these—that enterprise called the Magnetic Crusade. In Britain, the deputy leader was Edward Sabine, an Irish geophysicist we have already encountered. In 1818 and 1819, Sabine took magnetic observations while sailing as a Royal Artillery captain, first with John Ross and then with Edward Parry. He attributed changes in magnetic intensity to either a fluctuation in the Earth's magnetic intensity or the shifting of the north magnetic pole. Sabine called for more observations to be taken at both the north and south magnetic poles.

Bent on producing as complete a magnetic survey of the globe as possible, Sabine orchestrated the building of magnetic observatories throughout the British Empire, from Hobart to Cape Town and Toronto. As well, he recruited Royal Navy officers to the quest. During the 1818 Ross expedition, William Edward Parry had written excitedly that "an amazing increase" in compass variation had taken place since the 1600s, when William Baffin took readings at the entrance to Lancaster Sound. And when Parry led his own breakthrough voyage in 1819, he and Sabine paid "unremitting attention" to magnetic readings, which were "likely to prove of almost equal importance" with locating a northwest passage. Parry was committed. Yet of all those Royal Navy officers influenced by Sabine, James Clark Ross stands tallest.

Born in 1800, the son of a London businessman, J. C. Ross joined the Royal Navy as he turned twelve. He served with his uncle, John Ross, for six years, rising steadily through the ranks. In 1818, as we have seen, he sailed to the Arctic with his uncle. The next year, with Edward Parry, he reached Winter Harbour. Young Ross sailed again with Parry in 1821, taking part in land surveys and serving as a naturalist. In 1825, his third expedition with Parry nearly ended in disaster. After spending one winter in Prince Regent Inlet, one of the expedition's two ships, the *Fury*, was driven onto rocks and smashed beneath a cliff on Somerset Island. The sailors managed to get home in the other vessel.

In June 1829, with five Arctic voyages behind him, James Clark Ross sailed as second-in-command to his uncle, who had secured private financing for yet another Northwest Passage expedition. The men departed from Loch Ryan, on the west coast of Scotland, with two ships, the side-wheeler *Victory* towing the smaller *Krusenstern*. None of the sailors had any idea that they were about to be tested on an epic scale.

In southern Greenland, with the *Victory*'s engines giving no end

James Clark Ross in 1834, soon after he arrived back in England after pinpointing the north magnetic pole. The artist: John R. Wildman.

of trouble, the Rosses plundered an abandoned whaler and rigged the vessel as a schooner. The ships entered Lancaster Sound on August 7 and swung south into Prince Regent Inlet five days later. The officers investigated "Fury Beach," site of the 1825 wreck, and found the stores surprisingly intact, with tins of preserved meat and vegetables and much else. The expedition proceeded into the southern reaches of the Inlet and in October, settled in for the winter at "Felix Harbour," which John Ross named after his sponsor, gin merchant Felix Booth. So far, so good.

The men built a wall of snow blocks around the ship, which was roofed as per standard naval practice. They rigged up piping over the steam kitchen and baking oven to carry rising vapour into tanks. This kept the inside of the ship dry and comfortable at lower temperatures. The men also built an antechamber where they could remove wet clothing and prevent cold and wet from reaching living quarters.

In January, a party of about thirty Inuit turned up and established friendly relations. The ship's carpenter fashioned a wooden leg for a one-legged man. The Inuit came from a village of about one hundred who were living three kilometres away in a temporary village of eighteen snow huts. An Inuk named Ikmalick drew a remarkably accurate map of the whole Gulf of Boothia.

Travelling with various Inuit, James Ross made day trips along the coast by dogsled. He determined that, as the locals said, Boothia was not an island but a peninsula. In April and early May, he made several longer journeys. Later in May, he crossed what is now James Ross Strait and named King William Land, Victory Point and Cape Felix.

At Victory Point, Ross built a massive cairn. From the cape, the northern tip of King William Land, he looked out and marvelled at the heaviest pack ice he had ever seen, noting that lighter floes had been "thrown up, on some parts of the coast, in a most extraordinary

Ikmalick and Apelagliu were among the Inuit who sojourned near the bottom of Prince Regent Inlet. Here we have Ikmalick drawing a map of the Gulf of Boothia. John Ross painted the watercolour, which is reproduced here.

and incredible manner." This was the region where, in 1846, John Franklin would get trapped. Now, in 1830, magnetic readings told James Ross that he was within fifteen to twenty-five kilometres of the ever-shifting north magnetic pole. But he lacked the instruments to verify its location.

During the winter of 1830–31, with the *Victory* still trapped in the ice off the east coast of Boothia, Ross carried out endless observations and calculations. Late in the spring of 1831, hauling an enormous dip circle on his sled, and travelling with a party of Inuit, Ross followed his compass to the west coast.

On June 1, 1831, near a few abandoned huts, he made careful observations using that rudimentary dip circle. He kept moving until his dipstick indicated that he stood precisely atop the north magnetic pole. Here, having become the first man to "fix" the pole at a specific location, he built "a cairn of some magnitude." Beneath it Ross buried a canister containing a written record.

In his journal, Ross wrote that he could have pardoned "anyone among us who had been so romantic or absurd as to expect that the magnetic pole . . . was a mountain of iron, or a magnet as large as Mont Blanc. But nature had here erected no monument to denote which spot she had chosen as the centre of one of her great and dark powers." He turned to the half dozen men with him: "Amidst mutual congratulations, we fixed the British flag on the spot, and took possession of the North Magnetic Pole and its surrounding territory, in the name of Great Britain."

James Clark Ross built his cairn at latitude 70°5′17″ north and longitude 96°46′45″ west. In 1998, a search expedition found it there in ruins, little more than a circle of stones. The north magnetic pole is long departed. As of 2015, the pole was in the Arctic Ocean (at 86°3′ north, 160° west), zigzagging towards Russia.

Now came one of those ordeals for which the Arctic is feared. Summer arrived but failed to melt the pack ice. The *Victory* could go nowhere. The sailors, bitterly disappointed, settled in for a third cold, dark winter. John Ross kept most of his men free from scurvy by ensuring that they ate an Inuit diet, featuring plenty of fat. The Inuit themselves had moved and did not return—another disappointment.

In January 1832, one man died, having caught a severe cold during a fishing expedition. All of the men were suffering. In the dead of winter, they began preparing to abandon ship. J. C. Ross supervised the loading of boats and provisions onto sledges, and late in April, the sailors began hauling these northward in relays towards Fury Beach, where they knew supplies remained. John Ross summarized from the ship on May 21, noting, "We had travelled three hundred and twenty-nine miles to gain about thirty in a direct line; carrying the two boats with full allowance of provisions for five weeks; and expending, in this labour, a month."

Eight days later, the sailors hoisted the colours, drank a toast and abandoned the *Victory* to the ice. Man-hauling heavy sledges is known to be terrible work. With more than 240 kilometres still to go to Fury Beach, the exhausted men asked to abandon the sledges. John Ross "ordered the party to proceed, in a manner not easily mis-understood, and by an argument too peremptory to be disputed."

The men reached Fury Beach on July 1, "worn out completely," as John Ross admitted, "with hunger and fatigue." They erected a timber dwelling, "Somerset House," and repaired and rigged the three available boats. On August 1, with clear water at the beach, the party set out in the boats, carrying provisions for six weeks. Driven onto a rocky beach, they were marooned for six days beneath a cliff. Late in the month, they reached the mouth of Prince Regent Inlet,

The wreck of HMS Fury *in 1825, which left supplies on what has since been called Fury Beach, would prove to be the salvation of the 1830s expedition led by John Ross. Here the wreck is depicted in* Arctic Expeditions from British and Foreign Shores, *an 1877 book edited by David Murray Smith.*

a sixty-five-kilometre-wide expanse with ice blocking the way out to the north.

On September 25, the party turned around and, with ice appearing along the coast, started back towards Fury Beach. After reaching it on October 7, they began preparing to spend an unprecedented fourth winter in the Arctic. In January 1833, John Ross would write that, with ice and snow piled high around the rough house, "we have become literally the inhabitants of an iceberg." The following month, one man died of scurvy. The Rosses worked on their journals, but most of the men "dozed away their time in the waking stupefaction which such a state of things produces."

Late in April 1833, James Ross started carrying supplies forward fifty kilometres north, where the men had stored the boats. The party left Somerset House on July 8, with three of the sailors unable to walk and needing to be hauled. At the boats, gale-force winds pinned the men to the shore for another month. Finally, on August 14, a lane of water opened to the north. By eight the next morning, the party was underway in three boats. This time, the way forward remained relatively open.

The men crossed Prince Regent and continued eastward, camping from time to time. On the morning of August 26, off the north coast of Baffin Island near Navy Board Inlet, they spotted a ship that sent out a boat. John Ross asked the name of the vessel and was told: "The *Isabella* of Hull, once commanded by Captain Ross." This extraordinary coincidence brought an enthusiastic welcome as sailors hung from the rigging and cheered the shipwrecked sailors aboard.

When John Ross landed in England on October 18, 1833, one newspaper reported: "The hardy veteran was dressed in sealskin trousers with the hair outwards, over which he wore a faded naval uniform, and the weather beaten countenances of himself and his companions bore evident marks of the hardships they had undergone." Having survived more than four years in the Arctic, the Rosses were feted by King William IV. In October of 1834, James Clark Ross was promoted to post captain in recognition of his achievements—notably that of having pinpointed the elusive north magnetic pole.

II.

Two HBC Men Map the Coast

What was George Simpson thinking? The governor of the Hudson's Bay Company scorned caprice and whimsicality. His contemporaries called him "the Little Emperor." By June 1836, certainly, with sixteen years of dictatorship behind him, Simpson had earned his reputation as the Machiavelli of the fur trade. So when, at a meeting of governing council, he announced an Arctic expedition whose leadership would yoke his temperamental younger cousin, Thomas Simpson, with the "mixed-blood" veteran Peter Warren Dease, he undoubtedly thought the idea brilliant.

This was five years after James Clark Ross, at age thirty-one, had located the north magnetic pole. Like George Simpson himself, Thomas Simpson, not yet twenty-eight, had been born and raised in Dingwall, in northern Scotland. At King's College, Aberdeen, he had earned a master of arts degree with first-class honours, winning an award in philosophy. He was fond of the outdoors and, after his older cousin George brought him into the HBC, he spent five years working as the governor's secretary at Red River Settlement, the administrative centre of which was at Upper Fort Garry in the middle of present-day Winnipeg.

The younger Simpson was ambitious, competent and hard working. But he was also egotistical, outspoken and aggressively racist. At one point, he wrote that if smallpox thinned the Métis population, it "would be no great loss to humanity." At another, he confessed that he felt "not the least sympathy with the depraved and worthless half breed population." And again, speaking of native people, "for my part I owe them hatred and not pity."

Thomas Simpson was brilliant and persevering, but also headstrong and racist. This posthumous portrait by George Pycock Green is held in the Baldwin Collection at the Toronto Reference Library.

An incident from around Christmas 1834 brought matters to a head. A Métis worker had requested a standard advance on his next season's wages. Thomas Simpson had refused and insulted the man. When the worker answered in the same spirit, Simpson hit him with a poker, drawing blood. A mob gathered, warning that if Simpson was not handed over, or at least publicly flogged, they would destroy the HBC fort.

A priest defused the situation by paying off the offended worker and distributing ten gallons of rum and tobacco among those who had gathered. But George Simpson, himself no paragon of racial tolerance, could see that his ambitious young cousin needed to change his attitude, or at least learn to control his temper and keep his mouth shut.

Meanwhile, the HBC was under pressure to explore the North Country as part of its charter. The governor proposed to dispatch a two-part expedition to the Arctic coast to complete the coastal survey that Franklin and John Richardson had begun. The head-strong Thomas Simpson had been clamouring to lead this sortie. But in 1836, the governor decided to make him second-in-command to Peter Warren Dease, who had won praise for assisting Franklin on his second expedition.

At forty-eight, Dease had worked in the fur trade for thirty-five years. He was the son of an Irish immigrant administrator and a Mohawk woman from Caughnawaga (Kahnawake), near Montreal, and so, strictly speaking, was himself "a half breed." George Simpson knew that Dease had been among the Métis Nor'Westers who, in 1820, ambushed the HBC man Colin Robertson and carried him off to Lower Canada.

Yet since the fur-trade amalgamation that Simpson had engineered, Dease had risen steadily through the HBC ranks to become a highly respected chief factor. To John Franklin, before he embarked on his second expedition, the governor had written urging "that you do not part with Mr. Dease under any circumstances." Dease, he added, was "one of our best voyageurs, of a strong, robust habit of body, possessing much firmness of mind joined to a great suavity of manners, and who from his experience in the country . . . would be a most valuable acquisition to the party in the event of its being unfortunately placed in trying or distressing circumstances."

Dease was also a "most amiable, warm-hearted, sociable man," according to one of his subordinates. While in charge of the profitable New Caledonia District, he hosted feasts, organized game nights and led musical soirees at which he played fiddle and flute "remarkably well." Simpson knew, also, that Dease had taken a Métis woman as his country wife, and that together they had half a dozen children. On June 21, 1836, both Dease and Thomas Simpson were present when, at a meeting of the HBC council at Norway House, just north of Lake Winnipeg, George Simpson announced his decision. He must have reasoned that the mature, unflappable Dease would have a beneficial effect on his impulsive, hard-driving cousin.

From Norway House, having received their marching orders, Peter Warren Dease and Thomas Simpson initially went their separate ways. Late in the summer, Dease led a small group of men northwest along a well-known fur-trade route, a succession of rapids and portages, to Fort Chipewyan on Lake Athabasca. Thomas Simpson, meanwhile, remained at Fort Garry in Red River Settlement, where he applied himself to physical conditioning while mastering surveying and navigation.

Early in December, young Simpson set out with a few men to join Dease. He covered 2,043 kilometres in sixty-three days, including eighteen given over to stops, and arrived at Fort Chipewyan on February 1, 1837. As the winter unfolded, Dease supervised the construction of several boats, including three for the expedition. One of these, the massive *Goliath*, would sail the rough waters of Great Bear Lake, still farther north, where men would build a winter dwelling. The other two, *Castor* and *Pollux*, were small enough for hauling—each twenty-four feet long and six feet wide—and featured washboards to keep waves from rolling over the gunwales. He had all three ready and tested by the end of May.

From Fort Chipewyan on June 1, accompanied by Dene hunters, the explorers started down the Slave River. Over the next four months, they would travel non-stop. They would reach the Arctic coast, and then retrace and radically extend the mapping that Franklin and Richardson had accomplished on their second expedition. Hampered by ice, especially on Great Slave Lake, they reached Fort Resolution in ten days—they were now roughly one-third of the way to Great Bear Lake. They set out again on June 21, and were soon canoeing down the Mackenzie River.

Battling mosquitoes, the expedition passed Fort Simpson and reached Fort Norman on July 1. Dease sent four HBC men, plus a number of guides and hunters, east up the Great Bear River to begin building winter quarters (Fort Confidence) on Great Bear Lake. With a dozen men, Dease and Simpson continued north down the Mackenzie, reaching the coast on July 9. In their two boats, they started west, mostly rowing, and battling fog and ice.

They met a few small groups of friendly Inuit as they retraced Franklin's route. On July 23, they reached Return Reef, where that naval officer had turned back. In 1826, coming from the west in a Royal Navy ship, Captain Frederick Beechey had navigated the stretch eastward from Icy Cape, Alaska, to Point Barrow. Now, in 1837, Dease and Simpson were bent on closing the gap between Return Reef (Franklin's farthest) and Point Barrow, a distance of 280 kilometres. This would complete the survey of the western end of the coastal channel. But on July 31, having accomplished two hundred kilometres, they hit a solid barrier of ice that precluded further progress. Dease agreed to guard the boats while Simpson proceeded on foot with five men and a collapsible canvas canoe. These six travelled quickly until they reached "Dease Inlet," which was too broad and rough for their portable craft.

But here, by chance, they encountered a few Inuit who were willing to lend them an umiak, a traditional craft that could carry half a dozen people. In this, they crossed the inlet and continued west until, on August 4, 1837, they reached Point Barrow. Later, apparently

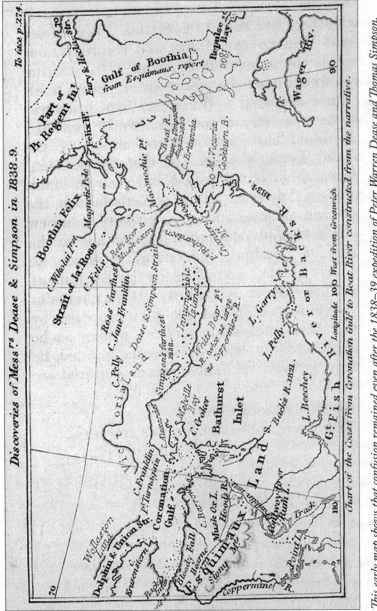

To face p. 274.

Discoveries of Mess.rs Dease & Simpson in 1838-9.

Part of Pr. Regent In.t

Gulf of Boothia from Esquimaux report

Repulse of Bay

Wager Riv.

Boothia Felix

Fury & Hecla str.

C. Nikolai I.st

Strait of Ja.s Ross

C. Teliar

Magnetic Pole Felix H.r

Macomochie P.t

Boat R.

Cape & Strap.ton Esquim.x do

C. Briarmia

M. Victoria Colburn B.

Ross' farthest

Reindeer & Muskoxen

C. Jane Franklin

C. Pelly

Victoria Land

Dease & Simpson strait

Christianson

Simpson's farthest 1838.

Invincible Islands.

White Bear P.t R. twice as large as Coppermine R.

Melville Bay

C. Alexander

C. Groker

Bathurst Inlet

L. Garry

Charnington

BACK R. 1834.

River or Back

Longitude 100 West from Greenwich

L. Pelly

S. Back's R. 1821.

L. Beechey

G.t Fish

C. Franklin

Ft Turnagain

Coronation Gulf

C. Barrow

C. Kater

W.r Iloston Land

C. Kruenstern

Dolphin & Union Str.

Back Inlet

Bloody Fall

Hood's R.

Musk Ox L.

E.s QUIMAUX Land

Stony Mts

Fort Enterprise

Point L.

Track

Fort Providence

Rum L.

Coppermine R.

Chart of the coast from Coronation Gulf to Boat River constructed from the narrative.

This early map shows that confusion remained even after the 1838–39 expedition of Peter Warren Dease and Thomas Simpson.

forgetting how Dease had got him down the Mackenzie and then to within five days of that location, Simpson would write to his brother, that "I, and I alone, have the well-earned honour of uniting the Arctic to the great Western Ocean, and of unfurling the British flag on Point Barrow."

The return journey unfolded without incident. On September 25, the men reached Great Bear Lake and the site of their winter quarters, still under construction. They had completed the first half of their two-part expedition. They lived in tents for the next month, when finally they moved into the wooden Fort Confidence. Now came a fierce Arctic winter, with short days, long nights, blowing snow and temperatures hovering between thirty and forty degrees below zero Celsius. The men turned trees into firewood, hunted caribou and muskox, and did plenty of ice fishing. One man got lost and died in the snow while bringing mail from Fort Simpson.

Near the end of March, Thomas Simpson located a viable route eastward to the Coppermine River. Early in April, he deposited six sledges worth of supplies on a tributary called the Kendall. By mid-May, the men were ready to attempt part two of their expedition: the eastern leg. In 1826, while Franklin had journeyed west with Tattannoeuck, John Richardson had surveyed the coast eastward from the mouth of the Mackenzie to the mouth of the Coppermine. On their first expedition, which had ended so disastrously, Franklin and Richardson had pushed eastward beyond the Coppermine to Point Turnagain on Kent Peninsula.

Eight years later, still farther east, George Back had descended to the Arctic coast down the Great Fish River, now called the Back River, and explored Chantrey Inlet and Montreal Island as far north as Ogle Point. Beyond that, the Arctic map grew vague. In 1830, James Clark Ross had visited the northern tip of King William Island (Cape Felix) by crossing ice from the west coast of Boothia Peninsula. But in fog and snowy weather, peering southward, he had failed to discern Rae Strait. Instead, surmising that the two land masses, the island and the peninsula, were connected by land, he drew a tentative map linking them across the bottom of a non-existent "Poctes Bay."

Eight years later, the geography of the area remained unclear. With the second part of their expedition, Dease and Simpson wanted to clarify matters and fill in the blank stretches. They proposed to travel from Franklin's Point Turnagain to Back's Ogle Point, a distance of at least 320 kilometres. The first time they tried, during the summer of 1838, they ran up against heavy ice. Halted near Point Turnagain, Simpson made a final push on foot. Accompanied by the two hunters and five HBC men, he trekked along the ice-choked channel to Cape Alexander, at the northeast corner of Kent Peninsula.

Some men might have decided that adding another 140 kilometres to the Arctic chart represented success. Thomas Simpson was not one of them. Instead of heading for home, as the men had fondly imagined they might, they found themselves preparing for another winter. Again they reduced trees to firewood. Again they set their fishing nets and hired locals to help with the hunting. Again, they insulated their lodgings as best they could.

This second winter proved harder than the first. Two native girls were murdered and the hunters grew fearful, afraid to head

Ouligbuck had served with Tattannoeuck on Franklin's second overland expedition. Lieutenant George Back drew this sketch, reproduced here courtesy of Kenn Harper.

out with their usual daring. The fishing was less successful and the caribou had migrated south. With many native people facing possible starvation, Dease had to dispense meat originally intended to make travel-ready pemmican.

Early in the spring came one positive development—the arrival of Ouligbuck, an outstanding Inuit hunter and interpreter who had served on Franklin's second expedition, mainly with John Richardson. Born around 1800, Ouligbuck was a younger friend of Tattannoeuck, who had brought him along from their home at Churchill. From the mouth of the Mackenzie River, when Tattannoeuck travelled west with Franklin, Ouligbuck had journeyed east with John Richardson.

He "was not of much use as an interpreter," Richardson wrote later, "for he spoke no English; but his presence answered the important purpose of showing that the white people were on terms of friendship with the distant tribes of Esquimaux." Richardson added that, "as a boatman [Ouligbuck] was of the greatest service, being strongly attached to us, possessing an excellent temper, and labouring cheerfully at his oar." His "attachment . . . was never doubtful, even when we were surrounded by a tribe of his own nation."

In 1827, having completed that expedition, Ouligbuck had returned to the HBC fort at Churchill, where he worked as a jack-of-all-trades. He harpooned whales, made canoe paddles and even weeded turnips. He also improved his English. In 1830, while waiting to join an HBC expedition into Ungava, Ouligbuck worked farther south, at Moose Factory. That September, he played a key role in opening trade at Fort Chimo (now Kuujjuaq), where he remained for the next six years.

The HBC summoned Ouligbuck to accompany the coastal expedition led by Dease and Simpson. With his wife and children, the Inuk reached Fort Confidence on April 13, 1839. Given his much improved English, and his exceptional abilities as a hunter, Thomas Simpson dubbed him a "valuable and unhoped for acquisition."

The month of May was colder than usual, which delayed the spring melt on the rivers and lakes. But then June brought warmer weather. Peter Dease took to breaking out his fiddle, and soon the men were ready to set out once more. This time, they hoped to extend their coastal survey at least to Ogle Point. On June 15, 1839, the men left Fort Confidence and made their way to the boat depot in four days. They ran the rapids down the Coppermine to Bloody Falls, where they retrieved their cached supplies.

On the twenty-fifth, Ouligbuck brought two Inuit back to camp, one of whom was elderly. They could provide only local information, but the old man, observing that Dease desperately needed new boots, promised to make him a pair for pick-up when he returned that way in September. The explorers ran the river to the sea, where ice kept them from leaving until July 3. Then they set out and at first made fitful progress.

Halted by ice just east of Port Epworth, the men spent four days building a fifteen-foot-long cairn. They reached Franklin's Point Turnagain on July 20, three weeks earlier than the previous year, and Cape Alexander on the twenty-eighth. Now they began charting new territory, pushing east through a scattering of islands until, on August 10, they reached Adelaide Peninsula and the western end of what would soon be called Simpson Strait.

They continued east, and two of the voyageurs, who had descended the Great Fish River with George Back in 1834, thought they recognized Ogle Point. They confirmed this about fifty kilometres south when, on August 16, they led the way on Montreal Island to a cache deposited by that earlier expedition. The men managed to salvage some aging chocolate, and the leaders preserved some gun powder and fish hooks "as memorials of our having breakfasted," Simpson wrote, "on the identical spot where the tent of our gallant, though less successful, precursor [George Back] stood that very day five years before."

Having reached Chantrey Inlet, Dease and Simpson had technically attained their objective. They could have headed for home. But the weather was fine, they had plenty of food and they agreed to press eastward to determine whether Boothia Felix was a peninsula or an island divided from the mainland by a strait leading to Lord Mayor Bay. They crossed Chantrey Inlet to Cape Britannia and then pushed north until headwinds forced them ashore. Early on August 20, they reached the mouth of a small river. They named it Castor and Pollux, after their two boats, and built another massive cairn, this one ten feet high. Simpson and Dease walked five or six kilometres farther north to a vantage point and stood gazing out.

Simpson believed—wrongly—that, just to the north of where he stood, a strait led eastward into Hudson Bay. "The exploration of such a gulph, to the Strait of the Fury and Hecla, would necessarily demand the whole time and energies of another expedition, having some point of retreat much nearer to the scene of operations than Great Bear Lake; and we felt assured that the Honourable Company, who had already done so much in the cause of discovery, would not abandon their munificent work till the precise limits of this great continent were fully and finally established."

Simpson had the details wrong. He surmised that a navigable strait ran west-east rather than south-north. But certainly he was bent on leading another expedition to this area—one that would have enabled him to find the as-yet-undiscovered Rae Strait, which runs between Boothia Peninsula and King William Island. "It was now quite evident to us," Simpson wrote, "even in our most sanguine mood, that the time was come for commencing our return to the distant Coppermine River, and that any further foolhardy perseverance could only lead to the loss of the whole party."

Despite headwinds, the expedition made steady progress. Back through Simpson Strait, the men hugged the south coast of King William Island. When, on August 25, they found it veering northward, they stopped and built a fourteen-foot-high cairn at "Cape John Herschel." Proceeding west through Queen Maud Gulf, they reached Melbourne Island and then, instead of retracing Kent Peninsula, continued west along the south coast of Victoria Island, identifying and naming Cambridge Bay.

They crossed Dease Strait to Cape Barrow on September 10, and from there battled snow showers. "We pursued our way unremittingly night and day, fair and foul," Simpson wrote, "whenever the winds permitted; and on the 16th, in a bitter frost, and the surrounding country covered with snow, we made our entrance into the Coppermine, after by far the longest voyage ever performed in boats on the Polar Sea, the distance we had gone not being less than 1,408 geographical, or 1,631 statute miles [2,625 kilometres]."

On reaching Bloody Falls, Dease wrote, "I found to my surprise . . . that the old man from whom I bespoke a pair of Boots, has punctually performed his promise. They were tied at the End of a Pole and put up in a Conspicuous place with some Seal Skin line." The men left one boat here, along with some supplies that would be useful to the Inuit, and tracked or towed the other to the previous boat depot. In his journal, Dease mentions several occasions along the way when Ouligbuck or another hunter shot a welcome buck.

Dease also offers an amusing anecdote about how, while helping several men haul the boat upstream, Ouligbuck got stuck halfway up a steep cliff, its rocks coated with ice and hung with icicles. After scuttling along after a smaller, lighter Dene hunter, he "got upon a narrow ledge of rocks, beyond which he thought it dangerous to proceed, and equally so in his now alarmed mind to retrace his way back. He therefore laid down and began to bawl out lustily for assistance, which was rendered him after the Indian had run about 1/2 mile after the boat. Some of the men went back and with a line extricated him from his awkward position, to his great joy, at finding himself again in safety."

After a final trek over snow-covered ground, the men arrived at Fort Confidence on the evening of September 24, 1839. Two days later, they were beating south across Great Bear Lake. And Governor George Simpson stood vindicated. With Peter Warren Dease handling logistics and keeping the crew well supplied and happy in their work, and Thomas Simpson driving obsessively to achieve geographical objectives, the expedition had exceeded expectations, accomplishing the longest boat voyage yet in what was essentially the Arctic Ocean. But now the co-leaders went separate ways.

Dease spent the winter at Fort Chipewyan. In August 1840, he formally married Elizabeth Chouinard, his Métis country wife of many years, and the mother of his eight children. Both Dease and Simpson had been granted a pension of one hundred pounds a year by Queen Victoria "for their exertions towards completing the discovery of the North West Passage." Dease undertook his first-ever trip to London, mainly to address vision problems, and was honoured at HBC headquarters. Writing from York Factory, the relatively progressive Letitia Hargrave reported hearing a rumour that Dease would be knighted. In the charming parlance of the day, she noted that this "diverts the people here as they say Mrs. Dease is a very black squaw & will be a curious lady." Later she added that Dease, "with that modesty which was part of his nature," declined the knighthood.

Dease remained on medical furlough until he retired officially in 1843. By then he had settled on a farm near Montreal, where, according to another chief factor, James Keith, he was governed "by his Old Squaw & Sons. She holding the Purse strings & they spending the Contents *par la Porte et par les fenetres.*" There he remained, comfortable and respected, until, having outlived three of his four sons, Peter Warren Dease died in 1863 at age seventy-five.

Thomas Simpson, meanwhile, spent the late autumn of 1839 at Fort Simpson, where he completed his narrative of the expedition for publication. He had sent a letter to his cousin, Governor George Simpson, seeking permission to lead an expedition to locate the final link in the Northwest Passage. To his brother Alexander, who was working for the HBC at Moose Factory, he wrote, "Fame I will have but it must be *alone.*" He would achieve more, he wrote, alluding to Dease, when he was free of "the extravagant and profligate habits of half-breed families."

On December 2, with the Mackenzie River frozen solid, Simpson set out travelling south by dogsled. He reached Red River Settlement on February 2, 1840, having travelled more than 2,800 kilometres. Back in October, Simpson had written to his cousin, the governor, and to the London committee of the HBC, proposing to investigate the area he had just visited. He was confident that there he would discover that elusive final link.

Simpson intended to use George Back's old base at Fort Reliance, and to descend the Great Fish (Back) River. He would return via the same route, or else, if he located an eastward strait, head south through Fury and Hecla Strait to York Factory. Again, this plan would have failed in its particulars but would undoubtedly have led him to discover Rae Strait. He would have corrected the map that, a few years later, in 1846, would encourage Franklin to turn west when he approached Cape Felix, and so to get trapped in the perennial pack ice flowing south from the polar ice cap.

At Fort Garry, the high-strung Simpson waited impatiently for a response from either the governor or from England. He received nothing with the next two mail packets, which arrived on March 24 and on the second day of June. On June 3, Thomas Simpson began preparing his proposed expedition, arranging for boats and supplies. He did not know it, but on that same day, the London committee approved his proposal. On June 4, George Simpson drafted a letter to him, adding detailed instructions. That was also the day Thomas set off southward from Fort Garry, bent on travelling via Minnesota to England to convince his HBC superiors to make a decision they had already made.

Thomas Simpson set out with two Métis. Next day, this trio joined up with a larger group of Métis. On June 10, Simpson insisted on pushing ahead with four men. What happened next has spawned no end of speculation. Certain it is that Thomas Simpson and two fellow travellers ended up dead. According to one version, Simpson became unhinged, shot the two Métis without reason and then committed suicide. According to another, more fanciful rendition, one Métis believed Simpson was carrying the secret to the Northwest Passage and, while trying to steal it, provoked a shootout. A third scenario, still more ludicrous, presented George Simpson as having masterminded the killing so that he could claim the glory of discovering the final link.

A friend of Thomas Simpson, Chief Factor John Dugald Cameron, offered the only credible explanation in a letter to James Hargrave of York Factory: "I am sure there must have been a quarrel between him and the others before the work of blood began. Mr. Simpson was a hardy active walker. Anxious to make an expeditious journey, he would have found fault with the slow pace of his fellow travellers." He would have made harsh remarks, Cameron added, prompting fellows as fiery as himself, and who had no great love for him, to respond in kind. This "would have soon led into quarrels—and from quarrels to the work of death."

The man's bigotry, impatience and egotism proved his undoing. If Thomas Simpson had lived to lead his 1841 expedition, he would have found Rae Strait—a discovery that would almost certainly have precluded the tragedy that engulfed the Franklin expedition. The fact remains that, in concert with Peter Warren Dease, he added roughly six hundred kilometres to the map of the southern channel of the Northwest Passage. He also identified the area where crucial discoveries were yet to be made. And when, in 1854, John Rae embarked on his last great Arctic expedition, he started its crucial final leg from the mouth of the Castor and Pollux River, where Simpson and Dease had left off.

12.

What If This Inuk Had Sailed with Franklin?

In September 1839, when Peter Warren Dease and Thomas Simpson were completing their epic boat journey along the northern coast of the continent, a nineteen-year-old Inuk went looking for a visiting whaling captain. Far to the east of the two Hudson's Bay Company explorers, on tiny Durban Island off the east coast of Baffin Island, Eenoolooapik had heard that Captain William Penny was asking questions about the whale-rich bay called Tenudiakbeek (Cumberland Sound). Eenoolooapik had grown up in that bay on Qimisuk (Blacklead Island). He had already explored much of the east Baffin coast, which faced towards Greenland, and yearned to venture farther.

He located Penny, who was rightly worried about the decline of the Arctic whale fishery. Three times, Penny had tried and failed to find this particular bay. Now, Eenoolooapik or "Bobbie," as he came to be called, convinced the captain that he could lead him directly to it. When Penny sailed for home in the *Neptune*, Eenoolooapik went with him. He would become the second Inuk to make his mark in Scotland. In *Some Passages in the History of Eenoolooapik*, Alexander McDonald—a doctor who later sailed with the adventurer—wrote

This portrait of Eenoolooapik, dressed in the latest British fashion, graces A Narrative of Some Passages in the History of Eenoolooapik, *published in 1841. Author Alexander McDonald would soon sail as a doctor with the Franklin expedition.*

The Castle of Mey, built around 1570, is situated on the north coast of Scotland, roughly ten kilometres west of John o' Groats. Eenoolooapik was denied entry in autumn 1839, but the castle and garden are now open to the public most days between May 1 and September 30. The castle featured in episode eight of the Netflix show The Crown.

that Penny brought home a "young Esquimaux of considerable intelligence, from whom, he had reason to think, much additional information might be obtained, not only on the subject of the whale fishery, but also concerning the geography of those partially explored regions."

The *Neptune* landed on the Scottish coast of Caithness, McDonald writes, near an edifice called the Castle of Mey. Eenoolooapik thrilled to the sight, and asked to see inside the building. "This, however, was denied him by the keeper of the mansion," McDonald continues, "who, with true Cerberus-like obstinacy, refused to allow the party even to walk round it."

On the morning of November 9, when Eenoolooapik debarked in Aberdeen, crowds gathered in the harbour to get a glimpse of him. A few days later, on the River Dee, the Inuk gave a display of his kayaking ability. He over-extended himself in the cold water and contracted pneumonia. McDonald, who had graduated from Edinburgh's Royal College of Surgeons five years after John Rae, declared Eenoolooapik to be suffering "an inflammatory affection of the lungs. It was extremely severe, but it presented no other remarkable peculiarity."

For the next few months, the young man hovered on the brink of death. Penny had become aware of his intelligence and ability, and had intended to teach him boat building. This plan fell by the wayside. But even from his sick bed, Eenoolooapik showed a sense of humour. The *Aberdeen Herald* of November 16, 1839, reported that "one of the men at the *Neptune*'s boiling-house drew the outline caricature of a broad face, and said, 'That is an Esquimaux.' Bobbie immediately borrowed the pencil, and, drawing a very long face, with a long nose, said 'That is an Englishman.'" Eenoolooapik was a gifted mimic. Having recovered from his illness, he demonstrated by behaving like a born gentleman at the theatre, at dinner parties and at two balls in honour of the Queen's wedding.

Captain Penny tried to interest the British Admiralty in a map he prepared with Eenoolooapik of the whale-rich bay. The governing board took no interest in whaling but, remembering the usefulness of John Sakeouse, did send a small sum to assist the Inuk. On April 1840, the young adventurer sailed with Penny and McDonald on the *Bon Accord*, carrying numerous gifts for distribution, among them a china teacup and saucer for his mother.

Penny spent the summer whaling, and then, guided by Eenoolooapik, brought the *Bon Accord* into Tenudiakbeek, which

John Davis had called Cumberland Gulf (now Sound). The information Eenoolooapik shared with Penny would transform the Arctic whaling fishery, and launch the colonization by Scottish whalers of Baffin Island.

Meanwhile, McDonald wrote of his friend Eenoolooapik: "If he had ever entertained any thought of returning to Britain with us, it was now evident, from the manner in which he employed himself, that he had abandoned such intention." Eenoolooapik married and settled at Tenudiakbeek. For several years, he traded baleen with Penny. In these years, too, among his own people, he became a renowned storyteller.

As such, he had still more impact on the story of Arctic discovery, mainly because he profoundly influenced one of his younger sisters: Tookoolito. Inspired by his example, she set out to master the English language and, after sojourning in England, would return to the Arctic to become one of the most crucial figures in determining what happened to the lost expedition of John Franklin. Eenoolooapik died of consumption in the summer of 1847. A brief biography of him, the first ever written about an Inuk, had appeared in 1841. Four years after that, its author, Alexander McDonald, sailed on the Franklin expedition as an assistant surgeon on the *Terror*.

The question arises: What if? What if, when Penny and McDonald returned to Britain on the *Bon Accord*, Eenoolooapik had come back with them? Had he been available to the Admiralty, then he, too, would almost certainly have sailed in 1845 with John Franklin. Would his presence have made a difference? Some of the final survivors interacted with Inuit hunters. What if Eenoolooapik had been present to communicate with them?

13.

Lady Franklin Sends Her Husband to Conquer the Passage

In 1843, with Eenoolooapik unavailable to the Royal Navy, several influential figures submitted a proposal to the British Admiralty for "an attempt to complete the discovery of a Northwest Passage." Designed by John Barrow and Edward Sabine, the presentation struck a nationalistic chord, alluding to Russia in highlighting "the unwisdom of yielding the palm of discovery to other nations active in the North." It also stressed "the importance of such a voyage for the completion of the magnetic survey of the globe."

This last provision gained the enthusiastic support of the Royal Society and the British Association for the Advancement of Science. The Society stressed that time was of the essence, because an international cooperative program of simultaneous geomagnetic observation—an initiative that had evolved out of the work of Alexander von Humboldt—was nearing its end. The association underscored the importance of building a global network of permanent magnetic observatories—one would be established in Toronto—and welcomed the prospect of more observations near the north magnetic pole.

Edward Sabine, the prime mover behind British involvement in the Magnetic Crusade, won over the Admiralty with his argument that the instruments and methods of observation had improved greatly in recent years. He pointed out that the only magnetical observations obtained from the Arctic were a quarter of a century old, and not nearly as reliable as could now be taken. And, he concluded, according to the Admiralty, "the passage through the polar Sea could afford the most important service that now remains to be performed towards the completion of the magnetic survey of the globe."

In a 2009 biography, Royal Navy historian Andrew Lambert uses this idea to explain how Sir John Franklin gained the leadership of the 1845 Northwest Passage expedition. He insists that "magnetic science dominated the genesis and direction of the Franklin expedition," adding that "without a magnetic impulse there would have been no arctic mission." Franklin had been "at the heart of the magnetic crusade from the outset." He was "not an explorer, a traveller or a discoverer," Lambert writes, but "a navigator." He argues that Franklin gained command "because he had impeccable credentials, extensive Arctic experience, proven leadership and above all because he was a first-rate magnetic scientist."

The Admiralty, in its instructions to Franklin and others, reiterated that "the effecting of a passage from the Atlantic to the Pacific is the main object of this expedition." Yet Lambert is right to insist that the expedition's secondary purpose was geomagnetic observation. *In Science and the Canadian Arctic*, Trevor Levere traces the formulation and advance of that objective. And Franklin did work, as Levere writes, "with the instrument maker Robert Were Fox to develop and promote an improved instrument for measuring magnetic dip and force."

It is interesting to note, however, given Lambert's insistence that

John Franklin was a master of geomagnetic science, that Edward Sabine opposed his appointment to lead the 1845 expedition. Although he was a friend of Franklin, and had travelled in Ireland with him, Sabine wanted James Clark Ross to assume the leadership. As leader of the Magnetic Crusade, he argued against appointing Franklin. Instead, he fought long and hard for Ross, and strove to make him change his mind. How, then, did Franklin gain command of the prestigious expedition? The answer can be stated in two words: Lady Franklin.

In Great Britain, a woman wed to a knighted male could take on the courtesy title of "Lady," provided she coupled it with her husband's surname. As the wife of John Franklin, Jane Griffin could style herself either Lady Franklin or Jane, Lady Franklin, but not, properly speaking, Lady Jane or Lady Jane Franklin—though today these formulations are popular. The young lady in question, who in 1818 had shown avid interest in the Royal Navy search for the Northwest Passage, had taken charge of the star-crossed Franklin in November 1828, when she married him.

John Franklin had expressed his interest in "Miss Jane" late the previous year, when as a recent widower he returned from his second overland expedition. After interviewing Franklin, Jane's father summoned his daughter to his study. How much did she know of this Captain John Franklin, who had, to his astonishment, inscribed the name "Griffin" on the map of the Arctic? And who had, it would appear, returned from that distant region with the intention of paying her court?

This sketch is based on a portrait done in Geneva when Jane Griffin was twenty-three. It is held in the Emmet Collection of Manuscripts at the New York Public Library.

Picture John Griffin striding around his study with his hands clasped behind his back. He had taken the liberty of making enquiries. John Franklin, born in 1786—five years before Jane—came of modest circumstances. His father had kept a shop in the market town of Spilsby, Lincolnshire. The ninth of twelve children, and lacking any obvious way forward, Franklin had joined the Royal Navy at twelve. With the husband of an older sister, Captain Matthew Flinders, he had sailed on a voyage of discovery to Australia.

Then, after serving at the battles of Copenhagen and Trafalgar, he had turned to Arctic exploration. For his service in the North, Captain Franklin would soon be awarded a knighthood. If Jane were to marry him, she would become Lady Franklin, gaining thereby both prestige and the freedom she coveted. On a previous occasion, he well remembered, Jane had demurred when a widower had offered to make her a lady—but that suitor, although wealthy and distinguished, had been far older. With Franklin, the difference was a mere five years. Presumably she could see the advantages of becoming Lady Franklin?

Jane Griffin had by this time rejected several proposals of marriage. Now in her mid-thirties, she might almost be considered a spinster—a deplorable situation. Franklin offered her a chance to trade her inherited wealth for increased status and carte blanche entrée into upper-echelon drawing rooms around the world. By making her Lady Franklin, this projected marriage would give her the freedom she had always craved—a range and autonomy approaching that enjoyed by men of her station.

As well, because she had befriended Franklin's first wife, Jane Griffin had discerned a special quality in the widower. Unlike the vast majority of middle-class British males, this man could take instruction from a woman. He had grown up with several older sisters, all of whom inevitably knew more than he did, and some of whom almost certainly bossed him around. As a result, Franklin could be guided by a powerful female. To a strong-minded, adventurous woman of this era, few things could be more attractive. On November 5, 1828, in the picturesque village of Stanmore, roughly twenty-five kilometres from her home in the heart of London, Miss Jane Griffin, one month shy of thirty-seven, married Captain John Franklin, forty-two.

The honeymoon did bring the occasional shock. While celebrating their marriage in France, the newlywed Franklins were welcomed at court by King Louis Philippe, an old friend of Jane's uncle. There, an aristocratic French woman openly expressed her astonishment at the size and rotundity of the famous explorer, who already, at five foot six, weighed 210 pounds. Jane Franklin could scarcely believe the woman's rudeness. But never mind. In April 1829, when Franklin received his knighthood, she became Jane, Lady Franklin, and at last the world lay open before her.

With Arctic exploration at a low ebb, Jane Franklin encouraged her husband to accept the captaincy of the *Rainbow*, a twenty-eight-gun frigate assigned to patrol the Mediterranean. That gave her reason to visit him. She left England on August 7, 1831, bringing with her a maid, a manservant and a four-posted iron bedstead that functioned like a tent. With these, after visiting Franklin at the naval base in Gibraltar, she went travelling around the Mediterranean. Over the next three years, Lady Franklin rode a donkey into Nazareth, sailed a rat-infested boat up the River Nile and explored the Holy Land with a handsome missionary given to serenading her by moonlight. I detail her adventuring in *Lady Franklin's Revenge*.

In October 1834, when finally she rejoined Franklin in England, his Mediterranean mission long since completed, she found him languishing as just another naval officer on half-pay. John Barrow of the Admiralty had sent the captain's former subordinate, George Back, to lead a search expedition for John Ross and James Clark Ross, who had disappeared into the Arctic. The Rosses had resurfaced to widespread astonishment in October 1833, but by then George Back had reached North America. Naturally, he proceeded to the Arctic coast. Late in 1835, having charted the Great Fish River (later called the Back River), he arrived back in London and became the toast of the town.

This former subordinate had recently begun suggesting that the Admiralty could complete the survey of the northern coast of the continent with one more naval expedition—led by himself, of course. After sailing through Hudson Strait to Wager Bay, he proposed to haul boats overland to the west coast of Chantrey Inlet. He and his men would then make their way westward to Point Turnagain. Nobody in England, not even the Arctic experts, appreciated the difficulties of such an undertaking—the distances involved, the harshness of the terrain.

But the proposal resembled one Franklin had advanced a decade before, and at Jane's urging, he pointed this out. He lobbied hard to gain the looming commission. Early in March 1836, however, rumours began swirling that George Back had carried the day. And soon enough, Lord Glenelg, the recently appointed secretary of state for War and the Colonies, confirmed the worst: George Back would lead the next Arctic sortie. To assuage Franklin's disappointment, Glenelg offered him a posting to Antigua, an island in the Caribbean, where the captain could serve as lieutenant governor. This would put him in the diplomatic line, as Glenelg said, and might lead to another appointment. Nor would it harm his naval prospects.

In Dover, where she was visiting relatives, Jane Franklin analyzed the offer. Was she prepared to live on a pittance in Antigua, a tiny island in the southern group of the British West Indies? Antigua was one of several Leeward Islands, which collectively had their own governor-in-chief. Sir John would therefore be a subordinate—or, as she put it to him in naval terms for clarity's sake, "little more than first lieutenant of a ship of the line." She told Franklin to refuse the offer, and to make it clear, politely, that he regarded such a position as beneath him.

John Franklin did precisely as Jane instructed. Lord Glenelg graciously accepted his refusal, admitting that, official rank aside, Franklin enjoyed "a high station in public regard and in private society." Glenelg was an eminent colonial administrator who, as president of the Board of Trade, had altered the constitution of the government of India. Yet he understood only vaguely that by marrying Jane Griffin, Franklin had acquired powerful allies.

In the south of England, Lady Franklin went to work. Among her influential friends, who had the ear of King William IV, she could scarcely conceal her shock and outrage. To think that a man of the stature of Sir John Franklin, an Arctic hero who had served his country so well, and at such cost to himself and those he loved, should be offered such a trifling position—why, the very idea was scandalous! What was England coming to? Every time she thought about it, and she could think of little else, Jane Franklin felt faint and had to lie down.

News of the staggering insult to England's Arctic hero reached King William IV, the "sailor king," and the former lord high admiral was not slow to make his feelings known. On April 1, 1836, scarcely two weeks after dismissing Franklin from both the Colonial Office and his own mind, seemingly forever, Lord Glenelg found himself writing humbly to the captain, and leaving no doubt as to who was directing him: "Dear Sir—You will think me a persecutor—but an occasion now presents itself which may not be unpleasing to you. Col. [George] Arthur is about to quit the government of Van Diemen's Land—and I am authorized by the King to offer you the succession to that Government. The salary is 2,500 a year. I shall be very happy if you feel yourself enabled to accept this important and interesting Station."

This was the offer, Franklin realized, for which his wife had been lobbying. The position carried a salary more than double that of the Antigua posting, and commensurate authority and prestige. He accepted with alacrity. Van Diemen's Land! That distant island colony to the south of continental Australia! To be sure, the place was a penal colony where England was incarcerating tens of thousands of unwanted convicts. But John Franklin would be the man in charge. On the far side of the world, he and his wife would begin a fantastic new life. And even the far-seeing Lady Franklin had no inkling whatsoever that this adventure might culminate not in glory and exaltation, but in shame, defeat and devastation.

As lieutenant governor of Van Diemen's Land, later to become Tasmania, Sir John Franklin was out of his depth. The captain had shown that he could command a sixth-rate frigate with a complement of 175 sailors, all of whom shared the same background and understood the rules. If you talked back to an officer, you might receive a dozen lashes. Unfortunately for Franklin, directing a small naval vessel did not prepare a man to govern a penal colony of 42,000 people, among them not just convicts but also settlers, aboriginal peoples and a ruling class of civil servants, all with different agendas. John Franklin was a decent man known to tremble at naval floggings, a devout Christian who revelled in delivering sonorous readings of the scriptures. He had no business trying to run a penal colony.

In *Lady Franklin's Revenge*, I devote 117 pages to what happened in Van Diemen's Land. Basically, the story is one of increasing estrangement between the Franklins and the powerful colonial secretary, John Montagu. By early 1841, the parties could scarcely exchange a civil word. Their mutual antipathy, exacerbated by proximity, became a ticking bomb with a short fuse. The spark came on January 7, 1842, when Franklin confronted Montagu over a newspaper article he had planted in the *Van Diemen's Land Chronicle*.

Already, claiming long tolerance for Franklin's "evident incapacity, his demonstrated feebleness," that newspaper had alleged that Sir John was an indolent time-server who had "long outlived respect." As for Lady Franklin, she had offended by climbing Mount Wellington, which at 1,271 metres in height, overlooks the capital of Hobart; and by travelling almost 900 kilometres through rough-country Australia from Melbourne to Sydney. The newspaper opined that her ramblings meant that immense sums had been "wantonly and disgracefully lavished upon ridiculous journeys and fantastical deviations from the beaten paths of men." Now, the two men called each other liar. As only the Colonial Office could fire Montagu, John Franklin suspended the man.

Ruthless, unprincipled and diabolically clever, Montagu took his case to England. He believed himself wronged, and so justified in transgressing any boundary. When truth contradicted convenience, Montagu would lie; where evidence proved lacking, he would fabricate. To support his allegation that Sir John was "little removed from an imbecile," he concocted damaging scenes and shaming anecdotes. And Lady Franklin? Montagu described her thus: "A more troublesome, interfering woman I never saw—puffed up with the love of Fame and the desire of acquiring a name by doing what no one else does." Her interference "in everything is so great, and her mode of proceeding so extraordinary, that there is scarcely any subject she is not so prominently conspicuous in as to render it unavoidable."

In an age when woman's place was in the home, and even courageous female authors would shelter behind male pseudonyms, rightly fearing ridicule and worse, Montagu alleged "corrupt, unbecoming, and malignant female interference in the affairs of state." Montagu was a vindictive liar who conducted a revolting smear campaign. But he had the backing of George Arthur, now lieutenant governor of Upper Canada, whose investments he handled and whose niece he had married. And in England, his campaign of denigration succeeded beyond his wildest imaginings. The Colonial Office, headed now by Edward Lord Stanley, accepted that Franklin was "a man in petticoats" and recalled him from Van Diemen's Land. The once-celebrated explorer returned home in disgrace.

Lady Franklin clung to the hope that Londoners would grasp

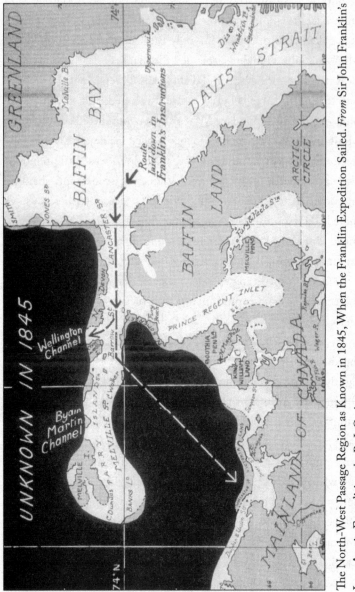

The North-West Passage Region as Known in 1845, When the Franklin Expedition Sailed. *From* Sir John Franklin's Last Arctic Expedition *by R. J. Cyriax.*

nothing of what had transpired. But in June 1844, soon after the couple debarked in Portsmouth, a relative made an insensitive allusion to the scandal of Franklin's recall. The remark reduced Jane Franklin to tears. To the mortification of everyone present, she filled the house with the sounds of her weeping.

On arriving in London, the Franklins learned that the British Admiralty was showing renewed interest in the riddle of the Northwest Passage. With the Russians making headway in the Arctic, and trade routes and national pride at stake, the overlords of the Royal Navy proposed to dispatch a two-ship expedition to discover a north-south waterway linking Lancaster Sound with Simpson Strait, so joining the discernible northern and southern channels of the Passage. How difficult could it be?

One question remained: Who would lead this epochal expedition? The aging Sir John Barrow, still controlling exploration as second secretary of the Admiralty, had settled upon James Fitzjames, an early-thirties naval officer who was also a friend of the family. Barrow had broached the subject to Fitzjames as early as March 1844. Eventually, of course, the Admiralty board—seven lords, all political appointees—would have to approve any appointment.

Whoever led the expedition, which was expected easily to "achieve the Passage," would receive £10,000—a princely sum to share as he chose among officers and crew members. Equally important, if not more so, that expedition leader would be celebrated internationally as Discoverer of the Northwest Passage. And so there ensued a fierce behind-the-scenes competition—precisely the kind, involving secret machinations and friends in high places, that suited Jane Franklin.

In this contest, despite Barrow's support, young Fitzjames suddenly stood no chance. Ultimately he would sail as third-in-command. James Clark Ross, now Sir James, headed the original list of leadership candidates. He had accepted a knighthood after returning from his last Antarctic expedition. Ross had taken part in more polar voyages than any of his contemporaries. But at forty-four, and recently married, he wished to live as a country gentleman on his estate southeast of London. And so he demurred, explaining that, before marrying, he had promised his father-in-law to undertake no more polar voyages.

Yet, as the first choice of many, Sir James wielded singular influence—and he had grown close to both Franklins, and especially Jane. While visiting Van Diemen's Land during his four-year Antarctic expedition (1839–1843), he had entrusted her with purchasing a 640-acre estate for him. Now, Jane Franklin moved quickly to ensure that Ross should exercise his influence on behalf of her husband.

Originally, both John Franklin and Edward Parry, who was four years younger, had been disqualified from consideration as too old for further Arctic rigours. Under normal circumstances, Franklin himself would probably have accepted this assessment. But since Van Diemen's Land had devastated his reputation, he felt driven to seek the leadership of this momentous expedition to exonerate himself. Later, when published reports insinuated this motivation, Lady Franklin protested too much, insisting, for example, that "nothing can be more false and more absurd than the idea that he went on his Arctic expedition from any other motive than the pure love of Arctic discovery and enterprise."

Apart from young Fitzjames, two veteran officers still in their forties remained in contention: George Back, who had distinguished himself as an Arctic overland traveller, and Francis Crozier, who had sailed on significant voyages with both Edward Parry and James Clark Ross, and who would sail, ultimately, as second-in-command. Left to his own devices, John Franklin would never have bested Crozier.

But behind him, he had the inexorable Jane, driven by the same desperate need for vindication. To James Clark Ross, Lady Franklin wrote with her usual astute mix of flattery and forthrightness. If Ross, who was clearly "the right person," chose not to lead the expedition, then she hoped Sir John would not be overlooked because of his age. After being "so unworthily treated by the Colonial Office," she wrote, "he will be deeply sensitive if his own department should neglect him, and that such an appointment would do more perhaps than anything else out of the Colonial Office to counteract the effect which Lord Stanley's injustice and oppression have produced. I dread exceedingly the effect on his mind of being without honourable and immediate employment, and it is this which enables me to support the idea of parting with him on a service of difficulty and danger better than I otherwise should."

Soon after receiving this missive, Sir James Clark Ross went public, declaring that the only possible leader for this definitive expedition was Arctic veteran Sir John Franklin. At the Admiralty, John Barrow could only shake his head in dismay. Barrow tried one final time to lure Ross into taking on the leadership, holding out a baronetcy and a massive pension. He even offered to postpone the mission for a year, if that would persuade him. J. C. Ross stood firm.

George Back visited Ross and pleaded for his support. Having twice travelled in the Arctic with Franklin, he insisted that the older man did not tolerate cold well, and argued that he was not physically fit to undertake such an adventure. Ross remained adamant. Sir Francis Beaufort, the Admiralty mapmaker, urged Ross to think again. And Edward Sabine, the man driving the Magnetic Crusade, did the same.

James Clark Ross was feeling the heat when Lady Franklin brought up reinforcements. Drawing on family connections and moral suasion, she had got through not only to the Royal Geographical Society, which sent a ringing endorsement of Franklin's candidacy, but to the redoubtable Edward Parry, who told Thomas Lord Haddington, the First Lord of the Admiralty, that Sir John was a better man than any other he knew: "If you don't let him go, he will die of disappointment."

On February 5, 1845, Haddington summoned Franklin to Admiralty House, in the heart of London. In the first-floor boardroom, splendidly furnished with mahogany bookshelves, two colourful globes, a powder-blue device that indicated wind direction and numerous charts hanging in great rolls, the two men talked at a table that could comfortably seat ten. Lady Franklin, who was not there, later offered a detailed recreation of what transpired, which has been dismissed as too literary to be completely credible.

Her account does provide a vivid approximation, however. As tactfully as he could, Lord Haddington raised the question of physical hardship. The decidedly overweight Franklin insisted that if he didn't think himself equal to the expedition, he would not have sought the leadership: "If it had been a question of walking, my lord, then I would not be the right man. I'm rather heavier than I used to be. But this is a sailing expedition—something quite different. And to that I feel entirely equal."

Franklin offered to submit to a physical examination (immediately afterwards, acting on Jane's advice, he sent a letter attesting to his good health, written by their close friend Dr. John Richardson). The First Lord, slightly embarrassed, said he was thinking also of mental toughness. He wondered if Franklin might not be exhausted by his recent ordeal in Van Diemen's Land. Franklin told him that the stress of an Arctic voyage would be nothing as compared with governing a penal colony.

"Look here, we'd like you to be our man," Haddington said. "But at fifty-nine, your age is against you."

Franklin, his birthday two months away, responded, "But, my Lord! I am only fifty-eight!"

On February 7, 1845, Thomas Lord Haddington announced his decision. The leader of this epochal Northwest Passage expedition would be that Arctic veteran Sir John Franklin. And three months later, on Sunday, May 18, 1845, at a village called Greenhithe, six kilometres above the main docks at Gravesend, Jane Franklin stood on the dock admiring the *Erebus* and the *Terror*. Freshly painted black and yellow, with a wide stripe running the length of each vessel, the two refurbished ships sparkled like success in the sun. Had not James Clark Ross sailed these same vessels to the Antarctic? Jane herself had boarded them more than once when Ross had sojourned in Van Diemen's Land.

Since then, the two former bomb-ships had been refitted yet once more, supplied with adapted railway engines and retractable screw propellers and a heating system that drove hot air through twelve-inch pipes. In a letter to a friend in Van Diemen's Land, John Franklin expressed satisfaction with the ships, and added that his appointment to the leadership of this significant expedition demonstrated that the slanders of a certain civil servant "have failed to injure me." Franklin was well satisfied, too, with his eager officers—"a fine set of young men, active, zealous, and devoted to the Service." As for the crew, he observed that "many say that no ships could go to sea better appointed than we are."

One minor incident darkened the final days before Franklin sailed. Following naval tradition, and like Sir John's first wife two decades before, Jane Franklin had stitched a British flag to give her husband as a parting gift. One afternoon, while he napped, she

From Disko Bay, Greenland, where he called in to obtain fresh water, John Franklin sent what would be the last letter to reach his wife. He reported that his men remained in high spirits, and that he had opened the ship's library to everyone on board.

placed it gently over him. Sir John opened first one eye, and then the other: "Why, there's a flag thrown over me!" He leapt to his feet, flinging it off: "Don't you know that in the Royal Navy we lay the Union Jack over a corpse?"

Shocked and hurt, Jane rose and left the room. John Franklin followed to apologize. "Forgive me, Jane. I was half asleep." She relented, seeing his dismay: "As if my loving gesture, John, could be anything but a harbinger of your success."

And so at Greenhithe, on the last Sunday before Franklin sailed, and less than one year since arriving back in England from Van Diemen's Land, Jane Franklin boarded the *Erebus* to hear Sir John read his first divine service on that vessel. She did not go dockside next morning, knowing that she would invite close scrutiny. But on May 19 she watched from a window at their lodgings as, starting around 10:30 a.m., the steamboat *Rattler* towed the ships into open water. From there, they sailed away.

Over the next few weeks, Jane Franklin received several letters. The last of these her husband dispatched from Disko Bay, Greenland, via a whaling ship. The men remained in high spirits. To all those aboard, Franklin had opened the ship's library. The 1,700 volumes included Arctic reference books and many tomes on religion, but also novels by Charles Dickens and William Makepeace Thackeray, collections of plays by William Shakespeare and bound volumes of the magazine *Punch*. Jane could easily imagine Franklin conducting religious services and providing slates to illiterate crewmen who attended evening classes.

Later in the year, she proposed to sail to North America via the West Indies. She would land in the south and, when she received word that Franklin had accomplished the Passage, cross the North American continent to greet him on the west coast of America. She would share in his moment of glory.

Part Four

LEARNING FROM FIRST PEOPLES

14.

An Orcadian Scot Joins the Search

When after two years Sir John Franklin had failed to emerge into the Pacific Ocean trailing clouds of glory, his wife, friends and naval colleagues grew worried. They began discussing search-and-rescue operations. Sir John Richardson, formerly Franklin's second-in-command, volunteered to lead a small search party down the Mackenzie River to the Arctic coast. He had served with Franklin on his two overland expeditions and had married a niece of the missing captain. The Admiralty approved Richardson's plan and sent four boats and twenty men to York Factory on Hudson Bay.

Now in his late fifties, Richardson had not expected to return to the Arctic, which he had last visited two decades before. For years he had lived ninety-five kilometres south of London, near Portsmouth, where he was chief medical officer at Haslar, the largest hospital in the world. Richardson knew he would need a competent travelling companion to serve as second officer. He found himself sifting through applications from hundreds of gentlemen of various ranks and professions, all of them eager, none of them especially well qualified.

Then, on November 1, 1847, while reading the *London Times*, Richardson discovered a report by Dr. John Rae, who had recently returned to Britain and Orkney after fourteen years in the North Country. In that report, written originally for the Hudson's Bay Company, Rae described how he had led a dozen men north to map the Arctic coastline. He had wintered at Repulse Bay, living off the land. And he had demonstrated that "Boothia Felix" was a peninsula, not an island, and confirmed that—contrary to the surmise of Thomas Simpson and others—no northwest passage flowed west out of the bottom of the Gulf of Boothia. On reading Rae's account at his home, a separate residence situated within the hospital grounds, Richardson jumped to his feet and to his wife cried out: "I have found my companion, if I can get him."

John Rae had been born in the Hall of Clestrain at Stromness, Orkney, in 1813. The son of a prosperous land agent, he had spent his youth climbing, fishing, hiking, hunting and sailing. In his midteens, this Orcadian Scot had trained as a doctor at the University of Edinburgh. At nineteen, he sailed with the Hudson's Bay Company as a surgeon. Ice prevented the ship from returning home, and Rae spent a winter near the bottom of Hudson Bay at tiny Charlton Island—the very island where, two centuries before, Henry Hudson had endured one horrific winter.

There, Rae survived food shortages, freezing-cold temperatures, and an outbreak of scurvy that killed two men. In the spring, realizing he was well suited to "the wild sort of life" available with the HBC, he signed on to serve two years as a company doctor—and

Orcadian photographer James Grieve created this image. It combines two photos: one of a statue of John Rae erected in Stromness in 2013 to mark the 200th anniversary of the explorer's birth, and another of the Hall of Clestrain, Rae's birthplace, as it looks today. The John Rae Society is working to restore the Hall and turn it into a visitor attraction.

ended up remaining at Moose Factory, the HBC's second-largest fur-trading post, for more than a decade. Here, Rae went on countless hunting trips with a Cree hunchback named George Rivers. A tall, well-built, powerful fellow in his youth, Rivers had injured his spine and remained so bent over that he stood little more than five feet tall. That didn't stop him.

With Rivers, Rae hunted moose and caribou, which provided the Cree not only with a staple food but also with hide that, once tanned, they fashioned into jackets, trousers and skirts. Rae had arrived as an excellent outdoorsman. But Rivers taught him native techniques of hunting and trapping, showing him how to cache meat under heavy stones to protect it from predators, and how to clean, skin and butcher large game, securing the blood in a bag made by turning the stomach inside out. He taught Rae to remove the gullet of a carcass, explaining that if this was not done, the meat would quickly become unfit to eat.

Rivers proved to be a fearless canoeist, an admirable shot and an excellent cook. The young doctor repaid the Cree for his tutelage by getting him a double-barrelled shotgun from England, with which he then made remarkable shots. With the help of Rivers, Rae mastered canoeing and snowshoeing. Still in his twenties, he became legendary as a survivalist and snowshoe walker. Once, making a long-distance home call, he covered 167 kilometres in two days—119 on the second.

In 1844, while Sir John and Lady Franklin lobbied to secure the leadership of that epochal Royal Navy expedition, John Rae visited Montreal from Moose Factory. There, he had convinced George Simpson, governor of the Hudson's Bay Company, that he was the man to complete the geographical survey of the Arctic coast of North America. He needed to learn the latest surveying techniques, and the following year, as Franklin sailed into the Passage, Rae accomplished an extraordinary overland journey. First, he paddled from Moose Factory to Red River (Fort Garry), a distance of 1,175 kilometres. When his intended instructor grew ill and died, Rae added another 2,230 kilometres. First he donned snowshoes and spent two months trekking to Sault Ste. Marie, hunting as he went. After sojourning there, he continued mostly by canoe to Toronto. There, at the magnetic observatory, a simple log structure (long gone) built six years before on the present-day grounds of the University of Toronto, he studied with the distinguished scientist John Henry Lefroy, learning how to use a sextant and take magnetic observations.

During the autumn of 1845, as Franklin prepared to winter on

The Hudson's Bay Company made John Rae a chief factor in 1850. Eight years later, J. Scott created this mezzotint of the explorer after a painting by S. Pearce. It is at the Wellcome Library, London.

Beechey Island, John Rae made his way back to Red River, mostly by canoe, and then beat east and north in a York boat first to Moose Factory (1,176 kilometres) and then to York Factory (992 kilometres). He arrived in a freezing gale on October 8, and there spent the ensuing winter, supervising the building of two boats and hiring men for his expedition. In June 1846, with two twenty-two-foot-long sailboats, John Rae set out from York Factory with a dozen men—six Scots (including four from his native Orkney), two French Canadians, one Métis and one Cree.

After sailing north for two weeks, Rae arrived at Churchill. Here he rounded out his party by adding two Inuit interpreters: Ouligbuck and one of his sons, a boy of thirteen or fourteen called William Ouligbuck Jr. The senior Ouligbuck had travelled with John Richardson on Franklin's second overland expedition. He had later ventured along the coast with Peter Warren Dease and Thomas Simpson.

The younger Ouligbuck had entered the written record in 1843, when he visited York Factory with his parents. Letitia Hargrave, wife of Chief Trader James Hargrave, wrote of him: "The boy is about 12, and speaks ten languages. He is otherwise a little scamp, but very smart & hideously fat and husky-like, tho' very well dressed." Two years later, Hargrave wrote to his opposite number at Fort Churchill that Ouligbuck Sr. "has been retained in the service solely with a view towards [going north with Rae] . . . As his son appears to be such a useful lad, he will likewise be included in the party—an opportunity which must be gratifying to his father."

Since the youth would "act as the second interpreter," Hargrave asked that "all the people at the Fort should be directed to address him in the English language only." Before the expedition was over, Rae would run out of patience with young William, describing him as an "incorrigible thief . . . [who] was twice caught with the old man's bale open, eating sugar; some tobacco was also taken, and the trousers of most of the men . . . completely cleared of buttons by the same hands." The young rascal, given to filching his father's sugar and tobacco, and of playing practical jokes, sounds almost like a contemporary teenager.

In his published journal, *Narrative of an Expedition to the Shores of the Arctic Sea*, Rae described how, on reaching Repulse Bay on July 24, 1846, he felt relieved to see four Inuit on the rocky shore. Their presence meant that he would find animals to hunt, and might be able to trade for fuel, cooking oil and perhaps even sled dogs. With the help of Ouligbuck, Rae inquired about the geography of the region. He would have to see for himself, of course, but now he learned that Thomas Simpson had been wrong: no channel led westward from here, or even from Lord Mayor Bay, to anywhere near the mouth of the Castor and Pollux River.

Rae had yet to discover the virtues of Inuit igloos or snow houses, and he supervised the building of a stone house, twenty feet by fourteen, which he named Fort Hope. As winter deepened, he visited a nearby Inuit camp. He found the snow house of an old man named Shishak so cozy and warm that his waistcoat, which had frozen stiff, actually thawed.

Rae sought instruction in how to build an igloo. After a few trials, he and a couple of his men became proficient ice-masons. By December 1846, they had built four snow huts, linked by tunnels, in which to store provisions. Later, as the cold and continuous darkness took hold, they constructed two observatories of snow, with an ice pillar in each—one for meteorological readings, the other to study the magnetic effects of the aurora borealis, or northern lights.

Using Ouligbuck and his son as interpreters, Rae collected Inuit stories from a communicative Inuk named Arkshuk. He learned, for example, that after the creation of the world, a mighty conjuror had raised himself up into the heavens, taking both fire and his beautiful sister with him. When the two argued, he scorched one side of her face. She escaped and formed the moon. "When it is new moon," Rae wrote, "the burnt side of her face is towards us; when full moon, the reverse is the case."

Dr. John Rae at Repulse Bay, 1846 *by Charles Fraser Comfort* (1932).

In April 1847, having survived temperatures as low as minus forty-three degrees Celsius, Rae set out westward with five men on a surveying expedition. Heading north, he chanced upon the snow-huts of two Inuit families who were fishing for trout. He hired one of the men, Kei-ik-too-oo, to help haul supplies for two days. The man harnessed his dog team, took on a heavy load and, after applying a mixture of moss and wet snow to his sled runners, glided away rapidly over the snow. Rae immediately noted the superiority of the iced runners over the bare ones he had been using, and adjusted his practice accordingly. Rae also described how he and his men built snow houses each night, raising "a good roomy dwelling" in an hour. A second party erected a kitchen, a necessary addition, "although our cooking was none of the most delicate or extensive . . . had it been only to thaw snow" for drinking water.

Travelling north and periodically caching provisions for the return journey, the party arrived at Committee Bay and followed the coast for four days. Bad weather slowed progress, but on April 17, Rae climbed a rise and looked out over a glorious expanse. From where he stood, he could see "a large extent of ice-covered sea studded with innumerable islands. Lord Mayor's Bay was before me, and the islands were those named by Sir John Ross" in the early 1830s. Rae could also see that, to the west, land connected Boothia Felix to the mainland, making it not an island but a peninsula.

On the return journey, Rae and two Orcadian men struck out overland across several ranges of ice hills. This meant climbing one hummocky ridge after another. One of his men, Flett, was suffering snow blindness. He "got many queer falls," Rae wrote, "and was once or twice placed in such situations with his head down hill, his heels up, and the strap of his bundle around his neck, that it would have been impossible for him to get up by his own unaided exertions."

Having travelled non-stop for thirty days, Rae arrived back at Repulse Bay, terminating "a journey little short of 600 miles [965 kilometres], the longest, I believe, ever made on foot along the Arctic coast." Nor was Rae finished. After resting for one week, he took four men and trekked to the west coast of Melville Peninsula, battling fierce winds, drifting snow and more hummocky ice to come within a few kilometres of Fury and Hecla Strait, so named by Royal Navy explorer William Edward Parry.

Over the course of this first expedition, John Rae charted 1,055 kilometres hitherto unmapped coastline. More than a century later, when explorer Vilhjalmur Stefansson read of Rae's adaptations, and of the way he used local resources, he called him "a genius in the art of travelling." He insisted that Rae's innovations constituted a revolutionary advance in northern travel: "Rae was as new as Darwin." The man himself advanced no such claims. He was the chief hunter of every expedition he ever led, and also the first European to adopt Inuit methods of travel. But he never failed to credit those who taught him, whether they were Cree or Inuit.

On August 30, 1847, when Rae reached York Factory, he was surprised to find that 20 men had recently arrived from England. An advance party, they had brought four transportable boats to use in searching for Sir John Franklin, who had disappeared with two ships and 128 men. Rae doubted their fitness for undertaking an Arctic search, but that was none of his concern. In a letter from George Simpson, he learned that he had been promoted to chief trader, and that he was free to travel until the annual general meeting of June 1848. John Rae had not been home for fourteen years. On September 24, 1847, he boarded an HBC supply ship and sailed for Stromness.

On November 1, soon after he arrived home, his report about over-wintering above the treeline appeared in the *Times*. Not long after that, he received an invitation from Sir John Richardson. Then just thirty-four years old, Rae knew Richardson to be England's finest naturalist. He had read about the older man in Franklin's first published narrative, and vividly remembered the courage and generosity Richardson had demonstrated. Already the search for Franklin had become a *cause célèbre*. Who could refuse? He agreed to serve as second-in-command.

In London, talking with those concerned, Rae gleaned that Franklin and his men carried enough food to last probably until July of 1848. No assistance could reach them before that date, and the men would be on short rations unless they managed to obtain fresh provisions by hunting or fishing. But to anyone who cared to listen, Rae explained that caribou and muskox are wary of hunters, especially if they have migrated from the south. In winter, they are especially difficult to approach because snow fills the ravines and hollows, leaving even an expert hunter no means of concealing himself. The natives had learned to trap deer in pitfalls dug in the snow, a highly specialized technique. With seals, Rae would explain, the challenges were greater still. At Repulse Bay, while the Inuit were bringing in one or more seals a day, the excellent Cree hunter Nibitabo could not obtain even one: the animals always managed to plunge under the ice and swim away, even if they were mortally wounded.

Rae was well aware that Franklin was probably facing far worse difficulties than the British public could imagine. But where, exactly?

Late in 1847, the Admiralty augmented Richardson and Rae's proposed Mackenzie River expedition, adding two searches by sea. One ship, the *Plover*, would enter Arctic waters from the west through Bering Strait and send boats eastward along the top of the continent. The other expedition would sail from the east and include two ships, the *Enterprise* and the *Investigator*, under James Clark Ross, who felt compelled to break his vow and go searching. Meanwhile, on March 25, 1848, Rae and Richardson sailed out of Liverpool on the mail steamer *Hibernia*. They were bent on finding John Franklin. And in this, soon enough, they would be far from alone.

15.

Voyagers Find Graves on Beechey Island

Late one morning in August 1850, while talking on the bow of a ship trapped in the ice off Beechey Island, speculating about what route John Franklin might have taken, an American searcher, Elisha Kent Kane, was startled by the sound of a voice yelling, "Graves!" A sailor was stumbling breathless across the ice from shore. "Graves!" the man shouted. "Franklin's winter quarters!"

Searchers had found what has since become the most visited historical site in the Arctic—the graves of the first three men to die during Franklin's final voyage. At this desolate spot in 1846, while still hoping to discover a northwest passage, the long-winded Franklin would have conducted sonorous funeral services for the dead men. Now, four years later, the Philadelphia-born Kane led searchers in scrambling across the ice and up a short slope to the makeshift cemetery. "Here, amid the sterile uniformity of snow and slate," he wrote later, "were the head-boards of three graves, made after the old orthodox fashion of gravestones at home."

Drawn by James Hamilton from a sketch by Elisha Kent Kane, this is a roman-ticized representation of the Beechey Island gravesite. In 1850, Kane was present at the discovery of the site.

Born in 1820, the oldest son of a patrician family based in Philadel-phia, then called "the Athens of America," Elisha Kent Kane trained as a doctor. Despite recurring illness and health problems—his heart condition would kill him within a decade—he became what today we would call an extreme adventurer. While still in his twenties, he descended into a volcano in the Philippines, infiltrated a company of slave traders in West Africa and narrowly survived a stabbing during hand-to-hand combat in the Sierra Madre.

While sailing as an assistant surgeon in the American Navy, ranging from the Mediterranean to South America, Kane felt revolted by the brutality of shipboard discipline. After seeing one man flogged three times and another receive fifty lashes, he sought and gained a transfer to the United States Coast Survey, which had been created to map harbours and coastlines.

This government-run department had become the leading proponent of "Humboldtean science" in America. At the turn of the nineteenth century, Alexander von Humboldt had established a new model for geographical studies. While exploring the interior of South America, Humboldt had forged a stellar reputation as a scientific truth-seeker who would risk his life to advance the causes of science and humanity.

By entering the Coast Survey, as David Chapin observed in *Exploring Other Worlds*, Kane found a model of exploration worth emulating. He liked the idea of men working outdoors, subordinating individual interests to the common good, and sleeping in tents for weeks at a time. Assigned to the steamer *Walker*, Kane helped survey the southeast coast of North America.

By January 1850, when he sailed into Charleston, South Carolina, Kane had become keenly interested in the search for Sir John Franklin. The previous April, Lady Franklin had written to American president Zachary Taylor, asking that the United States "join heart and mind in the enterprise of snatching the lost navigators from a dreary grave." A New York shipping magnate, Henry Grinnell, perceived that the search for Franklin could be combined with a quest to test a scientific hypothesis attracting attention among American geographers—the idea that, at the top of the world, there existed the Open Polar Sea, teeming with fish and mammals.

After exchanging letters with Lady Franklin, Grinnell decided to sponsor an American search expedition. To keep expenses within reason, he needed the U.S. Navy to supply manpower and provisions—and so he told Jane Franklin. In December 1849, this persuasive woman wrote again to President Taylor. She stressed that the lost sailors, "whether clinging still to their ships or dispersed in various directions, have entered upon a fifth winter in those dark and dreary solitudes, with exhausted means of sustenance."

In a January newspaper, Elisha Kent Kane read that President Taylor had brought Lady Franklin's request to Congress, and asked that the U.S. Navy supply Grinnell with two vessels. Soon afterwards, while still aboard the *Walker*, Kane wrote a letter to the secretary of the Navy, volunteering to serve with any Arctic search expedition that might be mounted. When he received no reply, the young officer abandoned hope.

But then, on Sunday, May 12, while swimming in the Gulf of Mexico at Mobile, Alabama, Kane was called ashore to receive a surprising telegram. It was "one of those courteous little epistles from Washington," he would write, "which the electric telegraph has made so familiar to naval officers." It detached him from the Coast Survey and ordered him "to proceed forthwith to New York, for duty upon the Arctic Expedition."

Kane exulted in this development. His mother was less enthusiastic, but recognized that "it is vain to grieve. Elisha cannot live without adventure." His father, a judge and backroom politician, wrote: "I cannot rejoice that he is going on this expedition; his motive is most praiseworthy, but I think the project a wild one, and I fear inadequacy in outfit. I wish most sincerely that Sir John Franklin was at home with his wife again, leading dog's lives together as they used to do . . . But it is as it is and we must make the best of it:—Oh! this Glory! when the cost is fairly counted up, it is no such great speculation after all."

As he travelled to New York City, Kane never doubted he would join one of two impressive ships. After all, the lost vessels of Sir John Franklin, the *Erebus* and the *Terror*, weighed 370 and 326 tons respectively, and could together accommodate more than 130 men. Nor was he alone in his expectations. Another officer who would sail with the expedition, Robert Randolph Carter, had just left the *Savannah*—a massive 1,726-ton ship with a complement of 480 men. This was the kind of vessel, surely, that would lead the United States Grinnell Expedition in Search of Sir John Franklin.

But on Tuesday, May 21, when Kane reported at the Brooklyn Naval Yard, he discovered to his dismay that the grandly named Grinnell expedition comprised two vessels so small that only their masts showed above the edge of the wharf. The flagship *Advance* weighed only 146 tons, and the *Rescue* just 91. Expected to carry a total of thirty-three men between them, these tiny "hermaphrodite brigs"—square-rigged foremast, schooner-rigged mainmast— were designed for manoeuvrability and speed, but lacked anything resembling naval trim. Half-stowed cargo cluttered their decks, and Kane felt he "could straddle from the main hatch to the bulwarks." The ships looked "more like a couple of coasting schooners than a national squadron bound for a distant and perilous sea."

Kane soon realized that Henry Grinnell and expedition leader Edwin De Haven had worked hard to prepare the ships for Arctic service. The eighty-eight-foot-long *Advance*, on which Kane would sail as surgeon, had been doubly sheathed in thick oak planking and reinforced from bow to stern with sheet-iron strips. Seven feet of solid timber filled the space behind the bow. The rudder could be hauled aboard, and the winch, capstan and windlass "were of the best and newest construction." Kane also found the library well stocked, especially with books on polar exploration.

The Navy-supplied equipment impressed him less. The antiquated stoves had been stowed deep in the hold, and the firearms, mostly ball-loading muskets, proved a "heterogeneous collection of obsolete old carbines, with the impracticable ball cartridges that accompanied them." Kane worried that the food supplies, while possibly adequate for the projected three-year voyage, would not prove varied enough to ward off scurvy.

With the "zealous aid" of Mr. Grinnell, who provided the funds, Kane spent several hours dashing around New York City, purchasing thermometers, barometers and magnetometers. These "would have been of use to me if they had found their way on board," he wrote later. From home, where he had briefly stopped, he had brought a few books, some coarse woollen clothing and a magnificent buffalo-skin robe from "the snow drifts of Utah," a parting gift from his brother, Thomas, later a hero in the American Civil War.

On the *Advance*, Kane would share a below-decks cabin, smaller "than a penitentiary cell," with De Haven and the other two officers. This dank accommodation contained camp stools, lockers and berths for four men, as well as a hinged table and a "dripping step-ladder that led directly from the wet deck above." Kane shielded his berth—"a right-angled excavation" six feet long, thirty-two inches wide and less than three feet tall—with a few yards of India rubber cloth.

Inside, on tiny shelves, he placed his books and a reading lamp. Then, using nails, hooks and string, he suspended a few items along the wall: watch, thermometer, inkbottle, toothbrush, comb and hairbrush. When, with all this accomplished, Kane "crawled in from the wet, and cold, and disorder of without, through a slit in the India-rubber cloth, to the very center of my complicated resources," he revelled in the comfort he had manufactured. And at 1:00 p.m. on May 22, 1850, the day after Elisha Kent Kane reached New York City, the

Advance cut loose from the "asthmatic old steam-tug" that had towed it out of the Brooklyn Navy Yard and began its long voyage.

As the *Advance* sailed north, Kane battled seasickness and perused the analytical writings of Matthew Fontaine Maury, wrestling with ideas that the theoretician would later incorporate in his 1855 classic, *The Physical Geography of the Sea*. After years of study, Maury had become the leading exponent of the popular theory that, at the top of the world, there lay the Open Polar Sea.

Whales sometimes carried harpoons in their backs from the Bering Strait in the west to Baffin Bay in the east. Because these mammals cannot travel such a distance under ice, Maury deduced that "there is at times, at least, open water communication through the polar regions between the Atlantic and Pacific Oceans." And so he revived the theory that the Open Polar Sea lay beyond a northern ring of ice, an idea with roots in the sixteenth century.

Elisha Kent Kane, age thirty-five, with telescope.

Captain De Haven, a veteran sailor, dreaded writing reports and found no excitement in Maury. But the imaginative Kane showed such a passion for the scientist's musings that when he floated the idea of writing a book about the voyage, De Haven hailed the idea. Night after night, while others slept, Kane huddled in his berth and scratched away by lamplight, bent on producing "a history of the cruise under the form of a personal narrative."

By the time he reached Greenland, Kane had sailed past his first iceberg—a gigantic cube coated with snow that resembled "a great marble monolith, only awaiting the chisel to stand out . . . a floating Parthenon." He had watched his first school of whales tumbling like porpoises around the vessel—"great, crude, wallowing sea-hogs, snorting out fountains of white spray." And he had marvelled at the continuous sunlight of northern latitudes in summer: "The words night and day begin to puzzle me, as I recognize the arbitrary character of the hour cycles that have borne these names."

On July 3, 1850, after resuming the voyage and passing through what Kane described as "a crowd of noble icebergs," the two American ships encountered a berg-dotted expanse of pack ice. Prevailing currents usually pushed this so-called Middle Ice to the west, opening a channel along the Greenland coast. Whalers would follow this laneway as far north as Melville Bay—little more than an indentation—and then swing westward, crossing Baffin Bay north of the Middle Ice, through the relatively ice-free North Water.

Occasionally, to save valuable summertime weeks, voyagers tried to cross Baffin Bay by threading their way through the Middle Ice. In 1819, Edward Parry had succeeded in this; fifteen years later, he wasted two months trying. Now, in July 1850, Kane described the "vast plane of undulating ice" as creating an unspeakable din of crackling, grinding and splashing: "A great number of bergs, of shapes the most simple and most complicated, of colours blue, white, and earth-stained, were tangled in this floating field." One evening, while standing on deck, he counted 240 icebergs "of primary magnitude."

By mid-August, the Americans understood that they would have to winter, as Kane put it, "somewhere in the scene of Arctic search." On August 19, as the *Advance* neared the entrance to Lancaster Sound, its sailing master spotted two British vessels following in the ship's wake. Within four hours, the larger of the two drew alongside. It proved to be the *Lady Franklin*, engaged in the Franklin search under whaling captain William Penny. He, too, had run into problems in Melville Bay. Before sailing past the slower *Advance*, he reported that a four-vessel British expedition led by Captain Horatio Austin had recently passed that way, and also the provision ship *North Star*.

A couple of nights later, while sailing through Lancaster Sound, driving before a strong wind and taking water at every roll, the Americans overtook a different British vessel. This small schooner, towing a launch and "fluttering over the waves like a crippled bird," proved to be the *Felix*. Kane watched as "an old fellow, with a cloak tossed over his night gear, appeared in the lee gangway, and saluted with a voice that rose above the winds." Two decades before, John Ross had been shipwrecked and survived four winters in the Arctic. Now he roared joyfully: "You and I are ahead of them all!"

Ross came on deck, a vigorous, square-built man looking younger than his seventy-three years, and reported that Austin's four-boat squadron had taken refuge in various bays, and that Penny was lost in the gale. At thirty, Kane knew enough Arctic history to appreciate the encounter—to delight in meeting John Ross near Admiralty Inlet, where seventeen years before the old seadog had contrived to escape an icy incarceration. Kane also marvelled that, despite opposition and even ridicule, Ross had sailed in search of his old friend in "a flimsy cockle-shell, after contributing his purse and his influence."

On August 25, having fallen behind its partner ship, the *Rescue*, the *Advance* approached Cape Riley. From the deck, the Americans spotted two cairns, the larger marked with a flagstaff. They landed and, in the larger cairn, found a tin canister containing a note. Two days before, the British captain Ommanney had called there with the *Assistance* and the *Intrepid*, both from Austin's four-ship squadron. He had discovered traces of a British encampment nearby, and noted that similar findings had been reported on nearby Beechey Island, at the entrance to Wellington Channel.

Later, in his book, Kane would suggest that Ommanney had suppressed a significant aspect of his landing: "Our consort, the *Rescue*, as we afterward learned, had shared in this discovery, though the British commander's inscription in the cairn, as well as his official reports, might lead to a different conclusion. [The *Rescue*'s] Captain Griffin, in fact, landed with Captain Ommanney, and the traces were registered while the two officers were in company." To this theme—the exclusive nationalism of the imperial British—the proudly American Kane would return.

Now, he inspected Cape Riley, notebook in hand. He identified five distinct "remnants of habitation"—four circular mounds of crumbled limestone, clearly designed as bases for tents, and a fifth such enclosure, larger and triangular in shape, whose entrance faced south towards Lancaster Sound. He also found large square stones arranged to serve as a fireplace and, on the beach, several pieces of pinewood that had once formed part of a boat. In Kane's view, the evidence was meagre but conclusive: "All these speak of a land party from Franklin's squadron."

Next morning, the *Advance* sailed on towards Beechey Island, which "rose up in a lofty monumental block" of limestone, and which Kane insisted on identifying as a promontory or peninsula, because a low isthmus linked it to the much larger Devon Island. By August 27, five vessels under three commanders—William Penny, John Ross and Edwin De Haven—stood anchored within a few hundred metres. Not far from Beechey, Penny had discovered some additional traces of Franklin's expedition—tin canisters with the manufacturer's label, scraps of newspaper dated 1844 and two pieces of paper bearing the name of one of Franklin's officers.

After breakfast, Kane and De Haven visited Penny's ship, HMS *Lady Franklin*. On the deck, together with John Ross and Penny himself, they stood discussing how best to cooperate in continuing the search. Penny sketched out a rough proposal. He would search to the west. Ross would cross Lancaster Sound to communicate with the *Prince Albert* and prevent her from sailing south unnecessarily; and the Americans, with whom he had already consulted, would proceed north through Wellington Channel.

With this agreed, Ross left to return to the *Felix*. Kane was talking with the veteran Penny, who had speculated in print about the existence of the Open Polar Sea, when he heard a yell and saw a seaman hurrying across the ice. The sailor shouted against the noise of the wind and the waves: "Graves, Captain Penny! Graves! Franklin's winter quarters!"

The officers debarked onto the ice to meet the messenger. After responding to questions as best he could, the seaman led the way onto Beechey Island and along a ridge to three headboards and graves, their mounds forming a line facing Cape Riley. The boards bore inscriptions declaring them sacred to the memories of three sailors—W. Braine of the *Erebus*, who died April 3, 1846, at age thirty-two; John Hartnell of the *Erebus*, no date specified, dead at age twenty-three; and John Torrington, "who departed this life January 1st, A.D. 1846, on board of H.M. Ship *Terror*, aged 20 years."

In describing this scene, Kane drew attention to the words "on board." He added: "Franklin's ships, then, had not been wrecked when he occupied the encampment at Beechey."

The excitement of this discovery of graves would be felt down through the decades. Now, on August 27, 1850, Elisha Kent Kane copied the inscriptions and sketched the three graves against the desolate landscape. He then scoured the area, which abounded in fragmentary remains—part of a stocking, a worn mitten, shavings of wood, the remnants of a rough garden. A few hundred metres from the graves, he came upon a neat pile of more than six hundred preserved-meat cans. Emptied of food, these had been filled with limestone pebbles, "perhaps to serve as convenient ballast on a boating expedition."

Countless other indications, including bits and pieces of canvas, rope, sailcloth and tarpaulins, as well as scrap paper, a small key and odds and ends of brass work, testified that this was a winter resting place. Nobody turned up any written documents, however, nor even the vaguest hint about the intentions of the party. Kane judged this remarkable—"and for so able and practiced an Arctic commander as Sir John Franklin, an incomprehensible omission."

Others, given the benefit of hindsight and the accretion of evidence, have wondered whether Franklin was as competent as some of his contemporaries believed. In 1850, Kane noted only that it was impossible to stand on Beechey without forming an opinion about what had happened to the British expedition. Before offering his own, he reviewed the incontestable facts. During the winter of 1845–46, the *Terror* had wintered there. She kept some of her crew on board. Some men from the *Erebus* were also there. An organized party had taken astronomical observations, made sledges and prepared gardens to battle scurvy.

Beyond this lay speculation. Kane inferred the health of the expedition to be generally satisfactory, as only three men had died out of nearly 130. He puzzled over the abandoned tin cans, "not very valuable, yet not worthless," and speculated that they might have been left if Franklin departed Beechey in a hurry—as a result, for example, of the ice breaking up unexpectedly.

The main question, of course, was where had Franklin gone? Entranced by speculations of the Open Polar Sea, Kane imagined that in the early summer of 1846, Franklin had gazed out anxiously, waiting for the ice to open. The first lead or opening to appear in the ice would, he thought, almost certainly run northwest along the coast of Devon Island. Would Franklin wait until Lancaster Sound opened to the south, and then sail back to try the upper reaches of Baffin Bay? "Or would he press to the north," Kane asked, "through the open lead that lay before him?"

Anybody who knew Franklin's character, determination and purpose, Kane insisted, would find the question easy to answer. "We, the searchers, were ourselves tempted, by the insidious openings to the north in Wellington Channel, to push on in the hope that some lucky chance might point us to an outlet beyond. Might not the same temptation have had its influence for Sir John Franklin? A careful and daring navigator, such as he was, would not wait for the lead to close."

It did not occur, even to the imaginative Kane, that before making camp on Beechey Island, Franklin might already have investigated Wellington Channel. And that, with heavy ice to the west, he had only one way to go: south.

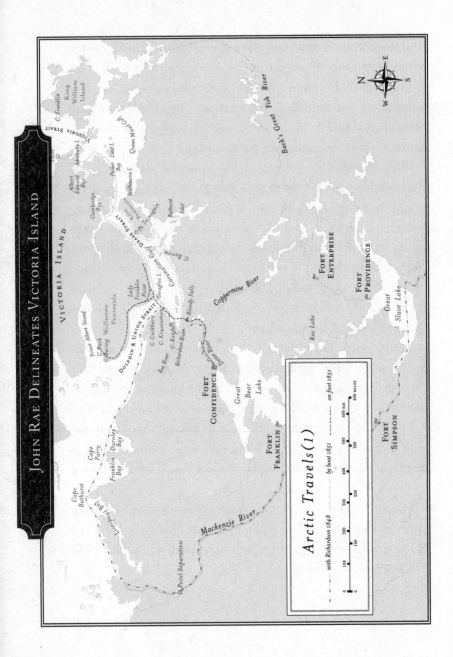

JOHN RAE DELINEATES VICTORIA ISLAND

VICTORIA ISLAND

Arctic Travels (1)

with Richardson 1848   by boat 1851   on foot 1851

FORT CONFIDENCE

FORT FRANKLIN

FORT ENTERPRISE

FORT PROVIDENCE

FORT SIMPSON

Mackenzie River

Coppermine River

Back's Great Fish River

Great Bear Lake

Great Slave Lake

Rae Lake

Dease River

Blue River

Richardson River

Bloody Falls

Coronation Gulf

DOLPHIN & UNION STRAIT

DEASE STRAIT

VICTORIA STRAIT

Queen Maud Gulf

Prince Albert Sound

Wollaston Peninsula

Kent Peninsula

C. Franklin

King William Island

Admiralty I.

Lind I.

Albert Edward Bay

Parker Bay

Melbourne I.

Cambridge Bay

Lady Franklin Point

Douglas I.

C. Colborne

C. Krusenstern

C. Baring

C. Back

Cape Bathurst

Cape Parry

Franklin Bay

Darnley Bay

Liverpool Bay

Point Separation

C. Barrow

Pt. Tinmulgan

Bathurst Inlet

206

16.

John Rae Mounts a Tour de Force

In May 1850, as the thirty-year-old American doctor Elisha Kent Kane sailed north out of New York City, Scottish doctor John Rae, seven years older, was canoeing down the Mackenzie River to the Arctic coast. Recently appointed head of district for the Hudson's Bay Company, Rae went to supervise the gathering of furs collected during the winter. As part of an annual cycle, traders stationed on the Mackenzie had to transport furs upriver in June to catch the HBC ships sailing for England from York Factory. Beyond Fort Simpson, to reduce blockages and traffic jams, those in charge would split the "Mackenzie Brigade" into two, giving half the boats a head start of several days.

On June 16, 1850, when off the coast of Greenland Kane was sailing amidst astonishing icebergs, Rae sent his second-in-command back upriver with four well-laden boats. Four days later, he followed with five more boats, portaging and tracking. For nine days, from two o'clock in the morning until eight or nine at night, Rae led his men up the Mackenzie, halting briefly for breakfast, eating dinner only after landing at night, and snacking on pemmican to keep going.

During the previous cold, dark winter, while based at Fort Simpson, Rae had written George Simpson requesting a leave of absence. After his recent hard work in searching for John Franklin, he anticipated that this would be granted. From York Factory, he intended to keep right on travelling, first to New York City and then to his beloved Orkney.

Just over two years earlier, on April 10, 1848, Rae and John Richardson had reached New York City from Liverpool. They had travelled north to Montreal by steamship, and spent three days with Sir George Simpson at his stone mansion in nearby Lachine. Anxious to begin their search, they left separately. Richardson travelled west in the steamer *British Empire*, and Rae took passage in the *Canada*, supervising eleven Iroquois and French-Canadian voyageurs who would form the backbone of a canoeing crew of sixteen.

In early May, reunited, Rae and Richardson paddled northwest out of Sault Ste. Marie, hugging the coast of Lake Superior, the so-called King of Lakes, which Richardson rightly described as occupying nearly as much space as the whole of England. The two Scots travelled in separate canoes, each with eight voyageurs, and followed the usual fur-trade route.

At Cumberland House, having travelled 2,237 kilometres from Sault Ste. Marie in forty-one days, Rae caught up with Chief Trader John Bell and the twenty British servicemen who, having arrived from York Factory, would accompany them to the Arctic. On June 13, 1848, after interviewing these men, Rae wrote to George Simpson expressing misgivings. None of the miners, sappers and sailors were accustomed to portaging, or to travelling in canoes and small boats. None were hunters. Neither the four boats nor the British servicemen were suited to the work ahead. The only positive development, Rae wrote, was that Albert One-Eye, a young Inuk interpreter, had joined the expedition.

Rae had met the youth in 1842 at Moose Factory. Since Albert had full use of both eyes, probably he was the son of a man who had lost an eye. He had been born around 1824 on the east coast of James Bay, in the so-called "Eastmain" of HBC territory. When he was eighteen, a visiting chief trader thought that Albert showed promise. He brought him across Hudson Bay to Moose Factory, the largest post in the south. John Rae was already there when Albert signed on to work for seven years as an apprentice labourer.

Within the year, however, he was seconded to work as an interpreter at Fort George, some distance north of Eastmain. He was still there early in 1848 when Rae had thought to request his services. From Fort George, HBC trader John Spencer wrote that he was "exceedingly sorry to part with him," adding that Albert was "a nice steady lad, and a favourite with his tribe." On June 13, from Cumberland House, Rae wrote to Simpson that he and Richardson were bringing no hunters to the Arctic coast. They would depend on Rae's own hunting, and on "the exertions of our Esquimaux interpreter . . . a fine active lad" who would "no doubt prove to be a good deer hunter."

While John Richardson was the nominal leader of the search expedition, John Rae, infinitely more capable in rough country, took charge. He led the party north through Great Slave Lake and, in August 1848, down the Mackenzie River. Albert One-Eye had no difficulty communicating with the Inuit of the Mackenzie Delta, as Richardson later attested. One local man, asked whether any white men were living on a given island, said yes. Richardson had visited that island the previous day and knew otherwise. He told Albert to tell the man he was lying. "He received this retort with a smile," Richardson wrote, "and without the slightest discomposure, but did not repeat his assertion." As historian Kenn Harper has noted, Albert would appear to have conveyed Richardson's assertion less confrontationally than the explorer himself.

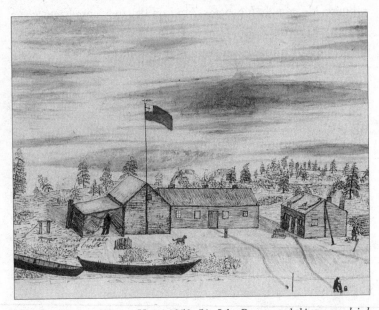

Fort Confidence, Winter View, 1850–51. *John Rae created this pen-and-ink drawing.*

From the mouth of the Mackenzie, Rae followed the coast eastward, retracing the route Richardson had followed two decades before. With winter coming on, and having found no sign of Franklin, he led the way up the Coppermine River and then to Great Slave Lake. He and Richardson spent the winter at Fort Confidence, which Dease and Simpson had built a decade before. They erected a small observatory and took meteorological readings sixteen or seventeen times a day. Decades later, weather historian Tim Ball would note that "no one kept more precise records than John Rae."

During the winter of 1848–49, Richardson turned sixty-one. He could see that, given Rae's abilities, he himself had become superfluous. In May 1849, he started the long journey home to England. Before he left, Rae elicited written instructions to seek Franklin along the shores of Wollaston Land and Victoria Land, and to abandon the quest at the end of the year. From Fort Confidence, Rae informed George Simpson that he would descend the Coppermine River, and then try to cross Dolphin and Union Strait to Victoria Island. The crew would include Albert, whom he described as "a very fine lad" and "fit for any of the duties of a labourer."

From Fort Confidence, Rae set out on June 7. On reaching the coast in early July, he found Coronation Gulf still clogged with ice. With half a dozen men, he pushed on to Cape Krusenstern, bent on crossing the fast-flowing Dolphin and Union Strait to Wollaston Land. Ice prevented any such crossing. Finally, on August 19, spying more open water than before, Rae pushed out into the swirling floes.

The men reached open water and rowed on through a soupy fog. They covered twelve kilometres, but then came up against a driving stream of rolling ice floes. With visibility approaching zero, Rae gave the order to turn back. After struggling for three hours, the men emerged from the fog and ran up onto an icy barricade. They hauled the boat for almost a kilometre, attaining land several hundred metres south of their original campsite. Rae hoped to try again, and waited two more days, but a northern gale blew up and jammed "our cold and persevering opponent in large heaps along the shore."

Finally, amidst howling winds and driving rain, Rae acknowledged that he had run out of time. Even if John Franklin waited just across the channel, nobody was going to reach him on this occasion.

Rae started leading the way up the Coppermine River. Then, on August 24, after getting past Bloody Falls, tragedy struck. The men had successfully manoeuvred their boat up the most treacherous part of the rapids and had reached an area where the current was strong but the river smooth.

Rae judged it safe to take a loaded boat up the river, with some of the men on shore hauling it along with a rope. "When halfway up some unaccountable panic seized the steersman," wrote Rae, and "he called on the trackers to slack the line, which was no sooner done sufficiently far, than he and the bowsman sprung on shore, and permitted the boat to sheer out into midstream [where] the line snapped, and the boat driving broadside to the current was soon upset."

John Rae and Albert One-Eye ran along the riverbank, hoping that the boat would get caught in an eddy. The boat passed close to where Albert stood waiting, and he managed to hook it by the keel with an oar. Rae ran to help him. He snatched a pole from the water and jammed it into a broken plank. He called to Albert to hold on with him. Either Albert didn't hear him or thought he had a better idea. He sprang onto the capsized boat just before the current swept it towards the head of a little bay. Rae thought Albert was safe there, but in seconds he saw the boat come out of the protection of the bay, driven by the current. It began sliding beneath the surface. Albert tried to leap from the boat onto the rocks. Rae wrote later that the young man slipped and tumbled into the water, "nor did he rise again to the surface."

For Albert's death, Rae never forgave the steersman, whom he described as "a notorious thief and equally noted for falsehood." He had hoped that, once this expedition was done, he would be able to keep Albert with him when he took charge of the Mackenzie River District. Rae had told Simpson that "he would be useful in the event of it becoming desirable to have any negotiations with the Esquimaux at the mouth of the Mackenzie," and he hoped "to make him in every way a most useful man to the Company."

At Fort Confidence, Rae mourned the loss of Albert One-Eye. "This melancholy accident has distressed me more than I can well express," he wrote. "Albert was liked by everyone, for his good temper, lively disposition and great activity in doing anything that was required of him. I had become much attached to the poor fellow."

Now, on June 25, 1850, one day shy of Great Slave Lake, and while dreaming of returning home to his beloved Orkney, Rae encountered two native canoeists carrying an "extraordinary express." He went ashore to accept delivery, then sat on the banks of the broad, fast-flowing river to read three communications. The first came from George Simpson at Lachine. Searchers had found no trace of John Franklin. England grew increasingly alarmed. Simpson wanted Rae to renew his search immediately, and to travel farther north than ever before. Reeling, Rae turned to the other two letters. From London, Lady Franklin wrote in a friendly, respectful and indeed flattering manner: "[My anticipations were not] so extravagant as other people's, for it has been the custom of people to throw upon you everything that others failed to accomplish—'oh Rae's in that quarter, Rae will do that'—as if you and your single boat could explore hundreds of miles NSE & West and as if no obstacles of any kind could interfere . . . Myself, I think that your quarter is by far the most promising of any, for it is the quarter to which my husband was most distinctly . . . directed to proceed, and where I have no doubt he directed his most strenuous efforts."

Also from London, Sir Francis Beaufort, the Admiralty's chief hydrographer—England's official mapmaker—contributed a final letter: "I cannot let the mail go without telling you how intensely fixed all eyes are upon you . . . [and] upon what is yet in your power, and in yours alone, to do next season . . . Let me then, my dear Doctor, add my voice to the moans of the wives and children of the two unfortunate ships, and to the humane and energetic suggestions of your heart, and implore you to save neither money nor labour in fulfilling your holy mission. Two ships will sail in ten days for Bering Strait—others in spring for Baffin Bay. The Americans are preparing an expedition but to you I look for the solution of our melancholy suspense."

Having read the letters through, Rae walked alone along the banks of the Mackenzie. He felt as low as he had ever felt in his life. On his last expedition, he had failed not only in his main objective, finding Franklin, but even in his secondary one of reaching Wollaston Land and perhaps discovering the final link in the Northwest Passage. About Franklin, missing now for five years, nobody could hope to discover good news. Rae had been dreaming not of returning to Arctic searching, but of travelling to Orkney and then London to seek a wife. Instead of strolling around Hyde Park with a pretty girl on his arm, he would soon be battling blizzards in the fierce, unforgiving North. He stood looking over the Mackenzie River, swiping at the mosquitoes that swarmed around his head. Why, oh why, hadn't Franklin stayed home?

On the Mackenzie River, while discharging his responsibilities as chief factor, John Rae organized a two-part expedition to resume the search for Franklin—a tour de force. Come autumn, he would return north to Fort Confidence with fourteen men (and a few country wives). During the ensuing winter, he would design and build two boats. Next spring, having secured enough food through hunting and fishing, he would set out. Before the ice thawed, he would lead a few men to the Arctic coast. On snowshoes, he would cross the Dolphin and Union Strait and explore the shores of Victoria Land. He would recross that strait before spring thaw and travel to a temporary provision station on the Kendall River near the coast. There he would meet a contingent of his men, who would have dragged the two boats to that location. Then, with a larger party, he would descend the Coppermine River and, as the ice broke up, sail the boats into Coronation Gulf and beyond.

Having envisaged this two-part search, John Rae set about making it real. At Fort Confidence during the ensuing winter, Rae taught John Beads and Peter Linklater—two men of Orcadian background born in Rupert's Land—how to build igloos. These two would accompany him on the first part of the expedition. Rae also gave Hector Mackenzie, his popular, fiddle-playing second-in-command, also from Rupert's Land, detailed instructions covering every contingency. He advised him what to do, for example, if Rae himself failed to return, if he sent word of some important finding or if letters arrived announcing that Franklin had been found.

The party would carry no useless weight. While naval officers sledding in the Arctic would haul bedding weighing almost twenty-five pounds per man, Rae had reduced this by limiting himself and his companions to one blanket, one deerskin robe and two hairy deerskins. Writing to George Simpson, he had described this as "rather luxurious, being 22 lbs. weight for all, but we can easily lighten it if required."

When travelling, Rae wore Inuit-style clothing: a fur cap, large leather mitts with fur around the wrist, and moccasins made of smoked moose skin, large enough to accommodate two or three blanket socks and with thongs of skin stretched across the soles to prevent slipping. He also wore a light cloth coat with its hood and sleeves lined with leather, a cloth vest and thick moose skin trousers. He carried "a spare woolen shirt or two and a coat made of the thinnest fawn skin with the fur on, weighing not more than four or five pounds, to put on in the snow hut, or when taking observations." His personal effects consisted of a pocket comb, a toothbrush, a towel and a bit of coarse yellow soap.

With preparations complete, Rae set out on part one of his expedition. He donned his snowshoes and, on April 25, 1851, led four men and four sledges east out of Fort Confidence. Dogs hauled three of the sledges, harnessed not in rows, as was British naval practice, but in an Inuit-style fan-out. Two men hauled the fourth sledge. For the snowshoe journey, Rae carried enough pemmican and flour to last thirty-five days and enough grease to serve as cooking fuel at a rate of one pound per day. Unlike government sledging parties, his would not stop for lunch but only for a moment to take what the Hudson's Bay men called "a pipe," eating a mouthful or two of pemmican before resuming the trek.

The weather turned ugly on April 27 as Rae arrived at the Kendall River station. After huddling in an igloo through two days of stormy weather, Rae led them with his men north. The fatigue party travelled to within sixteen kilometres of the Arctic coast, doing most of the heavy hauling, and turned back on May 2. Rae pressed on with Beads and Linklater, both of whom had been born in Rupert's Land and were in their early twenties: fit men and ideal travelling companions.

On reaching the Arctic coast at Richardson Bay eight kilometres west of the mouth of the Coppermine River, Rae found the ice

John Rae identified with and learned from the native peoples, both First Nations and Inuit. This watercolour portrait, Dr. John Rae, Arctic Explorer (1862) *by William Armstrong, comes from the Glenbow Museum in Calgary.*

ahead free of hummocks and pressure ridges and not unfavourable for travelling. In the afternoon, with the sun high in the sky, the glare off the ice and snow threatened the men with snow blindness, whose victims feel as if sand has lodged in their eyes. To avoid this, Rae decided to rest during the day and travel by night, when visibility would resemble that of twilight at the lower latitudes.

Two hours before midnight, he donned snowshoes and set out across Coronation Gulf towards Wollaston Peninsula on Victoria Island. In order to examine bays, rivers and inlets while his men drove the dogs straight ahead, Rae hauled a small sledge piled with bedding, instruments, pemmican, a musket and tools for building a snow hut. After slogging along the coast, he touched land at Point Lockyer and then crossed Dolphin and Union Strait by way of Douglas Island, where he cached provisions for the return journey.

Four days out, near Cape Lady Franklin, Rae reached Wollaston Land, believed at the time to be separate from Victoria Island. Searching for the lost ships of the Franklin expedition and for a non-existent strait between Wollaston and Victoria, Rae travelled east along the coast. At one point, between observations for time and latitude, Rae shot ten hares: "These fine animals were very large and tame, and several more might have been killed, also a number of partridges, had it been requisite to waste time or ammunition in following them."

When the temperature plummeted to thirty degrees below zero Celsius, the men—one of them badly frostbitten in the face—retreated with satisfaction to their latest igloo. On May 10, Rae ventured beyond where Dease and Simpson had reached in 1839, having passed this point from the east without encountering any north-south strait. From here, he would soon resume the search by boat. Now he turned around to retrace his steps, bent on searching to the west of his landing spot.

That night, a snowstorm reduced visibility to sixty feet. Fortunately, the snowshoers had the wind at their backs. Rae found their previous track and so didn't need repeatedly to take bearings: "After a very cold but smart walk of rather more than seven hours duration, we were very glad to find ourselves snug under cover of our old quarters, our clothes being penetrated in every direction with the finely powdered snow."

The storm that raged through the next night made travel impossible, but in the morning, accompanied by the panting of dogs, the creaking of sledges and the gentle *whump whump whump* of snowshoes, Rae again headed west dragging his sledge, which weighed over thirty-five pounds. Battling rough ice and blowing snow, following the coast as it swung north, Rae came upon thirteen Inuit lodges. He chatted amicably with the inhabitants. Timid at first, they soon gained enough confidence to sell him seal meat for the dogs and boots, shoes and sealskins for the men. These Inuit, living on the west coast of Wollaston Peninsula, had seen neither white men nor sailing ships.

By May 23, with spring thaw threatening to trap the boatless party on the wrong side of Dolphin and Union Strait, Rae realized he must soon turn back. Resting in the igloo as night came on, scribbling notes by candlelight, the explorer decided to make one last sortie northward. He would travel light, bringing only Peter Linklater, the faster of the two young men, and leaving the dogs and John Beads to rest in the camp before the long return journey.

After midnight, when finally the sun dipped below the horizon, Rae shook Linklater awake. He boiled water and sipped a cup of tea, then donned his snowshoes and led the way north along the unexplored coast of Wollaston Land. Having left camp with only a compass, a sextant and a musket for protection against wolves and bears, the two men travelled fast. They walked for six hours, stopping to rest only once, briefly, at the younger man's request. At last, as the rising sun heralded the dawn, Rae rounded Cape Baring. Linklater had fallen some distance behind but the explorer forged on ahead, excited now, climbing a promontory from which, in the distance, he could see a high cape.

This impressive landmark he named Cape Back, after George Back, who in 1821, by finding a band of Yellowknife-Dene, had saved Franklin and Richardson from starving to death at Fort Enterprise. Between that cape and the promontory on which he stood, Rae could see a large body of water (Prince Albert Sound), and wondered whether it might prove to be an east–west strait. Just ten days before, on May 14, 1851, a sledge party from Robert McClure's icebound *Investigator* had reached the other side of the sound, sixty-four kilometres north—though of course Rae could not know that. He yearned to keep walking, but knew that he had run out of time.

On May 24 Rae began to retrace his steps. He verified readings, retrieved caches and encountered a few friendly Inuit hunters. None of them had seen or heard of any Europeans. Six days after turning back, and having retrieved John Beads, Rae and his two men recrossed Dolphin and Union Strait to a high rocky point north of Cape Krusenstern. By June 4, when the trio reached Richardson Bay, a layer of water on the ice confirmed that they had concluded their snowshoe and dogsled journey just in time.

Rae and his men reached the Kendall River station by trekking for five days from the coast, "during some of which we were fourteen hours on foot and continually wading through ice cold water or wet snow which was too deep to allow our Esquimaux boots to be of any use." At one point Linklater slipped and lost all the cooking utensils, plates, pans and spoons. For the last two days, the men ate from large, flat stones. They survived on geese, partridges and lemming, these last proving especially tasty when roasted over the fire or between two stones.

In his official report, Rae praised his two travelling companions. He calculated that, starting from the Kendall River, he had covered 824.5 nautical miles, or 1,516 kilometres, and he speculated, in private correspondence, that this was "perhaps the longest [journey] ever made on the arctic coast over ice."

Now came part two of the landmark expedition. On June 13, 1851, Hector Mackenzie joined Rae at Kendall River, arriving as planned from Fort Confidence with eight men and two boats. Two days later, with Mackenzie and ten men, Rae proceeded down the Kendall towards the Coppermine. Ice forced the party to wait for almost a week at the confluence. After further delays, by portaging around the impossible stretches and running the merely difficult ones, the party made it to Bloody Falls. There, by placing a net in an eddy below the falls, they caught forty salmon in fifteen minutes.

At the mouth of the Coppermine, Rae set up camp and waited for the pack ice to melt farther out on Coronation Gulf. Finally, early in July, a breeze opened a narrow channel eastward. Seizing the moment, Rae sailed thirty-five kilometres by nightfall, when ice made further progress impossible. From that point on, he proceeded along the coast by taking advantage of any open water. Progress was slow and difficult. In many places, the ice lay against the rocks, forcing the men to make portages. This work, though arduous, had fortunately become routine for the steadily improving crew.

The weather remained changeable. On the morning of July 16, as Rae and his men rounded Cape Barrow, they found themselves sailing into a torrent of rain. After they put ashore for breakfast, the weather cleared and Rae climbed a promontory. The highest rocks afforded him a discouraging view north and east across Dease Strait. As far as the eye could see, the strait lay covered by an unbroken sheet of ice—ice so thick and strong that hundreds of seals cavorted along its edges.

Rae reboarded the boats and carried on, making slow progress by following crooked lines of water through the ice. Six days beyond Cape Barrow, a stiff southeasterly breeze opened a channel towards Cape Flinders at the western point of Kent Peninsula. Nearing that cape, which Franklin had named during his first disastrous expedition, Rae spotted three Inuit hunters and put ashore. Half a dozen other Inuit watched from a nearby island.

The explorer approached the hunters, noting that they looked thinner and less well-fed than the Arctic native people he had met around Repulse Bay. The men at first appeared alarmed and fearful, and again Rae regretted the loss of Albert One-Eye. He offered the strangers trinkets, a gesture that gained their confidence. These men had never before communicated with Europeans. Using gestures, sign language and Inuktitut words and phrases that he had picked up, Rae questioned the men for half an hour. They had lived here all their lives, but no, they had seen no great ships. Nor had they seen any foreigners. Rae was the first.

Disappointed but not surprised, Rae resumed his voyage eastward. He passed Point Turnagain, where in 1821—and far too late in the season—Franklin had finally turned around and begun his desperate overland retreat. Rae reached Cape Alexander, at the eastern end of Kent Peninsula, on July 24, two days earlier than Dease and Simpson had done in 1839. From here, where Dease Strait was narrowest, Rae proposed to cross to the southern coast of Victoria Land. Soon afterwards he wrote: "Had geographical discovery been the object of the expedition, I would have followed the coast eastward to Simpson Strait and then have crossed over towards Cape Franklin [on King William Island]. This course, however, would have been a deviation from the route I had marked out for myself, and would have exposed me to the charge of having lost sight of the duty committed to me."

Ironically, indeed tragically, had Rae carried on farther east, he would probably have discovered the fate of the Franklin expedition. He might have spotted the *Erebus* or the *Terror*, one or both of which were probably still afloat, and rescued some final survivors. If he did not see either one of those vessels, then almost certainly, on the southwest coast of King William Island, he would have found frozen corpses—some under boats, others in tents, still others face down in the snow. And he might well have found journals, diaries and last letters.

But on July 27, 1851, as the winter ice began breaking up, the dutiful Rae beat north across Dease Strait to Victoria Land. He put into Cambridge Bay and, when a storm blew up, stayed for two days. Early in August, the men reached Cape Colborne. From that point east, Rae began delineating coastline that had never been charted. After travelling more than 150 kilometres without stopping except to cook, Rae reached an insurmountable ice barrier.

The shore lay barren of vegetation and even of driftwood. A tract of light grey limestone had been forced up in immense blocks close to the shore by the pressure of ice. From the north came yet another gale, with heavy squalls and showers of sleet and snow. Finally the wind fell and a lane opened up along the coast, revealing reefs.

Rounding these, Rae emerged into open water, set close-reefed sails and beat onwards through an ugly, chopping sea. The slightly built boats strained and heaved as pounding waves washed over them, but eventually Rae entered a snug cove and secured them.

On August 5, in heavy weather, Rae passed high limestone cliffs rutted with deep snow. A thick, cold fog came on, encrusting the boats with ice, so he landed and broke out tents. As evening came on, the men forced their way forward for another five kilometres, pulling and poling against ever-thicker ice. Finally, just north of Albert Edward Bay, the boats ground to a halt.

For the next two days, a relentless northeast wind kept the ice close to the shore and showed no signs of changing. Rae decided to press ahead overland. What if Franklin had reached the coast directly ahead? Or what if the waterway Rae had seen on the west coast of Wollaston Land was in fact a strait that emerged just ahead, providing a final link in the Passage?

Just before noon on August 12, with three men, his trusty musket and enough food to last four days, Rae began hiking north. "Hoping to avoid the sharp and ragged limestone debris with which the coast was lined," he wrote, "we at first kept some miles inland, without however gaining much advantage, as the country was intersected with lakes, to get round which we had to make long detours. Nor was the ground much more favourable for travelling than that nearer the beach; in fact, it was as bad as it well could be, in proof of which I may mention that, in two hours, a pair of new moccasins, with thick undressed buffalo skin soles, and stout duffle socks were completely worn out, and before the day's journey was half done every step I took was marked with blood."

When Rae got back to the boats, he deposited a note in a cairn. It summarized his expedition and mentioned that he had explored the coast to thirty-five miles (fifty-six kilometres) north from this point. Two years later, in May of 1853, a sledging party from HMS *Enterprise*, wintering in Cambridge Bay under Captain Richard Collinson, would find it.

Early on August 15, 1851, with a fierce wind blowing from the north-northeast and the boats in danger if the wind shifted to the east, Rae sailed back a few kilometres to a safer harbour. There he waited for any favourable change in the wind and ice that would allow him to use the shelter of Admiralty Island (which he had named the previous week) to cross Victoria Strait to what he called "Point Franklin" on King William Land—by which he meant a promontory between Victory Point and Cape Crozier.

If Rae had managed to cross Victoria Strait to this point, again he would have discovered the fate of Franklin: this is the region in which many of Franklin's men died while struggling south along the coast of King William Island. It was not to be, however. Late that morning, Rae sailed out into the strait, but the breeze increased to a gale and shifted to the east. Facing a great accumulation of ice, Rae sought shelter in the lee of a point. The following morning, when the wind subsided, he tried once again to push across to Admiralty Island, but the ice was worse than ever.

Four days later and some kilometres farther south, Rae made a third attempt to force a passage eastward to King William Land. But after eight kilometres, he reached a wall of close-packed ice and that left him no choice but to turn back. Rae could not know it, but the conditions he encountered recur even today, because pack ice breaking off from the polar cap travels south down the broad McClintock Channel and jams into the narrower Victoria Strait. Ironically, the Canadian expedition that in 2014 located the *Erebus* did so only because heavy ice prevented its ships from searching this area.

In 1851, unable to reach King William Island, Rae proceeded southwest. On August 21, while creeping along the shore of what he called Parker Bay, Rae chanced upon a length of pinewood. He examined it with growing excitement. This was not driftwood but a piece of man-made pole. Almost six feet long, three and one-half inches in diameter, and round except for the bottom twelve inches, which were square, it appeared to be the butt end of a small flagstaff. It was stamped on one side with an indecipherable marking, and a bit of white line had been tacked to the pole near the bottom, forming a loop for signal halyards. Both the white line and the copper tacks bore the marks of the British government: a red worsted thread, the "rogue's yarn," ran through the white line, and a broad arrow was stamped on the underside of the head of the copper tacks.

Rae was still carefully describing this pole in his journal and had not travelled more than a few hundred metres when the two boats came upon another stick of wood lying in the water, touching the beach. This one was a piece of oak almost four feet long and three inches in diameter, with a hole in the upper end. This post or stanchion had been formed in a wring lathe. The bottom was square, and Rae deduced from a broad rust mark that it had been fitted into an iron clasp.

Anticipating a debate over the sources of these pieces of wood, Rae offered his analysis in his official report, and so became the first explorer to identify Victoria Land as an island. Citing the flood tide from the north, he argued that a wide channel must separate Victoria Land from North Somerset Island and that these pieces of wood had been swept down this channel along with the immense quantities of creeping ice. In his rough notes, though not in his report, Rae wrote of the two poles, "They may be portions of one of Sir John Franklin's ships. God grant that the crews are safe."

Like the vast majority of naval experts, Rae believed that the lost expedition would be found far to the north. His discovery of the two pieces of wood did not change his opinion. He correctly guessed the direction from which the broken pieces had come, but overestimated the distance they had travelled.

With these broken pieces of wood, John Rae became the first explorer to discover relics from one of the Franklin ships after it had got trapped in the ice. In his official report, he confined himself to description. After carefully stowing away the wood, the copper tacks and the line, Rae turned his attention to the wind and the waves.

From Parker Bay, Rae made excellent time sailing west. On August 29, he crossed Coronation Gulf and found the Coppermine River raging. When the water did not fall for two days, Rae proclaimed confidence in the skill of his men and started up the river. The ledges of rock that ran along the base of the cliffs lay hidden beneath the driving current, so tracking meant walking along the top of the cliffs. The men's strongest cord snapped four times, and so they entered the pounding river to shove the boat over the rocks. After five days of furious work, the party made camp at the Kendall River, the worst of the trek behind them.

A few days later, on September 10, 1851, Rae and his men regained Fort Confidence. Finding everything in order and more than three thousand pounds of dried provisions in store, Rae instructed Hector Mackenzie to close the post and pay the men, specifying bonuses and gratuities. Later, his superiors would complain of his generosity.

During his snowshoe sortie, Rae had trekked 1,740 kilometres, one of the longest such expeditions ever made over Arctic ice. He had immediately followed this with a second stunning achievement. His summer voyage east and then north along Victoria Island, during which he sailed 2,235 kilometres while charting 1,015 kilometres of unexplored coastline, stands in comparison with the Dease and Simpson voyage of 1838–39, which set an Arctic standard for small-boat travel. In addition to these physical and geographical accomplishments, Rae had discovered the first relics from the Franklin expedition.

The day after he arrived at Fort Confidence, having completed one of the most remarkable Arctic expeditions of all time, John Rae set out southward to enjoy his hard-earned leave of absence. He was bound for Orkney and nothing was going to stop him.

17.

Robert McClure Narrowly Escapes Disaster

On April 18, 1851, while John Rae was organizing his epic two-part expedition at Great Bear Lake, roughly five hundred kilometres to the north, with his ship *Investigator* locked in the ice of Prince of Wales Strait, Captain Robert John Le Mesurier McClure was dispatching three exploratory sledge parties. On May 14, 1851, when Rae was trekking westward along the south coast of Victoria Island, one of McClure's sledge parties—led by William Haswell—reached the north side of Prince Albert Sound. Ten days later, when Rae reached the south side of that same sound, McClure was compiling the data from his sledging team and waiting impatiently for the ice to clear so he could resume his voyage, complete the Northwest Passage and revel in the ensuing fame and fortune.

Robert McClure had been born in 1807 into an Irish family with military connections. He tried the army but at seventeen, seeing where the excitement was, moved to the Royal Navy. He served on anti-slavery patrols in the Caribbean and rose quickly through the ranks. In 1836–37, he ventured to the Arctic as mate on the *Terror* under George Back, an expedition that narrowly survived a sustained battle with Arctic ice. In 1848, after serving in North America and the Caribbean, he joined the Franklin search as first lieutenant on the *Enterprise* under captain James Clark Ross—an expedition that, impeded by heavy ice, spent one winter at Port Leopold, on the northeast coast of Somerset Island, and managed only to investigate 250 kilometres of coastline.

Two years later, the Admiralty decided to send two ships into the Arctic from the Pacific. Under the overall command of Richard Collinson in the *Enterprise*, McClure took charge of the *Investigator*. The ships ended up sailing separately, and failed to rendezvous in Honolulu, missing each other by a single day. McClure took a dangerous shortcut through the Aleutian Islands and, on July 31, 1850, arrived in Bering Strait ahead of Collinson. Instead of waiting, as a senior naval officer in another ship recommended, the ambitious McClure kept sailing. On August 7, the *Investigator* became the first exploring ship to round Point Barrow and enter the Beaufort Sea.

With the help of Moravian missionary Johann Miertsching, who had learned Inuktitut during five years in Labrador, McClure interviewed local Inuit, none of whom had any news of Franklin. The expedition's primary objective—though not McClure's—was to obtain intelligence about the lost expedition of Sir John Franklin. To that end, the men hoped to capture foxes alive in traps. They would fit them with special copper collars stamped with the positions of ships and supplies and then release them, hoping that one might be caught by Franklin's men.

Like other expeditions, this one carried gilt metal "rescue buttons" with words pointing to key locations. These the men would give to any Inuit they encountered, hoping they might wear them and attract the notice of any Franklin survivors. As well, McClure periodically released hydrogen-filled balloons that carried messages on pieces of brightly coloured paper. In short, the search was reduced to desperate measures.

Richard Collinson, nominal commander of the expedition, ran into heavy ice in Bering Strait and retreated for the winter to Hong Kong. McClure had already sailed eastward past the mouth of the Mackenzie River. Alone, he lacked the safety of a supporting vessel. With ice forming along the coast, he struck northeast between Victoria Island and Banks Island into Prince of Wales Strait.

The eastern end of that strait was (and often still is) blocked year-round by pack ice moving slowly south from the permanent polar ice cap. Halted by ice late in September, McClure settled in to winter in the strait. During the last ten days of October, with one other man, McClure sledged about fifty-five kilometres to the north coast of Banks Island. Looking out across an ice-choked channel a hundred kilometres wide (now called McClure Strait), he saw Melville Island, which William Edward Parry had reached from the Atlantic in 1819. This viewing across impenetrable ice, he would later argue—and, for its own reasons, the Admiralty would concur—constituted a discovery of the Northwest Passage.

Spring 1851 brought the sledge journeys cited above. Early in June, when John Rae was completing his snowshoe expedition across Dolphin and Union Strait, McClure and Miertsching travelled south to the entrance of Prince of Wales Strait and interviewed local Inuit, who assured them that Victoria Island was indeed one and indivisible. Back at the ship, after trying and again failing to push north, McClure retreated southward and then swung north around Banks Island.

At Mercy Bay on the northeast coast, his ship again became trapped by the same perennial flow of pack ice. The winter months

Created by Samuel Gurney Cresswell and William Simpson, this image— Critical Position of HMS *Investigator* on the North Coast of Baring Island, August 20, 1851—*speaks to the navigability of the Northwest Passage claimed by Robert McClure. This "passage" was not viable.*

did not pass quickly. In the spring of 1852, commencing on April 11, McClure and one other man sledged across the ice of McClure Strait to Melville Island, where Edward Parry had spent months at "Winter Harbour." He left a note at "Parry's Rock," a huge block of sandstone, giving his ship's coordinates. Back he went to the entrapped *Investigator*, which, while never a happy ship, now grew increasingly grim and desperate.

During the winter of 1852–53, with sailors already struggling to survive on reduced rations, the ship became a frozen hell of floggings, imprisonments, starvation, scurvy, and even, for a few, miserable deaths. Almost uniquely for this era, McClure was given to placing certain officers—notably, first lieutenant William Haswell—under arrest for extended periods. Several times, he ordered that men be given forty-eight lashes, the navy-mandated maximum.

Early in 1853, with his ship still beset and most of his hungry men suffering dreadfully from scurvy, McClure conceived a sinister plan to rid himself of his thirty sickest crew members, who insisted on consuming their short rations of food. He proposed to send them south and east to seek help in two separate sledge parties, both radically undersupplied. He and the healthiest men would remain with the ship to await further developments.

In April of that year, when he was mere days from enacting this plan, a sailor from HMS *Resolute*, part of a search expedition trapped ninety-five kilometres away off Melville Island, came upon the *Investigator*. Someone had found his note at Winter Harbour. McClure refused to abandon ship until he was ordered to do so by a senior officer, who gave the command only after a surgeon visited the *Investigator* and saw the shocking condition of those "volunteering" to remain. Then, McClure and his crew of walking skeletons sledged and stumbled across the frozen ice pack to the *Resolute*, which had entered Arctic waters from the Atlantic. The truth of the situation, as William James Mills writes in *Exploring Polar Frontiers*, "was that a disaster of near Franklinian proportions had been avoided only by the narrowest of margins."

Originally, as McClure well knew, a monetary reward had been offered for completing the Northwest Passage by actually sailing a ship from one ocean to the other, Atlantic to Pacific or vice versa. Having abandoned his ship under protest, McClure could later insist that he would have completed the Passage had he been left to his own devices. He argued, further, that walking and sledging across the ice for some distance, and then returning home in another ship, constituted a discovery of the Northwest Passage.

Of course it did—but only if we accept that walking across an impassable channel choked with heavy ice constitutes a legitimate fulfillment of the original objective. A century would elapse before anyone managed to sail through McClure Strait, as it was dubbed, north of Banks Island. In 1954, as part of the Canadian–U.S. Beaufort Sea Expedition, an American icebreaker, the USCGC *Northwind*, became the first ship to transit the Passage through there. Ten years before, while attempting that route, the Canadian schooner *St. Roch* had been forced to beat southwest through Prince of Wales Strait.

In 2010, Canadian archaeologists found the wreck of McClure's *Investigator* in Mercy Bay, precisely where he abandoned it. The ship sat eight metres below the surface. Today, first-time visitors to Beechey Island often puzzle over why they see four graves and headboards arranged in a line, given that only three men from the Franklin expedition are known to be buried there. The fourth marks the grave of able seaman Thomas Morgan, who died in 1854. He had managed to get off the *Investigator*, but was already so sick that he did not survive. He was one of the men McClure had earlier singled out to go on a death march.

18.

Greenlandic Inuit Save the Kane Expedition

L ate in May 1853, while Robert McClure was trapped in the western Arctic, Elisha Kent Kane sailed on his second voyage out of New York City. On returning from Beechey Island, the articulate, charismatic young doctor had secured the leadership of the Second Grinnell Expedition to sail in search of Franklin. In keeping with prevailing geographical theory, he believed that Franklin and some of his men might yet be alive in the mammal-rich Open Polar Sea at the top of the world. In September, he sailed the small, wooden *Advance*—26 metres, 144 tons—into Smith Sound, achieving a new farthest north and getting locked into the ice at a bay he named Rensselaer, after his grandmother's family.

Here, before he orchestrated a difficult escape, Kane would endure two horrendous winters of endless darkness and cold, with temperatures hovering around thirty-two degrees below zero Celsius. Starting with twenty men and fifty dogs on board, Kane sought to avert sickness with good hygiene. To avoid scurvy, he regularly mustered the men for health inspection, and also checked and cleaned the living quarters. Running low on meat, he relied on cabbage, and then raw potatoes and lime juice. Even so, men began

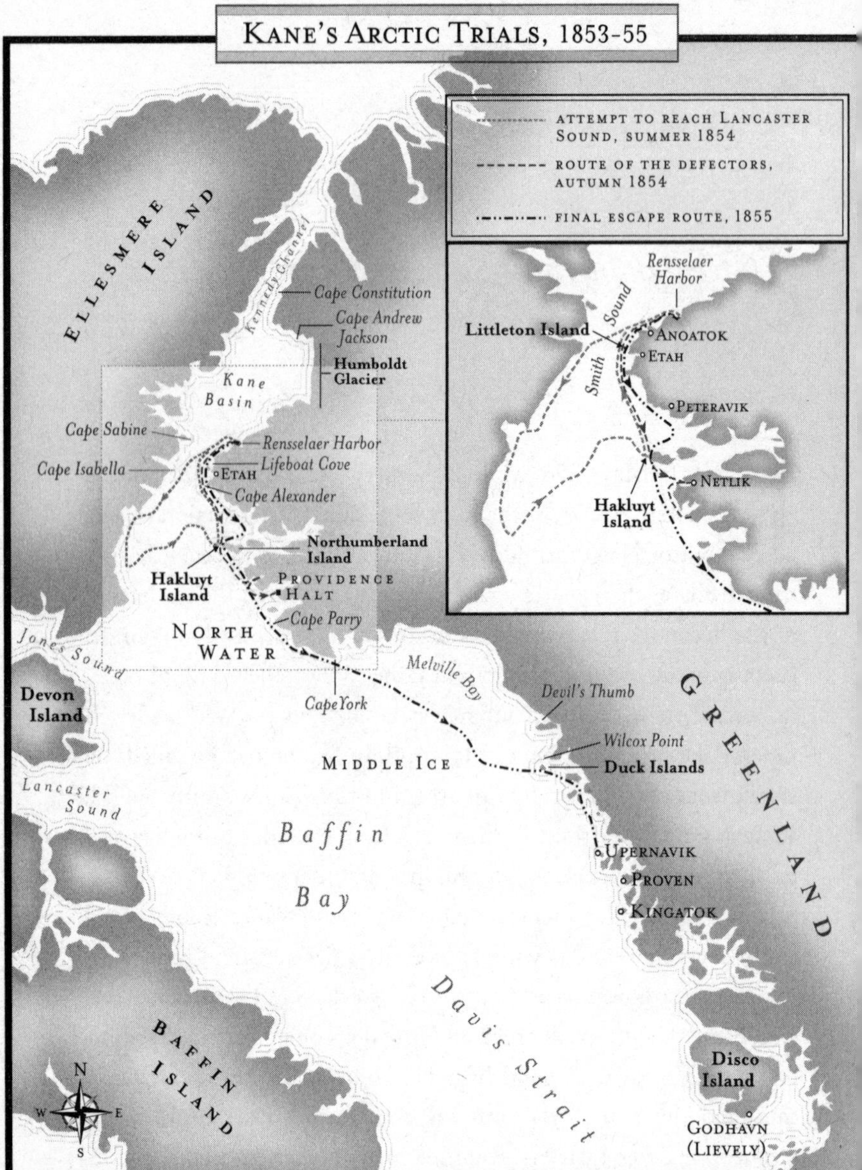

KANE'S ARCTIC TRIALS, 1853-55
ATTEMPT TO REACH LANCASTER SOUND, SUMMER 1854
ROUTE OF THE DEFECTORS, AUTUMN 1854
FINAL ESCAPE ROUTE, 1855
ELLESMERE ISLAND
Kennedy Channel
Cape Constitution
Cape Andrew Jackson
Humboldt Glacier
Kane Basin
Cape Sabine
Rensselaer Harbor
Cape Isabella
Lifeboat Cove
ETAH
Cape Alexander
Northumberland Island
Hakluyt Island
PROVIDENCE HALT
Cape Parry
NORTH WATER
Jones Sound
Devon Island
Cape York
Melville Bay
Devil's Thumb
Wilcox Point
Duck Islands
MIDDLE ICE
Lancaster Sound
Baffin Bay
UPERNAVIK
PROVEN
KINGATOK
GREENLAND
Davis Strait
BAFFIN ISLAND
Disco Island
GODHAVN (LIEVELY)
N
W
E
S
Rensselaer Harbor
Littleton Island
Smith Sound
ANOATOK
ETAH
PETERAVIK
NETLIK
Hakluyt Island

showing symptoms of scurvy—sore joints, swollen gums, patchy discolorations on the skin.

Kane lost two men after exposure and frost turned their feet black. After enduring amputations, one of them died of tetanus, the other of a bacterial infection. Kane buried them with due ceremony, walling them into a cave on a rocky island. He then had to deal with a near-mutiny. A number of malcontents defected in an attempt to scramble over the ice to Upernavik in northern Greenland. They abandoned him with a few active men and several ailing comrades. The defection, lacking leadership, ended in near-starvation and an ignominious return to the ship.

By then, thanks to the help of his Inuk interpreter, Hans Hendrik, Kane had established an enduring alliance with the Inuit who lived at Etah, roughly eighty kilometres south. Without that alliance, neither Kane nor any of his men would have returned alive to New York City.

Hans Christian Hendrik (Suersaq), born in 1834 in Fiskernaes, southern Greenland, would prove invaluable to several Arctic expeditions. He was nineteen years old when, in 1853, Kane called in at his hometown, looking to add an Inuit interpreter and hunter. The local superintendent recommended Hendrik as an expert with kayak and javelin. On meeting the chubby young man, Kane grew skeptical. But then the laid-back Inuk, he wrote later, "as stolid and unimpressible as any of our Indians," demonstrated his value by spearing a bird on the wing.

Kane not only agreed to pay Hendrik a modest wage, and to leave his mother two barrels of bread and fifty-two pounds of salt pork, but "became munificent in his eyes when I added the gift of a rifle and a new kayak." Years later, Hendrik would corroborate this account in *Memoirs of Hans Hendrik, the Arctic Traveller*. He wrote the manuscript "in tolerably plain and intelligible Greenlandish," according to first translator Henry Rink, and explained that he decided to join up when he learned that Kane would pay his mother. His father, assistant to the three priests in the community, had died the previous year. His mother begged him not to go, he reports: "But I replied, 'If no mischief happen to me, I shall return, and I shall earn money for you.'"

Kane sailed into Smith Sound and, as noted above, settled in for the winter, expecting to depart the next spring. The constant darkness took a toll. In mid-November, Hendrik declared that he could no longer tolerate such a confined and miserable existence. He bundled up his clothes, took his rifle and prepared to leave. Later, in his published memoir, he would write: "Never had I seen the dark

PORTRAIT OF HANS.

Hans Hendrik (Suersaq) was nineteen years old when he came aboard the Advance *at Fiskernaes, southern Greenland. He would prove invaluable. Sketch by Elisha Kent Kane.*

season like this. To be sure it was awful. I thought we should have no daylight any more. I was seized with fright, and fell a weeping. I never in my life saw such darkness at noon time. As the darkness continued for three months, I really believed we should have no daylight more."

Hendrik remained on the ship after talking with Kane. The commander ascertained that the young man yearned after "one of the softer sex at Fiskernaes," and noted that "he looked as wretched as any lover of a milder clime." Kane gave him a dose of salts and a key promotion: "He has now all the dignity of a henchman. He harnesses my dogs, builds my traps, and walks with me on my ice-tramps; and, except hunting, is excused all other duty. He is really attached to me, and as happy as a fat man ought to be." Kane's response to Hendrik, who had difficulty adjusting to a shipboard existence, led one jealous seaman to refer to the youth as "the captain's pet Eskimo."

In April 1854, while Kane sat below deck with a man dying of tetanus, he heard strange sounds coming from the nearby shore. He climbed into the sunlight to see figures "on all sides of the rocky harbor, dotting the snow-shores and emerging from the bleakness of the cliffs, wild and uncouth." Inuit hunters had climbed onto the highest fragments of land ice to stand waving and calling out "singly and conspicuously, like the figures in a tableau of the opera."

Hans Hendrik was away hunting. But soon he returned and found he could communicate with these people, who lived farther north even than those John Ross had encountered some four decades before. At first, Hendrik wrote later, "I feared they might be murderers, as they lived apart from any [Christian Greenlanders]; but, on the contrary, they were harmless men."

After some initial misunderstandings—pushing, shoving, pilfering, and then some brazen robbery—Kane negotiated a solemn treaty. Through Hendrik, the Inuit agreed to steal no more, and also to lead the sailors to finding animals. In return, the white men would release three hunters they had captured thieving, and use their guns to shoot game on joint expeditions.

As a result of this friendship treaty, the sailors and the Inuit began hunting together. "I can hardly say how valuable the advice of our Esquimaux friends has been to us upon our hunts," Kane would write. "Every movement of ice or wind or season is noted, and they predicted its influence upon the course of the birds of passage with the same sagacity that has taught them the habits of the resident animals."

Kane's vivid descriptions of Arctic wildlife resonate with contemporary implications. He describes hunting birds, seals and walrus, all now seriously depleted in numbers, and incidentally waxes eloquent about the strength of polar bears. He relates, for example, how several bears ravaged a cache of provisions, smashing open iron caskets, and tossing aside boulders that had tested the strength of three men.

During the second winter, with the ship still locked solid, the people of Etah retreated into two large huts buried in snow, completely enclosed except for vent holes. At one point, Kane lived among them for a week. While joining in settlement life, he also functioned as an ethnographer. In his book *Arctic Explorations*, Kane would devote more than twenty pages to describing habits and customs, touching on everything from eating utensils to mourning rituals, religious beliefs and the perquisites of the Nalegak-soak, or head chief, who enjoyed "the questionable privilege of having as many wives as he could support."

Kane's detailed depictions of clothes, sledges, weapons, housing and habits provide a unique opportunity to juxtapose today and yesterday. Unlike some others, this gentleman from Philadelphia proved humble enough to learn from hunter-gatherers who had been born into a tradition of Arctic survival.

An excellent artist, Kane drew sketches that later he developed into etchings for his book. At some point, using musical notation, and as evidenced in the archives at the American Philosophical Society, he went so far as to transcribe "An Eskimo Round" for six voices.

Over a period of several months, Kane would add to these sketches, producing detailed descriptions and drawings of life among the Inuit. One historian, L. H. Neatby, would suggest that these writings "make the most interesting part of his *Arctic Explorations*." For many southerners, in that age before even movies or photos, Kane created the conventional image of the "Eskimo."

During the second winter of entrapment, Kane wrote in his journal: "I have determined to borrow a lesson from our Esquimaux neighbours, and am turning the brig into an igloo." Praising Inuit housing and diet as "the safest and best to which the necessity of our circumstances invited us," Kane put his men to work prying moss and turf from the rocks and applying this material to the quarterdeck for warmth. Below decks, he created a large room roughly eighteen feet square, with interior walls again of moss and turf.

Having analyzed the functional ingenuity of the *tossut*, or narrow entrance-tunnel, to the conventional igloo, which keeps heat loss to a minimum, Kane got Christian Ohlsen, the carpenter, to create a similar entrance to the cabin from the much colder hold of the vessel. The winter quarters lacked "the dignity of a year ago," the captain wrote, but he and his men had become warriors under siege, hunkered down in a "casemate" or bunker, with all their energies "concentrated against the enemy outside."

Recognizing that Inuit attire suited the climate, Kane took to wearing bird-skin socks and fur boots; a fox-skin jumper, or loose-fitting shirt with an airtight hood; and bear-skin breeches, though he altered these to shelter those "parts which in the civilized countries are shielded most carefully." Outdoors, he learned to use "a fox's tail held between the teeth to protect the nose in the wind."

By forging a cross-cultural alliance with the help of Hendrik, Kane not only saved the lives of most of his men but set an example that is still remembered among the Inuit of Greenland. In the 1980s, after criticizing several other explorers for their arrogance and insensitivity, the Frenchman Jean Malaurie would hail the "extraordinary agreements" Kane made with the Inuit, and observe that "the favorable memory that Kane has left among my Eskimo friends is vague, certainly, but tenacious."

In the spring of 1855, when the ice showed no signs of breaking up, Kane developed a detailed escape plan. Around mid-May, when the cold grew less intense, he would lead the men in dragging boats along the ice-belt, and then over the pack ice of Smith Sound—a difficult trek of perhaps 110 kilometres. The men would then climb into boats and sail south, and so complete a journey "of alternating ice and water of more than thirteen hundred miles [two thousand kilometres]." At least four of the men would have to be carried—three because of amputations, and one as a result of a frost wound.

To the men, Kane offered an optimistic analysis. The hunting would soon improve, and collectively they would conquer scurvy with fresh meat. Warmer weather would enable them to reach Etah. It would also allow them to clean the cabin, filthy from lampblack, and to dry and air their fetid sleeping gear. Also, he exhorted the men to stick together. Only by doing so could they meet the challenges that lay ahead. Already he had begun sorting through documents and records, selecting those he must preserve. He set the men to working on clothing, boots, bedding and provisions, and kept them busy cutting up and stitching canvas and skins.

With the *Advance* still locked in the ice, Kane took Hendrik and a few others to check how far the ice pack extended. Near Littleton Island, they spotted a great number of ducks, and tracked their flight to a rugged little ledge so thick with wild fowl that a man could not walk without stepping on a nest. The men killed a couple of hundred birds for food. A rocky island crowded with gulls proved especially productive, and Kane named it "Hans Island."

Hendrik was by far the best hunter on the expedition. At one point, with most of the men sick and provisions nearly gone, Kane wrote: "If Hans gives way, God help us." Back on the ship, Kane sent Hendrik to seek help from Etah. Before long, he reported that the young man arrived with fresh food, three fellow hunters and much to relate: "To men in our condition," Kane wrote, "Hans was as a man from the cities." After spending one night at Anoatok, Hendrik had reached Etah late the next day. He was welcomed—but found himself surrounded by "lean figures of misery." The people of Etah, too, had endured famine, and been reduced even to eating twenty-six of their thirty dogs.

When Hendrik proposed a walrus hunt, his listeners rolled their eyes. They had tried repeatedly to kill walrus. But when the sea is frozen, that crafty creature can only be taken at an ice hole. With a harpoon, this was proving an insurmountable challenge, because even a struck walrus could escape into the water. In response, Hendrik showed the people Kane's rifle, and demonstrated what it could do. They dug out a sledge and harnessed the last four dogs. During the ensuing hunt, the men harpooned and shot not only a walrus, which took five musket balls, but also two seals.

Soon after the three hunters left, Hendrik approached Kane "with a long face" and asked permission to travel south to acquire some walrus hide for boots. He declined the offer of dogs, insisting that the weather was fine and that he could walk the eighty or ninety kilometres to Etah. The commander consented—but then waited in vain for his return.

For a while Kane worried. But from other visitors, he gleaned that Hendrik had formed an attachment to a young woman named Mersuk, the daughter of Shanghu. "Hans was a favorite with all," Kane wrote later, "the fair especially, and, as a match, one of the greatest men in the country." He continued to inquire after him, because "independent of everything like duty, I was very fond of him."

Later, Hans Hendrik wrote that he doubted his companions would ever reach Upernavik. While visiting Etah, he fell sick, and the local men "behaved so kindly towards me, I began to think of remaining with them." Still, he says that when he went off for the last time, he intended to return. But the men of Etah "began persuading me to remain. My companions would never reach Upernavik, they said, and they would take me along with them when they removed."

Still, he adds, "it was my intention to return. But I began to envy the natives with whom I stayed, who supplied themselves with all their wants and lived happily." Eventually, he writes, "I got a sweetheart whom I resolved never to part with, but to keep as my wife in the country of the Christians. Since then, she has been baptized and partaken of the Lord's Supper." This was Mersuk, who became the mother of his children.

Now, Kane wrote that some of his men were "fearfully down." But thanks to the meat provided by Hans and the other Inuit hunters, most began shaking off scurvy. Forced to burn even the ship's beams for fuel, Kane had preserved just enough wood to build two sledges seventeen and a half feet in length. Late in April, he set a departure date. Starting on May 17, using the new sledges, the men would drag the two whaleboats south to open water beyond Etah.

They would use a smaller sledge to haul the tiny *Red Eric*. From water's edge, they would set sail for Upernavik.

Kane himself would use a dogsled to ferry food and equipment as far as Anoatok, an abandoned Inuit hunting camp, halfway to Etah, that would serve as a staging post. Four of the other men could not walk. These Kane would transport by dogsled, first to Anoatok, and then to the edge of the ice pack. With preparations progressing, Kane assembled his officers and announced that he would make one final attempt to search northward for any trace of John Franklin, possibly still trapped behind a great ring of ice in the Open Polar Sea.

So far, the expedition had identified Kennedy Channel, which runs between Greenland and Ellesmere Island and today forms part of "the American route to the Pole." As well, Kane had discovered the largest glacier in the northern hemisphere, and named it after scientist Alexander von Humboldt. In April, after a final northward sortie, Kane closed "the operations of the search" for Franklin.

Focusing exclusively on the projected evacuation, and determined to avoid anything resembling the debacle that ended the mutiny, Kane organized everything from the cooking apparatus to the arms and ammunition. He put Ohlsen in charge of the boats. Despite the man's unparalleled abilities as a carpenter, however, and some capable assistance, nobody could confidently declare even one of the three vessels seaworthy.

The two whaleboats—twenty feet long, seven wide, three deep—had been battered by exposure to snow and ice. Ohlsen had reinforced the bottoms and fitted them with a neat housing of light canvas. And he had provided each of them with a mast that could be unshipped and carried with the oars, boathooks and ice poles. Yet the planking of both remained so dry that it could hardly be made tight by caulking. The third boat, the little *Red Eric*, was small enough to be mounted on the old sledge, the *Faith*, and could eventually be cut up for firewood.

With departure looming, Kane allowed the men twenty-four hours to select eight pounds of personal effects. Each man had woollen underclothes and a complete fur suit in the Inuit style, including *kapetah, nessak* and *nannooke*, or shirt, hood and trousers. Each had two pairs of boots, extra socks and a rue-raddy, a long canvas strap for hauling, adjusted to the proper length. Kane had also stipulated Inuit-style goggles to protect against snow blindness; sleeping bags of buffalo fur; eiderdown quilts covered in waterproof canvas; and canvas bags for personal effects, all of them numbered to avoid confusion.

On Sunday, May 20, 1855, Kane summoned all hands into the dismantled winter cabin to say a formal goodbye to the brig. The moss walls had been torn down and the wood supports burned. Most of the bedding had been stored on the boats and the galley sat cold and empty. In these bleak surroundings, Kane said a prayer, read a chapter from the Bible and took down the inspirational portrait of Sir John Franklin. Having removed the picture from its frame, he cased it for protection in an India rubber scroll. To a stanchion near the foot of the gangway, Kane fixed a note justifying the abandonment of the vessel, and explaining that "a third winter would force us . . . [to] give up all hope of remaining by the vessel and her resources. It would therefore in no manner advance the search after Sir John Franklin."

After saying a temporary goodbye to the four invalids who could not walk and would, for a while, remain on the brig, all the other hands went up on deck. Kane hoisted and saluted the American flag, and then hauled it down for the last time. He dispensed with further

Kane and his men had to haul their boats across a massive field of ice. As the weather warmed and the ice began to melt, the journey south became increasingly hazardous.

ceremony. He believed that cheers would be a mockery and, lacking alcohol, proposed no final toast. "When all hands were quite ready," he would write, "we scrambled off over the ice together, much like a gang of stevedores going to work over a quayful of broken cargo."

Determined to maintain discipline, the lack of which had doomed the defection, Elisha Kent Kane established clear lines of control. He assigned each man a fixed place in the drag lines, and ordered everyone except the whaleboat captains to take a turn at cooking. Recognizing that six worn-down men could not hope to haul the heavily laden sledges, Kane stipulated that the entire party would haul first one sledge and then the other. They would slog five kilometres to accomplish one, fifteen to advance three.

By May 24, the men had moved both whaleboats eleven kilometres south. That night, instead of returning to the brig, they began a routine of sleeping beside the boats beneath canvas housing. The next day, having patched and caulked the *Red Eric*, three men hauled it across the ice and entered it into the rotation. Temperatures remained below zero, though now the sun scarcely set. To avoid glare, the men slept by day and travelled through the twilight hours.

Kane began moving the four invalids to Anoatok, one by one. Using six dogs and a light sledge, he also shuttled provisions from the brig until the total weight reached fifteen hundred pounds— as much as the two whaleboats could carry. And now some Inuit friends from Etah, having discovered the evacuation in progress, had begun lending a hand without being asked. Already, an older man, Nessark, had used his dogs to transport supplies, and helped Kane bake bread on the brig.

With the sun climbing higher each day, temperatures rose and the ice-belt running along the coast grew soft. On June 5, the sledge carrying the *Hope* crashed through the ice and dragged six men into the water. They managed to crawl onto the ice, but Kane began to worry that he might be cut off from the relief hut at Anoatok. He set about moving the stores forward to two temporary stations.

Soon, heavy snow and widening chasms rendered the ice-belt almost impassable. Driven out onto the floes, Kane saw with growing concern that the ice had become sodden and stained with water from below. Besides the loads in transit, nearly nine hundred pounds of provisions remained at Anoatok, and two hundred pounds more, including shot and bullet bags, waited to be removed from another location.

Kane decided to ask the people of Etah to lend him two of their four dogs. He sent word ordering the invalids at Anoatok to be ready for instant removal and pressed on to Etah, arriving near midnight, with the sun low in the sky. Despite the temperature, twenty degrees below zero Celsius, he found thirty people gathered outside on the bare rocks. Melting snow had reduced their huts to a shambles, so now they camped out, variously socializing, sleeping, cooking auks or chomping on bird skins.

After spending the night, Kane left his tired dogs and took the settlement's only team in unequal exchange. Old Nessark piled Kane's sledge with walrus meat, and two young men came part way to assist him through a stretch of broken ice. Later, in *Arctic Explorations*, Kane would remember familiar figures with melancholy: "It pains me when I think of their approaching destiny—in the region of night and winter, where the earth yields no fruit and the waters are locked—without the resorts of skill or even the rude materials of art, and walled in from the world by barriers of ice without an outlet."

Kane also prepared a census, "exactly confirmed by three separate informants," that identified 140 souls scattered along almost a thousand kilometres of coast from the Great River near Cape Melville to the wind-loved hut of Anoatok. Within this narrow range, he wrote, the people exist "in love and community of resources as a single family." They situated their huts one dog-march apart. They named each rock and hill, so even the youngest hunter could go to retrieve a cache of meat deposited anywhere in the region.

But now, Kane had no time to reflect. From Etah, with fresh dogs and a sledge-load of meat, he raced back to the whaleboats, which had arrived within five kilometres of Anoatok. Warmer weather, improved hunting and diet, and increased exercise had made all the men healthier—but also hungrier. Some food remained on the brig, and Kane managed to retrieve that.

Increasingly fearful of getting cut off from Anoatok, Kane began shuttling invalids from there to the whaleboats. The next day, one of his men returned from Etah with several Inuit, sledges piled with meat and blubber, and every sound dog that remained. Once again, Kane controlled a serviceable dog team: "The comfort and security of such a possession to men in our critical position can hardly be realized," he would write. "It was more than an addition of ten strong men to our party."

From the *Advance*, Kane fetched the last bit of burnable pork fat, so necessary to the looming boat journey. Then, from Anoatok, he retrieved the sick men. Travelling along beneath the cliffs, he marvelled at the dramatic changes in the landscape. The hot sun released rocks that had been frozen into the ice, and they rolled down the debris-strewn slopes "with the din of a battle-field . . . clogging the ice-belt at the foot."

On June 16, 1855, after losing one man to the ice in a sledging accident, Kane and his crew began stowing cargo in their boats at the mouth of the bay near Etah, fewer than two kilometres from open water. The men had been steadily hauling for one month, except for a brief spell when, with a breeze blowing from the north, they had managed to sail across a stretch of smooth ice, using the long steering oars as booms. Thrilling to this new sensation, the men had broken into song: "Storm along, my hearty boys!"

But mostly they had slogged ahead, battling hummocks and snowdrifts with capstan bars and levers, or proceeding carefully over "salt ice marshes" scattered with threatening black pools. Without the help of the Inuit, Kane wrote, the escape might have foundered. The local people supplied the visitors with enormous numbers of small auks, which men and dogs together consumed at a rate of eight thousand a week. Once, when a sledge sank so deeply into the ice that the whaleboat floated loose, five Inuit men and two women worked with the sailors for more than half a day, asking for nothing.

Finally, at water's edge, moved by affection and gratitude, Kane distributed needles, thread, items of clothing and even his surgical amputation knives among the Inuit of Etah. His remaining sled dogs he donated to the community as a whole, taking only Toodlamik and Whitey into the boats: "I could not part with them, the leaders of my team."

Some of the Inuit wept, and Kane felt his heart go out to them— "so long our neighbors, and of late so staunchly our friends." Without these people, he wrote, "our dreary journey would have been prolonged at least a fortnight, and we are so late even now that hours may measure our lives." As the wind continued to blow, Kane gathered "these desolate and confiding people" around him on the ice beach and spoke to them as to brothers and sisters.

Kane told them that other groups of Inuit lived a few hundred miles to the south, where the cold was less intense, the season of daylight longer and the hunting better. He told them that, if they acted boldly and carefully, in a few seasons of patient march, they could reach that more welcoming environment. He implored them to make that march.

On the afternoon of June 19, the sea grew quiet and the sky cleared. At four o'clock, Kane and his men readied the boats, lashing the sledges and slinging them outside the gunwales. The three vessels were small and heavily laden. Split with frost, warped by sunshine and open at the seams, they would need to be caulked repeatedly. In these frail craft, Kane proposed to sail almost eight hundred kilometres. With the sea looking smooth as a garden lake, and despite overhanging black nimbus clouds, the captain and his men pushed off from the ice beach. Stars and stripes flying, they were making for home.

Contemporary Upernavik is a colourful town of 1,200. But in 1855, when Elisha Kent Kane and his men arrived in small boats, these few buildings constituted the entire settlement.

The voyagers had spent one month (May 17 to June 16) transporting supplies and dragging three small boats eighty or ninety kilometres south across ice to Etah. Now, having said a fond farewell to the Inuit who had helped him survive, Kane and his sixteen remaining men piled into tiny boats and began the eight-hundred-kilometre voyage to Upernavik. They survived seven storm-tossed weeks in those open boats, battling blizzards and threatening ice floes, and enduring near starvation.

But on August 1, Kane spotted the famous Devil's Thumb of Melville Bay. Approaching the Duck Islands, he decided to end the voyage, probably the most difficult in Arctic history, not with a reckless display of derring-do, but by wending cautiously through the labyrinth of islands along the coast. On August 6, Kane and his men rounded a cape and spotted the snowy peak of Sanderson's Hope, which rises above Upernavik. They heard the barking of the dogs, and then the six-clock tolling of the workmen's bells. Could this be a dream? Hugging the shoreline, they rowed past the old brew house, and then, in a crowd of children, hauled their boats ashore for the last time.

The people of Upernavik fitted up a loft for the Americans and shared their meagre stores. Now, Kane learned that two vessels had passed this way, looking for him. And from a German newspaper, translated by the local pastor, he gleaned news of the lost Franklin expedition. Some 1,600 kilometres to the southwest, on Boothia Peninsula, John Rae of the Hudson's Bay Company had retrieved relics. Apparently, the Franklin expedition had ended in disaster. Some of the final survivors had been driven to cannibalism. What? Surely not. Could this be true?

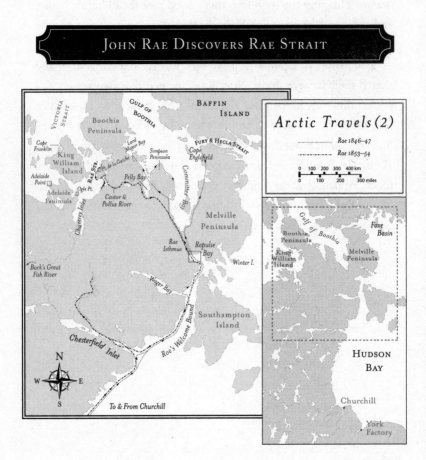

John Rae Discovers Rae Strait

Arctic Travels (2)

.... Rae 1846–47

– – – – – Rae 1853–54

0   100 200 300 400 km
0   100   200   300 miles

VICTORIA STRAIT

Boothia Peninsula

GULF OF BOOTHIA

BAFFIN ISLAND

Cape Franklin

King William Island

Lord Mayor Bay

Simpson Peninsula

FURY & HECLA STRAIT

Cape Englefield

Adelaide Point

RAE STR.

Pt. de la Guiche

Pelly Bay

Committee Bay

Adelaide Peninsula

Ogle Pt.

Castor & Pollux River

Chantrey Inlet

Melville Peninsula

Back's Great Fish River

Rae Isthmus

Repulse Bay

Winter I.

Wager Bay

Southampton Island

Chesterfield Inlet

Roe's Welcome Bound

N
W   E
S

To & From Churchill

Gulf of Boothia

Boothia Peninsula

Foxe Basin

King William Island

Melville Peninsula

HUDSON BAY

Churchill

York Factory

19.

The Scot, the Inuk, the Ojibway

L ittle more than one year previously, in the early summer of 1854, William Ouligbuck Jr. had sat in a tent at Repulse Bay, interviewing Inuit who arrived with relics from the lost Franklin expedition. As he elicited the story of what had happened and relayed the details to John Rae, the twenty-four-year-old Inuk more than redeemed himself for his youthful follies. As a boy of sixteen, young Ouligbuck had tried Rae's patience. During his expedition of 1846–47, Rae had twice caught the boy pilfering sugar and tobacco from his father's bale. Not only that, but young Ouligbuck had stripped the buttons from the men's trousers, probably thinking to use them as trading articles.

In November 1852, when from London Rae had begun organizing yet another expedition, he had inquired of the HBC man at York Factory if any interpreters other than Ouligbuck and his son William were available: "To Ouligbuck I have no particular objection," he wrote, "but the boy (his son) that I had with me formerly is one of the greatest rascals unhung—and by his falsehood and misconduct made his father sulky and discontented. I should prefer Ouligbuck's [other] son Donald, who, altho' he spoke but little English, was a good-tempered, hard-working fellow."

Ouligbuck Sr. had died in 1852. And when Rae arrived at Churchill the following July, on his way farther north, he learned that the designated interpreter, William Ouligbuck Jr., was out hunting porpoises, but was expected back any day. Rae discussed his options with a veteran HBC man named Omond, who insisted that young Ouligbuck, now several years older than the boy Rae remembered, was by far the best man available. Omond declared of the young man that "in addition to his own language he spoke English, Cree and French passably well, that he could be fully relied upon to tell as nearly as possible what was said, and no more, and give the Eskimo reply with equal correctness."

Under pressure from the lateness of the season, and seeing no sign of young Ouligbuck, Rae took aboard an Inuk named Munro, whose language skills were passable. Sixty-five kilometres north of Churchill, he encountered a group of Inuit hunters in kayaks, young Ouligbuck among them. Within five minutes, having seen for himself that Munro could not compare linguistically, Rae had engaged William Ouligbuck as interpreter. That young man quickly arranged for the disposal of his share of the game and transferred his possessions.

One month later when, after a setback at Chesterfield Inlet, Rae decided to change his itinerary and send back half his men, he did not hesitate in choosing an interpreter, but dispatched Munro and kept William Ouligbuck Jr. By September 1854, when Rae was on his way home, he would write: "My good interpreter William Ouligbuck was landed [at Churchill], and before bidding him farewell, I presented him with a very handsomely mounted hunting knife, entrusted to me by Captain Sir George Back, for his former travelling companion Ouligbuck; but as the old man was dead, I took the liberty of giving it to his son, as an inducement to future good conduct should his services be again required."

This image of William Ouligbuck was collected at York Factory by George Simpson McTavish (1863–1943), the great grandson of Sir George Simpson. It turns up in his privately printed book, Behind the Palisades.

In August 1853, in a cold, drizzling rain, and accompanied by just seven men, William Ouligbuck among them, John Rae sailed a small boat into Repulse Bay. He hoped to complete the survey of the west coast of Boothia early the following year, travelling overland before spring breakup. The previous year, after delivering those bits of wreckage he had discovered to the British Admiralty, Rae had received the Founder's Gold Medal from the Royal Geographical Society for making "many important additions . . . to the geography of the Arctic regions."

While visiting his mother in Stromness, Orkney, Rae developed a plan to complete the mapping of the Arctic coast of North America. He outlined it in a letter published in the *Times* on November 26, 1852. In a postscript, he added: "I do not mention the lost navigators as there is not the slightest hope of finding any traces of them in the quarter to which I am going." In January 1853, Rae returned to London. He visited Sir John Richardson, his former travelling companion, and dined with artist-explorer George Back, who entrusted him with that knife for Ouligbuck Senior.

Now, in mid-August, Repulse Bay looked more bleak and dreary, more forbidding, than Rae remembered. It also wore a more wintry and Arctic aspect than he had expected to face so early. Thick ice clogged the shoreline, and immense snowdrifts filled every ravine and every steep bank with a southern exposure. A mass of ice and snow several feet deep covered his old landing place.

Proceeding slowly up the North Pole River, Rae located a new, more amenable landing spot and moored the boat. Jumping ashore, awash in memories, Rae went directly to Fort Hope, the dwelling he had constructed in 1846. He found the stone walls exactly as he had left them. The little mud oven, although exposed to the weather, was still in perfect condition. Inuit hunters had used it to cache meat. In the woods, he found the path where, every night before going to bed, he had paced back and forth to warm his feet. Around the stone house, in the hard-packed mud, he found footprints tracing the outlines of his men's British-made shoes, the marks as clear and fresh as if they had been made seven days rather than seven years before.

Rae completed his reconnaissance with mixed feelings—wintering here had not been easy—and then returned to the river. He found the boat moored, the tents pitched, and the cargo partly unloaded. This pleased him enormously, "my fellows being all so well up in their work that they did not require my superintendence."

Since his first sojourn here at Repulse Bay, Rae had learned a lot, mainly from the Inuit, about wintering above the treeline. He did not even consider reoccupying Fort Hope, the stone house he had built seven years earlier. Instead, he and the men pitched tents. As soon as they had enough snow, then directed by William Ouligbuck, they erected igloos and moved into them.

November brought sunny weather and a mean temperature of minus twenty-seven degrees Celsius. But December brought gales, drifting snow and a mean of minus thirty. And February proved the harshest month of all, with temperatures falling as low as minus forty-seven and the sun never rising above the horizon. By then, the meticulous Rae had begun preparing for the looming spring journey. He had hired carpenter Jacob Beads, a relative of John Beads, who had previously snowshoed with Rae to Victoria Island, and was also attached to this expedition. In a workshop built of snow, Rae had the "very handy" Jacob Beads dismantle the party's four sledges, reduce their framing and put them back together more securely than before. Acting on Rae's instructions, Beads narrowed the runners and reduced the sledges' weight by a third.

To locate weaknesses and determine the speed at which he might travel, Rae timed his men hauling loaded sledges over a measured mile. He, too, practised over that distance, hauling his sledge with 120 pounds on it. He set aside the fixed ration he proposed to use and, along with the men, tested it for four days. He examined his "six-inch sextant by Dollard" and adjusted his two chronometers, which he wore inside a thick blanket belt around his waist to protect them from cold.

With spring arriving, and hoping still to buy sled dogs, Rae sent three men to search one final time for any sign of Inuit. They found none, and the explorer resigned himself to man-hauling. He would leave three men—Thomas Mistegan, Murdoch McLennan and John Beads—to guard the boat and other property. Next to himself, the Ojibway Mistegan was the expedition's best hunter, so those who stayed behind would not starve. Rae put Beads in charge, however, because during the winter he had taught the young man to read and write well enough to keep a rough journal.

On March 31, 1854, having lived off the land through yet another Arctic winter, forty-year-old John Rae left Repulse Bay, leading four men more than a decade younger. The five began their journey in bright sunshine and, despite the heavy work ahead, in excellent health and spirits. Two of the men who would remain behind accompanied them for twelve kilometres.

Rae at first headed northwest along the same route as he had taken in 1847. He proposed to cross Boothia Peninsula and chart its western coast from the mouth of the Castor and Pollux River, the farthest Dease and Simpson had reached, to Bellot Strait, identified in 1852. Two days out, Rae realized that one of the chosen four, already suffering fatigue and pains in his chest, would be unable to keep the pace. He sent him back to Repulse Bay in favour of Thomas Mistegan, who had been bitterly disappointed at being left. In addition to his other qualities, Mistegan was an admirable snowshoe walker and sledge-hauler who could tolerate cold. The Ojibway hunter caught up with the party on April 4. The men prepared him a special supper, to which he did ample justice after his forced march of fifty-five kilometres.

John Rae travelled Inuit-style, building igloos as he went. These snow huts remained impenetrable to stormy winds. They required, on average, one hour to build, but stood ready, with doors blocked up, for the return journey. Also, a traveller would not have the trouble of pitching, taking down, packing on a sledge and hauling a cumbrous tent, which, like bedding, would keep gaining weight from moisture. Another advantage was that moisture from the men's breath adhered firmly to the igloo's walls, instead of condensing and dripping onto the bedding as it did in a tent.

Unlike naval explorers, who cooked twice a day and stopped for lunch, Rae travelled non-stop, usually breakfasting on fruit, a piece of frozen pemmican and half a biscuit: "We never stopped to eat or drink, but put a small piece of our breakfast allowance of pemmican in our pockets, which we munched at our pleasure." Supper usually consisted of still more pemmican, boiled with flour and preserved potato into a porridge called rababoo.

At night, all five men "lay under one covering," Rae wrote, "taking our coats off, so that our arms might be more closely in contact with our bodies. This and the changing of our moccasins was all the undressing we went through. I always occupied an outside place, and the cook for the next day the other. Those inside were warm enough, but when either of the outsiders felt chilly on the exposed side, all he had to do was turn round, give his neighbours a nudge and we'd all put about, and the chilly party was soon warmed. We got so speedily accustomed to this that I believe we used to turn over from one side to the other when required without waking."

Rae had started out as early as he dared in the travelling season, and now the weather turned wintry again. Gale-force winds and heavy, drifting snow confined the men to snow huts or reduced them to travelling as little as nine kilometres a day. The temperature fell to minus fifty-two degrees Celsius, and Jacob Beads froze two of his toes. By April 10, when the party reached the point on the coast of Committee Bay from which the explorer intended to travel due west across Boothia Peninsula, all the men, including Rae, had endured some degree of snow blindness, their eyes stinging as if filled with sand.

Rae led the men forward through the zero visibility of a violent snowstorm, steering by compass. For a while the skies cleared, but at Pelly Bay, a dense fog descended and again the compass became necessary. Confronted by impassable mountainous terrain, Rae veered southwest across Boothia Peninsula and came across the fresh footprints of an Inuk hauling a sledge. Rae sent Ouligbuck and Mistegan to find the traveller. After eleven hours, they returned with seventeen Inuit, among them five women. Rae had met some of these people at Repulse Bay in 1847, but others had never seen Europeans before and behaved aggressively.

"They would give us no information on which any reliance could be placed," Rae wrote in his official report to the HBC, "and none of them would consent to accompany us for a day or two, although I promised to reward them liberally." The Inuit objected to the party's travelling farther west, protesting without explanation, so that initially, Rae was baffled. "Finding it was their object to puzzle the interpreter and mislead us," he wrote, "I declined purchasing more than a piece of seal from them, and sent them away, not however, without some difficulty, as they lingered about with the hope of stealing something; and, notwithstanding our vigilance, succeeded in abstracting from one of the sledges a few pounds of biscuit and grease."

The following day brought an odd incident. Early in the afternoon when the party stopped to cache seal meat, William Ouligbuck slipped away and tried to rejoin the Inuit he had met the previous day. Rae noticed his absence and immediately gave chase, determined not to lose his excellent interpreter. He and Mistegan overtook the Inuk after a sharp race of seven or eight kilometres. The young man, crying like a baby, pleaded illness as an excuse for his attempted defection. Rae accepted this, suggesting in his report that Ouligbuck had "eaten too much boiled seal's flesh, with which he had been regaled at the snowhuts of the natives."

This explanation would fail to satisfy many of Rae's contemporaries, and also some of his later readers. Perhaps the young man, while being entertained for several hours at the snow huts of the locals, had become interested in one of the women and wished to rejoin her. Perhaps Rae suspected or even knew this and chose not to report it.

Years later, one of the most reliable and articulate Inuit men, In-nook-poo-zhe-jook, would explain that the Pelly Bay entourage had deliberately frightened young Ouligbuck by claiming that hostile Inuit living farther west would probably murder the entire expedition. Yet nothing of the kind had ever occurred in this vicinity. Why the fabrication?

Rae had deduced that the hunters had cached meat to the west and did not want it stolen, so they frightened Ouligbuck, hoping he would persuade the party to change course. In any case, once overtaken, Ouligbuck wept and expressed his readiness to rejoin the expedition. The falsity of the assertion about hostile Inuit would be demonstrated almost immediately, because two men from Pelly Bay joined the party in travelling west, quite without fear.

Rae encountered the first of these, See-u-ti-chu, driving a team of dogs with a sledge laden with muskox meat. Rae hired the man, who cached his booty on the spot and recommended heading west along the route he had just travelled. The party had no sooner loaded the dogsled and started out than a second Inuk, In-nook-poo-zhe-jook, arrived with more dogs and offered to join the party. He would emerge, over time, as a key player in ascertaining the fate of the Franklin expedition.

Now, the observant Rae noticed that In-nook-poo-zhe-jook wore a gold cap-band and asked him where he had got it. The Inuk, who was notably expressive and articulate, replied that it came from the place where the dead white men were. He had traded for it. Rae

This painting captures one of the most significant moments in exploration history—the moment when, on Boothia Peninsula, John Rae first learned that a number of white men had starved to death some distance to the west. The 1949 painting by Charles Fraser Comfort is called Dr. Rae Meets Eskimos / Discovery of Franklin Expedition Relics. *William Ouligbuck speaks to a pointing Inuk in snow goggles, while Rae holds a utensil.*

proceeded to interrogate him with the help of William Ouligbuck. Later that day, he recorded field notes: "Met a very communicative and apparently intelligent Eskimo; had never met whites before but said that a number of Qallunaat [white people, often rendered 'kabloonas'], at least 35–40, had starved to death west of a large river a long distance off. Perhaps 10 or 12 days journey. Could not tell the distance, never had been there, and could not accompany us so far. Dead bodies seen beyond two large rivers; did not know the place, could not or would not explain it on a chart."

Given the advantage of subsequent revelations, we know that In-nook-poo-zhe-jook, who would later visit and investigate scenes of the Franklin tragedy, was himself not yet clear about what had happened where. The remains of thirty-five or forty sailors would eventually be found at Terror Bay on the west coast of King William Island. More remains would turn up on the North American coast near Starvation Cove. The discussion of what happened, where exactly and when would continue into the twenty-first century.

Rae bought the Inuk's cap-band on the spot. He wondered whether it might have come from the lost Franklin expedition, but dismissed that as unlikely. Half a dozen ships were searching the waters and islands far to the north. That, everybody agreed, was where the Franklin expedition would be found. Besides, what did he have to act upon? Some white men had died ten or twelve days away in a spot these Inuit hunters had never visited, and that now lay under a thick blanket of snow. The information was too vague. Rae told In-nook-poo-zhe-jook that if he or his companions had any other relics from white men, they should bring them to his winter quarters at Repulse Bay, where they would be well rewarded.

Both dog teams were tired, and the party made slow progress along a river to Simpson Lake. After a couple of days, the two Inuit who had joined them wished to leave for home. See-u-ti-chu feared that wolverines might plunder his cache of muskox meat. Rae paid both men well, repeated his promise regarding any relics and said goodbye. On resuming his journey, he noticed deer tracks and traces of muskox and realized that the surrounding tundra, frozen and snow covered, was a hunting ground in which game abounded.

Some weeks before, Jacob Beads had frozen two toes. On April 25, after a hard day's hike of more than thirty kilometres, he was scarcely able to walk. The slightly built Johnston also showed signs of fatigue. Rae decided to allow these two men to proceed at a slower pace to some rocks that lay directly ahead, where they could build an igloo and wait. The following day, with his two sturdiest men, Mistegan and Ouligbuck, the Ojibway and the Inuk, Rae took four days' worth of provisions and set out for the mouth of the Castor and Pollux River—the farthest point charted from the west, fifteen years earlier, by Peter Warren Dease and Thomas Simpson.

On April 27, 1854, Rae reached sea ice: a coastline. He passed several heaps of stones, evidently Inuit caches, before discovering a pillar of stones clearly intended more as a marker than for property protection. Its top had fallen down. He sent Mistegan to trace what looked like the frozen bed of a small river immediately to the west, while with Ouligbuck he dismantled the pillar in search of a document. He discovered none but, checking his latitude, found himself within a quarter mile of Thomas Simpson's 1839 reading on the cairn he had built at the mouth of the Castor and Pollux River. Mistegan returned and affirmed that the frozen bed was indeed a river. Rae had reached his first goal.

Now he prepared to carry out the main objective of his expedition. He would travel north and west along the coast of Boothia Peninsula to Bellot Strait, and so complete the mapping of the northern edge of the continent. He and his two men retraced their steps. After a tiring fifteen-hour march over fifty kilometres of rough, icy terrain, they arrived at the snow hut of Beads and Johnston. The two had shot nothing and had gathered little fuel. Beads could scarcely move, and, despite their protests, Rae insisted that the two men remain where they were.

At two o'clock in the morning on April 30, having loaded provisions for twenty-two days onto sledges for Ouligbuck and Mistegan, and himself dragging a third sledge piled with instruments, books and bedding, Rae set out to trace the last uncharted coastline of North America. Through fierce winds and heavy, blowing snow, he forced his way north along the coast of Boothia Peninsula.

Opposite an island to which he gave the name Stanley, gazing west across the ice, Rae noted a distant promontory and called it Matheson Island (later amended to Matheson Point). To his interested surprise, the coastline showed no sign of turning west, as the charts suggested it should, to link with King William Land. Rae continued north and, on May 6, 1854, arrived at a promontory he named Point de la Guiche (latitude 68°57′7″ north, longitude 94°32′58″ west). There, with his two men, Rae stood gazing out over the ice of a frozen channel where naval charts had suggested they would find land.

Fog and stormy weather had slowed their progress to this point. Given the distances involved, the time left before spring thaw and the condition of his men, Rae realized that he would not be able to reach Bellot Strait and so complete the whole survey of the coast as intended—not without risking lives. Decades later, in a book review, Rae would write: "Thus nearly 800 miles of the 1,000 left unexplored in 1839 [after the expedition of Peter Warren Dease and Thomas Simpson] . . . were completed by me, but there still remained about 200 miles [320 kilometres], between Bellot Strait and the Magnetic Pole on the west shore of Boothia, a blank on the charts, and these were explored by McClintock in his memorable journey [of 1859]."

Some commentators have misinterpreted Rae's reference to "unexplored miles." They confuse Arctic coastline with the open waterway (comprising Peel Sound and Franklin Strait) that extends south from Parry Channel (the extension of Lancaster Sound), and forms part of the first-sailed Northwest Passage. By 1891, when Rae wrote that review, everyone knew that John Franklin had sailed directly past this unmapped bit of coastline, so establishing that a navigable channel existed as far south as King William Island, where he got blocked by ice. His voyage rendered that short stretch of uncharted coastline irrelevant to any discussion of the Passage.

In May 1854, when John Rae stood on the coast of Boothia Peninsula, looking west across a frozen strait towards what he now perceived was an island, King William Island, he could not help but wonder: Was this channel the long-sought missing link? The ever-practical Rae put William Ouligbuck to work building a snow hut. Taking out his instruments and charts, he sent Mistegan north across the ice beyond Point de la Guiche. The hunter hiked eight or nine kilometres and climbed a hill of rough ice to gain a farther vantage point. The land was still trending northward, while to the northwest, at a considerable distance across the ice—perhaps nine-teen or twenty kilometres—more land appeared: "This land, if it was such," Rae wrote, "is probably part of Matty Island or King William Land, which latter is also clearly an island."

Rae had reached a point where, except for the unknown strait before him, his survey matched that made by Sir James Clark Ross in 1830, providing "a very singular agreement . . . considering the circumstances under which our surveys have been taken." In snowy weather, as noted in Chapter 11, James Clark Ross had missed the strait John Rae could clearly see, and charted an enclosed bay—albeit with a dotted line and a question mark. His uncle Sir John Ross, who had discovered the non-existent Croker Mountains, closed the line while preparing the final copy of the expedition map and applied the name "Poctes Bay"—possibly intending Poet's Bay. Either way, this supposedly enclosed bay was in fact an open strait.

Rae contemplated the frozen passage before him. It contained what he called "young ice," radically unlike the much rougher ice he had encountered three years before on the western side of King William Island. Clearly, that island protected this channel from the impenetrable pack ice that flowed from the north. This passage would be navigable when Victoria Strait was not.

Rae looked north towards where James Clark Ross had traversed the ice by dogsled. Ross had surmised, though with some hesitation, that no passage existed in this vicinity. Rae looked south down the strait. In 1835, George Back had looked north, wondering about this waterway, before reluctantly retreating to the mainland. Four years later, Thomas Simpson had sailed past south of this channel, believing that, somewhere in this vicinity, lay the secret of the Northwest Passage. Bent on returning to investigate further, Simpson had died the following summer.

Now, although he could not prove it, John Rae realized that here, running between Boothia Peninsula and King William Island, he had discovered the hidden gateway in the Northwest Passage. Together with Ouligbuck and Mistegan, he had solved the first great mystery of nineteenth-century exploration. Half a century would elapse before Roald Amundsen would prove him correct. That night, after building a cairn just south of the tip of Point de la

Guiche, a satisfied Rae and his two hardiest men, the Inuk and the Ojibway, began the long journey back to Repulse Bay.

On reaching the two men he had left waiting in a snow hut, Rae felt confirmed in his decision to turn back. Both were worn down, and Jacob Beads was losing one of his big toes at the joint. On other occasions, farther south, Rae had treated frostbite with great success by applying a poultice made of the inner bark of the larch fir. Now, under more difficult conditions, he could do little. Beads insisted on limping along, stoutly refusing to be hauled. The weather had cleared, the snow was hard-packed and the men made better time than coming out. They reached their Pelly Bay snow hut on May 17, shortly after midnight, with the bright sun low on the horizon.

Noticing tracks in the snow, Rae sent Mistegan and Ouligbuck, after they had rested, to follow those tracks. Eight hours later, the two returned with a dozen Inuit men, women and children. One of the Inuit produced a silver fork and spoon, which Rae promptly bought: "The initials F.R.M.C., not engraved but scratched with a sharp instrument on the spoon, puzzled me much, as I knew not at the time the Christian names of the officers of Sir John Franklin's expedition." Still convinced that Franklin had got lost far to the north, Rae speculated about Captain Robert McClure, who had sailed with a search expedition in 1850, and wondered whether the initials might be his, with the small "c" omitted—perhaps F. Robert McClure?

Two of the Inuit, one of whom Rae had met in 1847, offered for a price to accompany the party for two days with a sledge and dogs. Always anxious to spare his men, Rae accepted the offer. When the two visitors left them, he bought one of the dogs. He used it to help him to carefully chart the coastline of Pelly Bay, so settling once and for all the geographical questions—Was Boothia really a peninsula?

Did no hidden channel lead west?—raised after his 1847 expedition. Then he continued south.

John Rae arrived at Repulse Bay at five o'clock in the morning on May 26, having covered in twenty days the distance (minus fifty or sixty kilometres) that, going out in rougher weather, had taken thirty-six days. He found the three men he had left behind living on friendly terms with several newly arrived Inuit families who had pitched tents nearby. "The natives had behaved in the most exemplary manner," wrote Rae, "and many of them who were short of food had been supplied with venison from our stores, in compliance with my orders to that effect."

These Inuit had arrived from Pelly Bay with relics to trade and stories to tell. At last, Rae had an opportunity to glean answers about the white men who had died of starvation. Only now did Rae begin to realize and understand, with growing horror, that the visitors were almost certainly talking about men from the lost Franklin expedition, which had sailed nine years before.

While trading for relics, and then more thoroughly afterwards, Rae asked questions with William Ouligbuck as his interpreter. The Inuit visitors told him that all of the Qallunaat had died several years before, and the explorer had no reason to doubt this. No survivors had ever reached any HBC trading post, where Yellowknife-Dene had been sent to seek them with ammunition, clear instructions and promises of reward.

The Inuit newcomers explained that four winters earlier, in 1850, some Inuit families killing seals near the northern shore of a large island (which Rae now understood to be King William Island) had encountered at least forty Qallunaat dragging a boat and some sledges southward. None of these white men could speak Inuktitut, but they communicated through gestures that their ships had been crushed by ice and that they were travelling to where they hoped to hunt deer.

The men looked thin and hungry, and all except the leader were hauling on the drag ropes of sledges. The leader was a tall, stout, middle-aged man who wore a telescope strapped over his shoulder. The party, obviously short of provisions, bought seal meat from the Inuit, then pitched tents and rested. These Qallunaat then headed east across the ice towards the mouth of a large river—a river that, Rae now recognized by its description, could only be Back's Great Fish River.

The following spring, when the Inuit visited that river to fish, they discovered about thirty corpses. They found graves on the main part of the continent (*noon-nah*) and five dead bodies on an island (*kai-ik-tak*), a long day's journey northwest of the river. Rae surmised that these references were to Ogle Point and Montreal Island. The Inuit discovered some dead bodies in tents and others under the boat, which had been overturned to form a shelter. A few other bodies lay scattered about.

None of the Inuit he questioned had seen the Qallunaat alive or dead, but Rae had worked long enough in the North to appreciate the power and reliability of the Inuit grapevine. This was an oral culture. Sitting in his tent, he conducted repeated interviews through William Ouligbuck, checking the veracity of his informants against information he recalled from the narratives of George Back and Thomas Simpson.

The Inuit viewed it as strange that no sledges had been found among the dead, although the boat remained. Rae pointed out that the Qallunaat, having reached the mouth of the Great Fish River, would need their boat to proceed farther, but might have burned the sledges for fuel. "A look of intelligence immediately lit up their faces," he wrote, "and they said that may have been so, for there had been fires."

He continued: "A few of the unfortunate men must have survived until the arrival of the wild fowl (say until the end of May) as shots were heard and fresh bones and feathers of geese were noticed near the scene of the sad event. There appears to have been an abundant store of ammunition, as the gunpowder was emptied by the natives in a heap on the ground out of the kegs or cases containing it, and a quantity of shot and ball was found below highwater mark, having probably been left on the ice close to the beach before the spring thaw commenced."

One night, having gleaned all the information he could, Rae sorted through the relics he had acquired. Among them were pieces of telescopes and guns, and broken watches and compasses. Again he counted the identifiable items, those bearing the crests and initials of officers on Franklin's two ships. These totalled fifteen. They included a gold watch, a surgeon's knife, several silver spoons and forks bearing the Franklin crest, an order of merit in the form of a star and a small silver plate engraved "Sir John Franklin, K.C.B."

Rae studied the engraved plate by lantern light and marvelled: Franklin himself had eaten from it. The presence of this silver dish, together with the other relics, verified the Inuit story beyond doubt. He knew the answer to the second great mystery of nineteenth-century Arctic exploration: What had happened to the lost Franklin expedition?

But now Rae faced a difficult decision—probably the most important he would ever confront. He returned the silver plate to his leather bag, then stepped out the door of the tent. It was almost midnight, but here in the Arctic, the sky was merely grey and streaked with clouds. Beside the tent, Rae paced back and forth, his hands clasped behind his back. Should he return immediately to England to report what he had learned? Or should he wait here until next spring and then travel overland to see whether he could find the bodies?

With summer imminent, he could not hope to begin that prodigious trek for another eight or ten months. The ice would soon begin to melt, rendering distance travel impossible. Nor did he have a boat waiting at the far end of his journey that he could then use to reach King William Island and Back's Great Fish River. And he couldn't hope to haul the boat he did have several hundred kilometres.

On the other hand, he had enough pemmican to last three months. If he so decided, he could conceivably wait until winter. Should he do it? Staring up at the scudding clouds, John Rae decided not. At least half a dozen ships, and maybe more, were seeking John Franklin in all the wrong places. Their captains had orders to continue searching. Under the circumstances, Rae had a duty to communicate what he had learned as soon as possible, and so to reduce the risk of more lives being needlessly lost.

After countless difficult hours of interviewing Inuit and sifting through artifacts, John Rae had gleaned the essential truth about the Arctic tragedy of the century. Of course he felt driven to share it. On August 4, 1854, when at last the pack ice cleared, Rae sailed south out of Repulse Bay to begin his journey back to England. The explorer could not know it, but having made a career of testing himself, he was about to face the most difficult ordeal of his life.

Part Five

THE VICTORIAN RESPONSE

20.

Lady Franklin Enlists Charles Dickens

On October 23, 1854, the *London Times* published a front-page report quoting explorer John Rae, who had just arrived back from the Arctic. Rae related how, while crossing Boothia Peninsula with a few men, he had chanced to meet some Inuit hunters. From one of them, he learned that a party of white men had starved to death some distance to the west. Subsequently, he had gleaned details and purchased a variety of articles that placed "the fate of a portion (if not all) of the then survivors of Sir John Franklin's long-lost party beyond a doubt; a fate as terrible as the imagination can conceive."

Rae explained that, to secure information, he had offered substantial rewards. At his camp at Repulse Bay, with spring sunshine melting the Arctic ice, he had sat with William Ouligbuck and conducted interviews with visiting Inuit. From them, he collected spoons and broken watches, gold braid, cap bands, a cook's knife. And he determined that a large party of Franklin's men had abandoned their ships off King William Island in Victoria Strait. Contrary to all expectations, they had trekked south towards mainland North America, many of them dying as they went.

Some of the Franklin-expedition relics John Rae brought to England, as depicted in The Illustrated London News. *When Lady Franklin saw them, she knew that her husband was dead.*

One party of Inuit hunters had discovered thirty-five or forty dead bodies. Some lay in tents or exposed on the ground, others under an overturned boat. One man, apparently an officer, had died with a telescope strapped over his shoulder and a double-barrelled shotgun beneath him. Writing for the Hudson's Bay Company and the Admiralty, rather than a public readership, and accustomed to facing realities beyond the experience of most of his audience, Rae reported the unvarnished truth in words that would resonate around the world: "From the mutilated state of many of the corpses and the contents of the kettles, it is evident that our wretched countrymen had been driven to the last resource—cannibalism—as a means of prolonging existence."

Rae's report shook not just Britain but all of Europe. Sir John Franklin and his noble crew had been reduced in the frozen north

. . . to cannibalism? Historian Hendrik Van Loon, author of *The Story of Mankind*, would write that his father, who lived in Holland during this period, forever remembered "the shock of horror that . . . swept across the civilized world."

Lady Franklin took to her bed. Friends had prepared her, relaying rumours of a preliminary account that had appeared in a Montreal newspaper. That John Franklin had been personally involved in cannibalism she flatly rejected as inconceivable. Even the notion that some of his crew, the flower of the Royal Navy, could be reduced to measures so desperate—no, it exceeded credibility.

Yet, when at the Admiralty offices she examined the relics Rae had brought back from the Arctic—the ribbons, the buttons, the gold braid, the broken watch—Jane Franklin found herself confronting a terrible reality. For nearly ten years she had kept hope alive. Now, as she recognized an engraved spoon that had belonged to Sir John and felt its silver heft in her hand, she felt the truth crash over her like a dark wave. Never again would she see her husband alive.

Late in 1854, Jane Franklin rose from her bed. John Rae's allegations of cannibalism threatened her husband's reputation, and so her own. Those assertions could not be allowed to stand. Rae's relics had convinced her that Franklin had died, but never would she accept the narrative that came with them. When the explorer paid her the obligatory courtesy call, still wearing his full Arctic beard, Jane told him to his face that he never should have accepted the word of "Esquimaux savages," none of whom claimed to have seen the dead bodies. They were merely relaying the accounts of others. John Rae would not be cowed. He knew the truth when he heard it, and he had written his report not for the *Times*, but for the Hudson's Bay Company and the Admiralty. Jane Franklin replied that he should never have committed such allegations to paper.

Eventually, Rae would be vindicated. Down through the decades, researchers would contribute nuance and clarification. But none would repudiate the thrust of his initial report. Some of the final survivors had been driven to cannibalism. Such was the fate of the Franklin expedition.

In 1854, however, Lady Franklin refused to accept this reality. And she had no shortage of allies. These included the friends and relatives of men who had sailed with Franklin, and an array of officers concerned for the reputation of the Royal Navy—men like James Clark Ross, John Richardson and Francis Beaufort. But all of these, she realized, would be open to charges of special pleading.

The resourceful lady wondered about Charles Dickens. Hadn't his father had some connection with the Royal Navy? Surely he could be induced to strike the right attitude? The forty-two-year-old author had already published such classic novels as *Oliver Twist*, *David Copperfield* and *Bleak House*. More importantly, for her purposes, he edited a twice-monthly newspaper called *Household Words*—potentially the perfect vehicle. Through her friend Carolina Boyle—formerly a maid of honour to Queen Adelaide, the consort of King William IV—Jane communicated her wish that Dickens should call on her as soon as possible.

The desperately busy author dropped everything and, on November 19, 1854, turned up at her front door. No eyewitness account of their meeting has survived. But Jane Franklin wanted John Rae repudiated—especially his allegations of cannibalism—and the greatest literary champion of the age undertook to accomplish that task. The

After conferring with Lady Franklin, Charles Dickens decided that he was "rather strong on Voyages and Cannibalism." He proceeded to publish a shameful two-part screed repudiating John Rae's report and libelling the Inuit as "savages." This was probably the worst thing Dickens ever wrote.

very next morning, Dickens scrawled a note to one W. H. Willis, a sometime assistant. While until now he had paid scant attention to the issue, Dickens observed, "I am rather strong on Voyages and Cannibalism, and might do an interesting little paper for the next No. of Household Words: on that part of Dr. Rae's report, taking the arguments against its probabilities. Can you get me a newspaper cutting containing his report? If not, will you have it copied for me and sent up to Tavistock House straight away?"

Taking his cue from Lady Franklin, Dickens wrote a ferocious two-part denunciation entitled "The Lost Arctic Voyagers." He published Part One as the lead article on December 2, and Part Two the following week. Acknowledging that Rae had a duty to report what he had heard, and so seeming to demonstrate his even-handedness, Dickens castigated the Admiralty for publishing his account without considering its effects. While exonerating Rae personally, he attacked that explorer's conclusions, contending that there was no reason whatsoever to believe "that our wretched countrymen had been driven to the last resource—cannibalism—as a means of prolonging existence."

Given that he could present no new evidence, and had never got anywhere near the Arctic, Dickens argued by analogy and according to probabilities. He suggested that the remnants of "Franklin's gallant band" might well have been murdered by the Inuit: "It is impossible to form an estimate of the character of any race of savages, from their deferential behaviour to the white man while he is strong . . . We believe every savage to be in his heart covetous, treacherous, and cruel; and we have yet to learn what knowledge the white man—lost, houseless, shipless, apparently forgotten by his race; plainly famine-stricken, weak, frozen, helpless, and dying—has of the gentleness of the Esquimaux nature."

Dickens offered much more along these lines. He criticized Rae for having taken "the word of a savage," and, confusing the Inuit with the Victorian stereotype of the African, argued, "Even the sight of cooked and dissevered human bodies among this or that tatoo'd tribe, is not proof. Such appropriate offerings to their barbarous, wide-mouthed, goggle-eyed gods, savages have been often seen and known to make."

With all the literary skill at his command, Dickens presented an argument that, from the vantage point of the twenty-first century, can only be judged distressingly racist. In this instance, at least, the author failed to transcend the attitudes of his age. Time has proven his two-part essay to be a tour de force of self-deception and wilful blindness. But late in 1854, it engulfed John Rae like an avalanche. The explorer responded as best he could, but he had only truth on his side, and few writers in any time or place could have contended with Charles Dickens in full rhetorical flight. When Dickens was done, in the realm of Victorian public opinion, John Rae was deader than Franklin.

Early in 1855, Lady Franklin began clamouring for more search expeditions. Sir Edward Belcher, having sailed with five ships on what was supposed to be "The Last of the Arctic Voyages," had arrived back in London. Despite the protests of his senior officers, he had abandoned four of his ships in the Arctic, revealing himself to be both indecisive and cowardly. His outraged subordinate officers saw that he faced a court martial, but he escaped censure, narrowly, because he could point to equivocal orders. Belcher had rescued Robert McClure, but brought no further news of the Franklin expedition.

As for John Rae, Lady Franklin contended that he had left the search area prematurely. Never mind that the winter ice was turning to water and he had no boat on the west coast of Boothia or anywhere near King William Island. Surely the Hudson's Bay Company, which had sponsored his revelatory expedition, would undertake to complete the task Rae had begun. And what of the British Admiralty? Now that the correct search area had been precisely identified—she accepted the Inuit testimony that suited her—they had a moral obligation to search for more complete answers.

Rae's evidence that her husband had died in the Arctic intensified Lady Franklin's sense of urgency. The same was true of the claim, now being advanced even by certain "Arctic people" she counted as friends, that Robert McClure had discovered the Northwest Passage. No sooner had McClure arrived in England than he began asserting that sledging across the ice to a rescue ship constituted a "completion" of the Northwest Passage—and that this accomplishment entitled him to the £10,000 reward for the discovery of a navigable waterway.

Together with Rae's proof that Franklin had died in the Arctic, McClure's claim served to clarify Jane Franklin's course of action. Most of her contemporaries believed—and she encouraged them in this—that she had driven the search for her absent husband because she loved him more than life itself. But for her, determining "the fate of Franklin" was intertwined with the quest for the Northwest Passage—and with establishing that her husband had somehow "discovered" that elusive channel.

On July 20, 1855, the British House of Commons responded to the claim of Robert McClure by striking a parliamentary committee to enquire into Northwest Passage awards. It received several claims, but only those of two Royal Navy men—McClure and, in absentia, John Franklin—received serious consideration. McClure was claiming that he had succeeded by walking across that ice-choked channel, and so should receive the £10,000 award—a sum that, by conservative measure, is today worth more than US$1.3 million.

Lady Franklin faced a complex situation. She could advance a claim on behalf of her late husband only because of the testimony of John Rae. While rejecting his statements regarding cannibalism, she embraced his declarations that Franklin had sailed as far south as King William Island, and that some of his men had reached the North American continent.

To make her case, Lady Franklin realized that she needed to abandon the original criterion of navigability. She could not argue that McClure had failed to discover a passage because he had walked across the frozen sea to a rescue ship. Judging from Rae's testimony, Franklin had at best achieved something similar, though without the happy ending. The final survivors from his expedition had died, apparently of starvation, while trekking south from their ships to the coast of the continent.

Compelled to accept McClure's "walk a Passage" argument, Jane Franklin countered with characteristic ingenuity. She introduced the idea that there existed several northwest passages, not just one. She argued that Franklin had discovered his "more navigable" passage first—even though his ships had never emerged at the far end, but had got trapped in an ice-choked channel that would remain impassable for the rest of the nineteenth century and well into the twentieth. To advance this claim, as British author Francis Spufford observed in *I May Be Some Time: Ice and the English Imagination*, success in discovering the Northwest Passage had to be "carefully redefined as an impalpable goal that did not require one to return alive, or to pass on the news to the world."

To the awards judges, Jane Franklin wrote that she did not wish "to question the claims of Captain M'Clure to every honour his country may think proper to award him." She continued: "That enterprising officer is not less the discoverer of a North-West Passage, or, in other words, of one of the links which was wanted to connect the main channels of navigation already ascertained by previous explorers, because the *Erebus* and *Terror* under my husband had previously,

Lady Franklin as she looked in middle age, according to artist Thomas Bock, who drew this portrait in Tasmania using chalk on paper. A third portrait of Jane Franklin does exist, and depicts her sitting in a chair, but it has disappeared into a private collection in Australia.

though unknown to Captain M'Clure, discovered another and more navigable passage. That passage, in fact, which, if ships ever attempt to push their way from one ocean to the other, will assuredly be the one adopted."

Never mind that Franklin, too, had got trapped in an ice-choked channel, Victoria Strait, that would remain impassable until well into the twentieth century. The parliamentary committee, however, faced a dilemma. The only logical response would have been to admit that none of the "discovered passages" satisfied the original condition of being navigable. Logic decreed that nobody had yet proven successful in this quest.

Admitting that, however, implied renewing the adventure at considerable cost. At present, such spending was unthinkable: Britain was embroiled in an expensive war against Russia. Instead, the committee declared it "beyond doubt that to Captain McClure belongs the distinguished honour of having been the first to perform the actual passage over water—between the two great oceans that encircle the globe." One of McClure's junior officers, Samuel Cresswell, had been the first to reach England, but by Royal Navy convention, he didn't count. The government awarded McClure a knighthood and £10,000. By returning alive to England, he and his men had provided "a living evidence of the existence of a Northwest Passage."

Lady Franklin did not concede defeat. She had lost a skirmish, not a war. And she had recognized the wisdom of abandoning navigability as a criterion for discovery of the Passage. Indeed, this latest wrangle had introduced two useful concepts, notable amendments to the original challenge. First, McClure had established that one could "perform" or "accomplish" the Passage without sailing through it. True, by walking across the ice, he had at least completed a transit from one ocean to another—something nobody would ever be able to say of the Franklin expedition. Never mind. Lady Franklin herself had introduced the second corollary notion: several Passages existed, not just one. She would exploit both ideas—and, almost 170 years later, after the discovery of *Erebus* and *Terror*, avid apologists would revive both.

Initially, Lady Franklin and her allies held fast to the logic of "walk a Passage." Sir John Richardson, who had twice travelled with Franklin and later married one of his nieces, coined a poetic phrase to encapsulate the achievement of the expedition's men: "They forged the last link with their lives." But the clearest summation came from John Rae. In August 1855, he wrote to Richardson from Stromness, agreeing with his old travelling companion that McClure had been lucky. As for what was said of the matter in the House, Rae declared "it was all balderdash and could only go down with those who knew nothing of the subject."

Meanwhile, during the summer of 1855, in response to Lady Franklin's importunities, the Hudson's Bay Company sent fur trader James Anderson down the Great Fish River to Chantrey Inlet on the Arctic Coast. Acting on a plan devised by John Rae, Anderson travelled the only way he could on such short notice: by canoe. He encountered several Inuit and acquired a few more relics—part of a snowshoe, the leather lining of a backgammon board—but, having failed to acquire a requested Inuit interpreter, he elicited no new detail.

Given Britain's engagement in the above-mentioned Crimean War, the Admiralty grew increasingly desperate to cease spending on Arctic exploration. To staunch the financial bleeding, the Lords opened a second monetary-awards front. On January 22, 1856, they announced that, within three months, they would decide whether to award the £10,000 prize offered for determining the fate of Franklin. To do so would mean further expeditions were unnecessary. Once again, several claimants stepped forward, among them the whaling captain William Penny, present at the discovery of the Beechey Island graves, and the irrepressible Richard King, who had long ago travelled on one overland journey with George Back: "I alone have for many years pointed out the banks of the Great Fish River as the place where Franklin's claim could be found."

Soon after the Admiralty announcement, unaware that Lady Franklin had animated Charles Dickens to write his two-part repudiation of his championing of the Inuit, John Rae called on her once more. Here was a woman who, as Francis Spufford would later observe, "could blight or accelerate careers, bestow or withhold the sanction of her reputation. No other nineteenth-century woman raised the cash for three polar expeditions, or had her say over the appointment of captains and lieutenants."

John Rae informed Lady Franklin that in Upper Canada, with the help of two expatriate brothers, he had ordered a schooner built. He intended to use any reward money he received to mount yet another Arctic expedition, during which he would seek to acquire more evidence to confirm his report. Although he probably did not mention it, clearly the veteran explorer hoped during that same projected voyage to sail the entire Northwest Passage, using the strait he had discovered to the east of King William Island—the twenty-two-kilometre-wide channel, already known as Rae Strait, through which the Norwegian Roald Amundsen would sail in 1903–1906 while becoming the first to navigate the Passage.

Lady Franklin remained unimpressed. The meeting over, she observed, "Dr. Rae has cut off his odious beard but looks still very hairy and disagreeable." Nevertheless, she made use of the information she gleaned from the explorer when, in April, she dispatched a long, rigorous letter stressing that the reward had been intended to go "to any party or parties who in the judgement of the Board of the Admiralty should by virtue of his or their efforts first succeed in ascertaining the fate of the expedition."

Jane Franklin argued first that the fate of her husband's expedition had not been ascertained because too many questions remained unanswered. She insisted that, even if Rae had ascertained the fate—through those countless interviews and cross-questionings—he had done so not by his efforts, but by chance. By giving the award now, the Admiralty would deny it to those who would rightly earn it. This would create a check or block "to any further efforts for ascertaining the fate of the expedition, and appears to counteract the humane intention of the House of Commons in voting a large sum of money for that purpose."

Jane Franklin brought her epistle to a stirring climax: "What secrets may be hidden within those wrecked or stranded ships we know not—what may be buried in the graves of our unhappy countrymen or in caches not yet discovered we have yet to learn. The bodies and the graves which we were told of have not been found; the books [journals] said to be in the hands of the Esquimaux have not been recovered; and thus left in ignorance and darkness with so little obtained and so much yet to learn, can it be said and is it fitting to pronounce that the fate of the expedition is ascertained?"

The Lords of the Admiralty would have none of it. They had grown tired of receiving unsolicited advice from Lady Franklin. On June 19, 1856—three months beyond the promised date—the Board notified John Rae that he would receive the award. Rae himself would get four-fifths, and his men would receive the rest.

Lady Franklin had lost another skirmish. Over her protests, and despite her relentless opposition, first Robert McClure and now John Rae had received monetary awards. First the Passage, now the fate—how all occasions informed against her. Was she finished? Had the time come to concede defeat?

21.

The Lady Won't Be Denied

B y 1856, Lady Franklin had spent £35,000 searching for her husband—the equivalent today, by conservative estimate, of US$3.7 million. Some came from her own accounts and some she raised through public subscription. She inspired Americans to contribute as well—more than US$13 million in contemporary terms, two-fifths of that from shipping magnate Henry Grinnell.

Of three dozen expeditions that had sailed in search of Franklin since 1848, Lady Franklin had organized, inspired and financed ten. As well, using both public opinion and influential friends, she had exerted relentless pressure on the Lords of the British Admiralty, compelling them to spend between £600,000 and £675,000.

Meanwhile, during the two years ending in March 1856, the British government had spent massively on the Crimean War, battling Russia—in alliance with France and the Ottoman Empire—to reduce that country's influence around the Black Sea. Faced with increasing pressure to reduce expenditures, and as one expedition after another returned from the Arctic with nothing to report, the Lords of the Admiralty yearned to forget the long-lost Sir John. Jane Franklin was not going to let that happen.

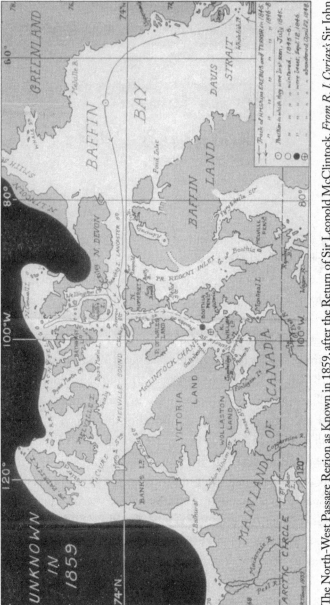

The North-West Passage Region as Known in 1859, after the Return of Sir Leopold McClintock. *From R. J. Cyriax's* Sir John Franklin's Last Arctic Expedition.

In spring 1856, she organized yet another petition. She solicited signatures from dozens of prominent figures, among them scientists, naval officers, presidents and past presidents of the Royal Society and the Royal Geographical Society. The signatories challenged the notion that Franklin's fate had been ascertained. They appealed for yet another search expedition "to satisfy the honour of our country, and clear up a mystery which has excited the sympathy of the civilized world."

In June, Lady Franklin sought support from the House of Commons. The president of the Royal Society informed her that she would receive assistance if she provided a ship and a commanding officer. She still owned the schooner *Isabel*, and thought she might return that ship to Arctic service. To command the vessel, and solidify her alliance with the Americans, she looked to Elisha Kent Kane.

During his recent expedition, Kane had displayed courage, wisdom and resourcefulness. A protegé of New Yorker Henry Grinnell, Kane was a gifted writer and artist. Jane had admired his published journal of the first Grinnell expedition. She had exchanged letters with him. Since re-emerging from the Arctic, Kane had been working sixteen hours a day, turning his detailed journal and vivid sketches into a two-volume classic: *Arctic Explorations: The Second Grinnell Expedition in Search of Sir John Franklin*.

As Kane put the finishing touches on this work, Lady Franklin wrote to him requesting his services in the Arctic. If he would consent to take the *Isabel* in search of Franklin, she would travel to New York City to discuss her hopes for this final expedition. Kane accepted with alacrity but gallantly insisted that he would come to England to discuss the undertaking.

Despite ominous indications that his chronic heart condition was worsening—weight loss, emaciation, physical weakness, lack of energy—the explorer convinced himself that he needed only rest. By mid-July, however, he realized that he would not be able to undertake a proposed lecture tour. To Jane Franklin, Henry Grinnell wrote from New York that Kane had visited him for an hour: "I never saw him look so bad; he is but a skeleton or the shadow of one; he has worked too hard." Kane wrote of travelling to France and Switzerland, and regaining his health among the glaciers before proceeding to England. But Grinnell noted: "He is every day attacked with the remittent fever, better known here as fever and ague."

Kane reached England in October 1856, soon after he published *Arctic Explorations.* Jane Franklin admired the work enormously, though it told so grim a tale that she feared it might discourage further searches for her husband. When Kane called at her home, she realized, with shock and dismay, that the heroic explorer had not recovered from his last Arctic voyage. She hoped that "the air of the old country" would restore his health and, over the next couple of weeks, plied him with cod-liver oil. Doctors advised Kane to make for more salubrious climes. Lady Franklin recommended Madeira, just off northern Africa.

With his health failing, the explorer opted instead for Cuba, nearer to home. He got that far and no farther. On February 16, 1857, Elisha Kent Kane died in Havana. Such was his fame throughout the United States that he was given an unprecedented state funeral. Possibly the detour to England had made no difference. Either way, Kane was dead. And Lady Franklin had to look elsewhere for a ship's captain.

By now, she was embroiled in a battle to acquire a British ship called the *Resolute.* In 1854, to his everlasting disgrace, expedition leader Edward Belcher had abandoned that ship and three others in the Arctic ice. The following September, an American whaler, James Buddington, had chanced upon the *Resolute*, by then floating freely off Baffin Island, some 1,900 kilometres east of where she started. With a skeleton crew of thirteen men, Buddington sailed the ship home to Connecticut, arriving on Christmas Eve. The American navy, encouraged by Henry Grinnell, bought and refurbished the salvaged vessel, and proposed to return it to Britain as a goodwill gesture. In conjunction with Grinnell, and having learned that her *Isabel* was in dubious condition, Lady Franklin launched a vigorous campaign to acquire the *Resolute* for yet another "final" search expedition.

Over the years, however, she had made enemies. The First Lord of the Admiralty, Sir Charles Wood, and the First Sea Lord, Sir Maurice Berkeley—tired of being bullied and browbeaten, sick unto death of communications from Jane, Lady Franklin—argued that the expense of another expedition could not be justified and that the Royal Navy had lost quite enough men searching for Franklin. In the end, they succeeded in denying her the *Resolute*.

By the time she heard the official response, Lady Franklin had devised a contingency plan. Within one week of the Admiralty rejection, she had arranged to purchase—for a special low price of £2,000—a newly available sailing ship of 177 tons. The vessel had belonged to Sir Richard Hutton, who had died after using it for a single cruise. Considerably smaller than the *Resolute*, the *Fox* was 124 feet long, 24 feet wide and 13 feet deep. Refitted for Arctic service, it would suit perfectly.

The former question remained: Who would command this search expedition?

22.

Leopold McClintock Retrieves a Record

After sounding out friends and naval officers, Lady Franklin offered the *Fox* to Captain Francis Leopold McClintock. Born in Dundalk, Ireland, in 1818, McClintock had joined the Royal Navy as a gentleman volunteer at the ripe old age of seventeen. In 1848, as a second lieutenant, he had sailed in search of Franklin with James Clark Ross. Their two ships had got repeatedly locked in the ice, and after eleven months, the expedition returned to England.

Five years later, serving with Henry Kellett, McClintock conducted a notable sledging journey, travelling 2,250 kilometres in 105 days and charting 1,235 kilometres of previously unmapped coast. He was a capable, deliberate officer who knew enough to write to James Clark Ross about serving Lady Franklin, wondering "how far the Admiralty sanction ought to be obtained, as I do not wish to be so impolitic as to act counter to their wishes."

In April 1857, from Dublin, McClintock sent the Lady a conditional acceptance. He enclosed, for forwarding, his application for a leave of absence from the Royal Navy. Jane wrote to Prince Albert's private secretary, asking that the prince intercede on McClintock's

Before sailing at the behest of Lady Franklin, Leopold McClintock had shown himself to be a capable, deliberate naval officer.

behalf so that he would not have to resign his commission—and so making the result a foregone conclusion. On April 23 she wired McClintock, "Your leave is granted; the *Fox* is mine; the refit will commence immediately."

Six days later, under the heading "Lady Franklin's Final Search," the *Times* carried an advertisement for subscribers to finance the expedition. Private companies contributed boats, food, stoves and tents, and the Admiralty came through with arms, ammunition and three tons of pemmican. Later, a newspaper report published by "friends of Lady Franklin" would indicate that the expedition cost £10,434. Subscribers included not only relatives of those lost with Franklin but the novelist William Thackeray and Peter Mark Roget, originator of the famous thesaurus and an old flame of Jane Franklin's. Allen Young, a wealthy captain in the merchant marine, contributed £500 and volunteered to serve as sailing master without pay.

McClintock proceeded to Aberdeen to sift through applications and oversee the refitting of the *Fox*. This involved replacing velvet furnishings, stowing provisions and making the pleasure craft an ice-worthy vessel. He was there when Jane Franklin, mindful always of appearances, summoned him to London to meet Queen Victoria at a public ceremony. With that accomplished, McClintock returned to Aberdeen.

Lady Franklin followed a few days later, travelling to that city by train. On the last day of June 1857, she and Sophy Cracroft, her niece and amanuensis, went aboard the *Fox* for a farewell luncheon. Later McClintock would write of Lady Franklin: "Seeing how deeply agitated she was on leaving the ship, I endeavoured to repress the enthusiasm of my crew, but without avail; it found vent in three prolonged, hearty cheers. The strong feeling which prompted them was truly sincere, and this unbidden exhibition of it can hardly have gratified her for whom it was intended more than it did myself."

On July 2, 1857, with a complement of twenty-five men, including seventeen Arctic veterans, Leopold McClintock sailed out of Aberdeen. He went to gather evidence of what had happened to the Franklin expedition. That was his primary objective. But in the weeks before sailing, he found time to consult with John Rae, to discuss whether he might sail the *Fox* through Rae Strait, which separated Boothia Peninsula and King William Island. If he could make his way through there, he could almost certainly proceed to the Pacific Ocean, and so become the first explorer to navigate the Northwest Passage.

In the mid-Atlantic, as ordered, McClintock opened a letter of instructions from Jane Franklin. In it, she laid out three priorities: he should rescue any survivors, recover any written records and seek confirmation that Franklin's men had travelled over water to the northern coast of the North American continent. This last affirmation would enable Jane to argue that her husband had preceded McClure as first discoverer of a northwest passage, even though he had got nowhere near the Pacific Ocean, and this alleged passage, the ice-choked Victoria Strait, was just as fictional as the one McClure discovered, and would remain impassable until the 1960s.

Confident that McClintock would strive to attain her stated objectives, and mindful always of posterity, Jane Franklin had added, "My only fear is that you may spend yourselves too much in the effort; and you must therefore let me tell you how much dearer to me even than any of them is the preservation of the valuable lives of the little band of heroes who are your companions and followers." In western Greenland, McClintock bought two dozen sled dogs and added an Inuk interpreter called "Christian" to assist Carl Petersen, who had sailed with William Penny and Elisha Kent Kane.

McClintock proceeded north along the west coast of Greenland to Melville Bay, a crescent-shaped indentation extending along the coast, south to north, for 240 kilometres. Like Kane before him, McClintock swung directly west into Baffin Bay and the Middle Ice—that floating mass of ice fields dotted with giant icebergs, scores of them larger than the *Fox*. The Middle Ice was almost always impenetrable, although a few ships had managed to get through. Six years before, Kane had done so while driving north into Smith Sound. He had hitched his ship to a massive iceberg and had it drag him along against the wind and the waves. He had discerned that the iceberg extended so far underwater that it was driven by a deeper current.

McClintock proved less lucky. He got trapped in the Middle Ice and spent eight months drifting south. Released on April 25, 1858, McClintock returned to Godhavn (Disko Bay), off present-day Ilulissat, and resupplied the ship. In mid-June, he sailed north again. This time, he got into Lancaster Sound and, without mishap, sailed west to Beechey Island. There, just above Northumberland House, he erected a splendid memorial tablet provided by Lady Franklin.

The Fox *got trapped in the Middle Ice and spent an agonizing eight months being driven south. Leopold McClintock resupplied the ship at Disko Bay and resumed his westward voyage.*

From Beechey, McClintock started due south down Peel Sound. But after travelling forty kilometres, he found himself blocked by ice. He retreated north and east and then swung south down Prince Regent Inlet. He hoped to sail west through Bellot Strait to King William Island. But when he reached the western end of that narrow channel, he encountered a wall of ice blocking Victoria Strait. He withdrew and, late in 1858, established winter quarters within easy viewing distance of a ridge overlooking present-day Fort Ross (so named by the Hudson's Bay Company in 1937, when it built a trading post there).

Today, at the highest point on that ridge, visitors can stand beside "McClintock's Cairn" while gazing out over Bellot Strait, Prince Regent Inlet and the Fox Islands. In the winter of 1858–59, anyone scrambling to that spot would have been able to see the *Fox* locked in the ice and battened down for the winter; and also a magnetic observatory nearly two hundred metres from the ship, "built of ice sawed into blocks," as McClintock wrote, "there not being any suitable snow."

Prevented by ice from sailing farther, McClintock took to sledges. On February 17, 1859, he set out with two dog teams on a reconnaissance mission to Cape Victoria, on the west coast of Boothia Peninsula, near where James Clark Ross had located the north magnetic pole. There, McClintock encountered some Inuit who had acquired and were happy to trade Franklin relics, among them forks, spoons, a medal and a gold chain. None of them had seen any white men, but one older man, Oo-na-lee, said the relics came from a place where some white men had starved on an island in a river containing salmon. Others spoke of a ship, McClintock wrote, that had been "crushed by ice out in the sea to the west of King William's Island."

Bad weather prevented further investigation until April. But then, after returning to Cape Victoria, McClintock met another group of Inuit, including a young man who sold him a knife. "After much anxious inquiry," McClintock wrote, "we learned that two ships had been seen by the natives of King William's Island; one of them was seen to sink in deep water, and nothing was obtained from her, a circumstance at which they expressed much regret; but the other was forced on shore by the ice, where they suppose she still remains, but is much broken. From this ship they have obtained most of their wood, etc.; and Oot-loo-lik is the name of the place where she grounded."

Most of this McClintock learned from the young man who sold him the knife. "Old Oo-na-lee, who drew the rough chart for me in March, to show where the ship sank, now answered our questions respecting the one forced on shore; not a syllable about her did he mention on the former occasion, although we asked whether they knew of only one ship? I think he would willingly have kept us in ignorance of the wreck being upon their coasts, and that the young man unwittingly made it known to us." The savvy Oo-na-lee was probably thinking of acquiring valuable trade goods.

Here the story grows more dramatic. The young man "also told us that the body of a man was found on board the ship," McClintock wrote; "that he must have been a very large man, and had long teeth; this is all he recollected having been told, for he was quite a child at the time." Both men said that the ships were destroyed in August or September; "that all the white people went away to the large river, taking a boat or boats with them, and that in the following winter their bones were found there."

Which of Franklin's two ships housed the body? Today, the best guess is probably *Erebus*, found in September 2014 at Oot-loo-lik, off the northwest coast of Adelaide Peninsula in Wilmot and Crampton Bay. What year was that ship grounded? Best guess, 1851—eight years before McClintock began asking questions. But most of this Inuit oral history would be set aside in light of what came next: a written document.

In April 1859, on Boothia Peninsula at Cape Victoria, McClintock divided his expeditionary team. He sent William Hobson, his second-in-command, to trace the northern and western coasts of King William Island. He himself headed south through Rae Strait. He crossed Simpson Strait to Montreal Island and the estuary of the Great Fish River (now called the Back River). Finding nothing but a few relics in an Inuit cairn, he recrossed Simpson Strait and travelled west along the south coast of King William Island. He came across an unburied skeleton and a number of Franklin expedition relics, and at Cape Herschel, he dismantled the cairn Thomas Simpson had built twenty years before, but found it empty.

Nineteen kilometres on, McClintock spotted a new cairn containing a note from his second-in-command. Hobson had made a

H. M. S.hips *Erebus* and *Terror*

{ Wintered in the Ice in

28 of May 1847 { Lat. 70° 5' N Long. 98° 23' W

Having wintered in 1846–7 at Beechey Island

in Lat 74° 43' 28" N. Long 91° 39' 15" W after having

ascended Wellington Channel to Lat 77° and returned

by the West side of Cornwallis Island.

Sir John Franklin commanding the Expedition.

All well

WHOEVER finds this paper is requested to forward it to the Secretary of the Admiralty, London, *with a note of the time and place at which it was found*; or, if more convenient, to deliver it for that purpose to the British Consul at the nearest Port.

QUINCONQUE trouvera ce papier est prié d'y marquer le tems et lieu ou il l'aura trouvé, et de le faire parvenir au plutot au Secretaire de l'Amirauté Britannique à Londres.

CUALQUIERA que hallare este Papel, se le suplica de enviarlo al Secretario del Almirantazgo, en Londrés, con una nota del tiempo y del lugar en donde se halló.

EEN ieder die dit Papier mogt vinden, wordt hiermede verzogt, om het zelve, ten spoedigste, te willen zenden aan den Heer Minister van de Marine der Nederlanden in 's Gravenhage, of wel aan den Secretaris der Britsche Admiraliteit, te London, en daar by te voegen eene Nota, inhoudende de tyd en de plaats alwaar dit Papier is gevonden geworden

FINDEREN af dette Papiir ombedes, naar Leilighed gives, at sende samme til Admiralitets Secretairen i London, eller nœrmeste Embedsmand i Danmark, Norge, eller Sverrig. Tiden og Stœdit hvor dette er funden önskes venskabeligt paategnet.

WER diesen Zettel findet, wird hier-durch ersucht denselben an den Secretair des Admiralitets in London einzusenden, mit gefälliger angabe an welchen ort und zu welcher zeit er gefundet worden ist.

Party consisting of 2 Officers and 6 men left the Ships on Monday 24th May 1847

Gm. Gore Lieut
Chas. F. Des Vœux mate

As of early 2017, the Victory Point record remained the only written document recovered from the Franklin expedition. It indicated that the two ships were "deserted" on April 22, 1848. Today, most analysts are convinced that at least some men returned to one or both of the vessels.

spectacular discovery. He had found two notes scrawled on printed Royal Navy forms and deposited in metal cylinders near Victory Point. The first message, written on May 28, 1847, indicated that the *Erebus* and the *Terror* had spent the previous winter in the ice at the northwest corner of King William Island, off Cape Felix. It said Franklin had spent the winter before that (1845–46) at Beechey Island after ascending Wellington Channel to latitude 77° and circling Cornwallis Island. All was well.

The second message, which was added to the page eleven months later, on April 25, 1848, said that the *Erebus* and the *Terror*, trapped twenty to twenty-five kilometres northwest of Victory Point since September 1846, had been "deserted" three days before: "The officers and crews, consisting of 105 souls, under the command of Captain F. R. M. Crozier, landed here [it gave geographical coordinates]. Sir John Franklin died on the 11 June 1847; and the total loss by deaths in the expedition has been to this date 9 officers and 15 men." Captain Francis Crozier had added a final few words: "And start (on) tomorrow, 26th, for Back's Fish River."

What had happened to reduce the expedition's numbers so dramatically, from 129 to 105? Why had such a high percentage of officers died? The Victory Point record raised more questions than it answered. Halfway down the west coast of King William Island, at Erebus Bay, Hobson had found a twenty-four-foot-long boat-sledge containing an array of unnecessary goods, as well as two dead bodies. McClintock, following Hobson north, also puzzled over the boat, which was facing north. Were the men trying to haul the boat back to the ship off Victory Point? That would be madness . . . an idea that would fuel theories of addled brains and lead poisoning.

Rivetted by the Victory Point record—a written document, after all—searchers and armchair experts would set aside Inuit oral history.

For decades, nobody gave much thought to the notion that all or at least some of the 105 men might have returned to the ships. Nobody suggested that, with men aboard, both vessels had been carried south by ice—one only as far as Terror Bay, the other to near Adelaide Peninsula. Nobody speculated that with one or both ships proceeding slowly south along the coast, the survivors would not need to drag that overloaded boat and sledge any great distance. When the ice melted, they would need only to haul it back into the water to make for the nearest ship. Who cared which way it faced?

From the boat, McClintock retrieved remnants of a blue jacket and a great coat, a clothes brush and a horn comb, a toothbrush, a sponge, some crested silver and a prayer book called *Christian Melodies*, frozen hard, along with a Bible and a copy of *The Vicar of Wakefield*. Back at his Boothia camp, he talked to an old Inuit woman, who reported, "They fell down and died as they walked along."

Having reboarded the *Fox* by the end of June, McClintock waited in the ice. He sailed at last on August 10 and reached London six weeks later. He had charted 1,280 kilometres of coastline and completed the mapping of the northern coast of the continent. He had found the only written record of the Franklin expedition that has yet turned up. To Lady Franklin, who was travelling in southwestern France when he arrived in London, McClintock sent a letter summarizing. He noted that Sir John had died on June 11, 1847: "I cannot help remarking to you what instantly occurred to me on reading the records. That Sir John Franklin was not harassed by either want of success or forebodings of evil."

This was precisely what Jane Franklin needed to hear. Her late husband stood personally absolved of cannibalism. As for no "want of success," McClintock had brought her more than enough to create an enduring mythology.

23.

Who Discovered the Fate of Franklin?

The Victorian establishment quickly decided, as William James Mills writes in *Exploring Polar Frontiers*, that with his voyage of 1857–1859, Leopold McClintock had confirmed "that Franklin's men, in making the journey from Point Victory to the Great Fish River, had completed the first crossing of the Northwest Passage."

Contemporary readers may find themselves scratching their heads. Wait, what? Say again? The Passage extends from Baffin Bay to the Beaufort Sea. Every last one of Franklin's men died roughly in the middle. They got trapped in the ice of an impassable strait. They did not return home with any geographical news. Obviously, they completed nothing. But never mind.

Building upon the Victory Point record, and ignoring the Inuit he had interviewed, McClintock himself articulated an oversimplification that would give rise to an erroneous "standard reconstruction." The starving crews, he wrote, had abandoned the *Erebus* and the *Terror* in April 1848. "The survivors, under Crozier and Fitzjames, numbered in all 105; they proceeded with boats on sledges to the Great Fish River. One of their boats was found by us, untouched by the Esquimaux, and many relics brought from her, as also obtained from the natives of Boothia and the east shore of King William Island."

Today, given the discoveries of both *Erebus* and *Terror*, and the additional information provided by Inuit testimony, we know that, while some men trekked south and east along the coast of King William Island, a few others returned to one or both of those ships and remained on board as the pack ice carried them south.

Subsequent searchers would find more relics, more bodies, more frozen bones. They would interview Inuit eyewitnesses and excavate gravesites and conduct forensic examinations. They would produce extrapolations and conflicting theories and draw attention to unexplored aspects of the Franklin legend. But nobody has yet turned up another written record—though that may change over the next few years as Parks Canada divers scour the two ships. Of the one-page document he presented to Lady Franklin on her arrival in London, McClintock declared, "A sadder tale was never told in fewer words."

With that characterization, few would argue. Yet what, exactly, was the truth of that tale? A decade would elapse before the American Charles Francis Hall would return from the Arctic, carrying notes from interviews he had conducted with numerous Inuit, including eyewitnesses—detailed testimonials, harrowing and convincing, that some final survivors of the Franklin expedition had resorted to cannibalism. And more than a century would go by before forensic studies would provide conclusive physical evidence that, with his initial report, the forthright John Rae had revealed a more profound truth about "the fate of Franklin" than the circumspect Leopold McClintock.

But in 1859, the complex truth of the expedition's "fate" did not matter much, if only because, in her sense of history and how to create it, Lady Franklin stood alone among her contemporaries. Her wide reading, unprecedented adventuring and obsessive visiting of historical sites had taught this astute Victorian that what actually happened at any given moment dwindles to insignificance in comparison with what is perceived to have happened. Jane Franklin understood that, as regards history and enduring reputation, perception creates the only truth that counts. And at controlling perception, she knew no peers.

Ignoring John Rae's report, so unpleasant and inconvenient, Jane Franklin hailed McClintock as discoverer of the fate of Franklin. She expected her influential friends to do likewise. The closest of them, cognizant of her aspirations, required no specific guidance. On October 11, 1859—not two weeks after McClintock arrived home—John Richardson would turn his back on Rae, his old travelling companion, to laud the captain of the *Fox*: "The intelligence procured by Dr. Rae was less reliable, as coming from a tribe who had seen neither the wrecks nor the crews themselves, alive or dead, but had got their information and the European articles they possessed through an intervening party. Some of their reports therefore are to be regarded merely as the habitual exaggerations of a rude people in repeating a story." In fact, McClintock's informants were also relaying secondhand information.

From the United States, Henry Grinnell sent excited congratulations, observing that McClintock "has acquired a just fame for himself, which the pages of history will never allow to be obliterated." He added that, as regards Lady Franklin herself, "it is better that I should say nothing, for I have not the command of words to define the estimate I entertain of your character. I am not alone in this; the whole community is with me. I am from all quarters congratulated

John Rae as depicted in 1854 in The Illustrated London News. *Notwithstanding the accolades bestowed on McClintock, Rae was the one who brought the first authentic tidings of the fate of the Franklin expedition.*

on the event, as though I had a part in bringing it about; it is you, however, that is intended, through me."

Within three months, encouraged by Jane Franklin, McClintock was proclaiming that he had ascertained the fate of the Franklin expedition. William Arrowsmith, a leading cartographer, responded to him by observing that John Rae had not only already ascertained the fate but had been recognized and rewarded for doing so. In March 1860, McClintock wrote to Rae complaining of Arrowsmith's tone.

Responding from London, Rae entered into what became a testy correspondence. By suggesting that McClintock had merely confirmed and clarified his own findings, and that, in future, other searchers would shed additional light on the fate of the Franklin expedition, he originated an argument that stands up in the light of subsequent history. Rae wrote:

It is very generally allowed that the information brought home by me in 1854, together with the numerous relics bearing the crests and initials of fourteen of the officers of the *Erebus* and *Terror*, were sufficient evidence that a large portion of both Franklin's ships had died of disease and starvation in the neighbourhood of the Back River and King William's Land on or previous to 1850, and that these were the last survivors of the party. I was told also that the ship or ships had been destroyed by ice.

Your information does not contradict that brought by me in any important fact, and proves the correctness of the Esquimaux intelligence even in regard to the route followed by the unfortunate people on their way to the Back River. You leave 102 persons out of 129 unaccounted for, except through information similar to that from which mine was obtained—my interpreter was perfectly acquainted with the dialect and language of the Esquimaux of Repulse Bay, many of whom I had known in 1846–47, and had always found with a few exceptions honest and truthful.

There are other more minute particulars that I might dwell upon, but the great fact that a large portion of Franklin's party died of starvation and (leaving little doubt as to the fate of the remainder) at a certain locality which I named correctly on or before 1850, was communicated by me in 1854 . . .

W. Arrowsmith showed me your note to him, after perusing which I scarcely think his note to you can be called intemperate. I write in perfect good feeling, as I hope people may do in a matter of opinion on a subject where there always will be two sides of the question, perhaps three, were another expedition to go out and find the journals of some of the latest survivors.

From Dublin, addressing his letter "My dear Rae," Leopold McClintock replied:

I quite agree with all you state as to the information and relics brought home by you in /54; they afforded circumstantial evidence as to the fate of a large party, probably the last survivors of Franklin's crews; and the impression was strong as to the sad fate of the whole. But positive proof was wanting, therefore in /55 Anderson was sent out by the government, but he was unable to do more than confirm your locality of Montreal Island. In /59 I confirmed more of your report and found such further traces and records as have cleared up the fate of the whole expedition. Now it is evident that as these traces were unknown to the natives themselves, no information respecting them could have reached you; therefore these skeletons, records, several cairns and a boat, besides articles innumerable, are my discovery.

Also, by having been able to judge of their equipment from specimens seen, of their state of health, and of the absence of game upon the coast they travelled, I have shown that they could not possibly have reached beyond Montreal Island and must have all perished . . .

This should not be confused with the information you received respecting those who died upon the mainland. All native information whether obtained by you or I must be limited to the SW shoreline of King William Island, since they have not visited the NW coast. But you will see that I have managed my work as to be independent of their testimony altogether.

My object in the *Fox* was to examine the whole of the unexplored area between the Barrow Strait beaches and Anderson and I did so. Had your information as to locality been conclusive this great labour would have been unnecessary. Now in spite of these additional and important facts, Arrowsmith does me the injustice of giving you credit for the whole, and simply mentioned me as having "fully confirmed" you, and talks of "the first intelligence of the Fate" as if anything could be discovered twice.

To this, John Rae responded: "I must confess that your able arguments do not in any material point alter my opinions, no more than any thing I could say would be likely to alter yours. Your information although of course fuller than that obtained by me does not account for 102 persons or about 3/4 of Franklin's party, except through Esquimaux testimony which you say you managed to be 'wholly independent of.'"

The exchange continued, wending into details of less relevance. John Rae had already presented the decisive argument, when he suggested that more differences would inevitably arise, especially "were another expedition to go out and find the journals of some of the latest survivors." The great hope today, of course, is that maritime archaeologists will find journals, letters, or other written documents aboard the *Erebus* or *Terror*.

Eventually, McClintock would stand revealed as the first of many investigators to add detail and nuance to Rae's original report, which had been based on Inuit accounts. But in 1859, that truth did not matter. Lady Franklin presented all of McClintock's sailors with a silver watch, engraved with a likeness of the *Fox*. To McClintock himself, at a dinner she held in his honour at her home in central London, she gave a three-foot-long silver model of the *Fox*, which he would keep under a glass in his drawing room.

McClintock had not been home three weeks before Lady Franklin relayed the relics and records he had brought home to Queen Victoria, using as a go-between Franklin's old friend Edward Sabine, now a major general in the army. From Windsor Castle, the monarch responded with a letter of thanks that paid homage to "the unremitting and praiseworthy efforts of Lady Franklin," a missive Sophy Cracroft rightly described as "the most charming message of thanks . . . and of sympathy."

On July 1, 1860, the Queen boarded the *Fox* with Prince Albert, who, on going below to inspect the cabins, expressed "surprise at the smallness of the apartments." Before the year was out, Leopold McClintock would be knighted—an honour that would forever elude the plain-speaking John Rae. As well, Sir Leopold would receive honorary degrees in London and Dublin.

Meanwhile, Lady Franklin had arranged for yet another motion to be brought before the House of Commons, this one to reward McClintock. The prime minister, Viscount Lord Palmerston, agreed that, although the official reward had already been paid to John Rae, "this was a fit occasion in which to make, within moderate limits, a grant, over and above the amount already sanctioned."

Then came a characteristic "Lady Franklin twist." Speaking in the House, the powerful Palmerston hoped that a monument would be erected to Sir John Franklin in commemoration of his achievement.

Another old family friend, the influential Benjamin Disraeli, leapt to support this idea, declaring that such a memorial would be "most gratifying for the country, as it evidently is most gratifying for this House." The well-rehearsed symphony reached a crescendo with a vote, passed unanimously, to award Leopold McClintock £5,000—and to set aside another £2,000 for a monument to Sir John Franklin.

The accolades accorded McClintock redounded to the credit of Lady Franklin, who, if she had not already done so, now achieved iconic status. The *Morning Advertiser* wrote of her that she would go to her grave clutching a miniature of Sir John, and the *Daily Telegraph* designated her "Our English Penelope." Jane's brother-in-law Ashurst Majendie exaggerated only slightly in observing, "She now holds the highest position of any English woman."

Lady Franklin would also treasure an afternoon in May 1860 when the Royal Geographical Society awarded her the Founder's Gold Medal—the first woman ever so honoured. The citation testified "to the fact that [Franklin's] expedition was the first to discover a North-West Passage." It hailed Lady Franklin's "noble and self-sacrificing perseverance in sending out at her own cost several Expeditions until at length the fate of her husband was entertained." On all this, Jane Franklin could build.

More than 130 years later, in *Unravelling the Franklin Expedition*, David C. Woodman would write: "The vague stories [Leopold McClintock] had collected were essentially uninteresting to the British public. They added detail to Rae's account, and confirmed it, but presented little that was new." McClintock carefully avoided explicitly confirming the most significant aspects of Rae's report. Having witnessed the excommunication of the HBC explorer, he wisely made no mention whatsoever of Englishmen eating Englishmen.

McClintock—or rather his second-in-command, Lieutenant William R. Hobson—did discover the only written document that has yet been salvaged from the expedition. But he could not have accomplished that if Rae had not returned with the original information. Sir Leopold certainly deserves recognition as one of the investigators who added detail to Rae's discovery.

But it was Rae who correctly reported in 1854 that all members of the Franklin expedition were dead. He revealed where many of them died and indicated where others had probably perished. Finally, because he knew enough to believe the Inuit, he divulged the least welcome, yet somehow most significant, truth of all: that some of the final survivors had resorted to cannibalism.

The fate of the Franklin expedition will never be known in every detail. Marine archaeologists may yet find another written record in a waterproof cylinder on the *Erebus* or the *Terror*. Louie Kamookak, who is based in Gjoa Haven, continues to seek the grave of John Franklin on King William Island. More searchers may yet add their names to the ever-growing list of those who have clarified the fate of Franklin. The first name on that list, however, will forever remain that of John Rae. The maverick Rae, not the circumspect McClintock, brought the world the first authentic tidings of the fate of the Franklin expedition.

Part Six

THE MYTH OF FRANKLIN

24.

Lady Franklin Creates an Arctic Hero

On November 15, 1866, three weeks before she turned seventy-five, an elegantly dressed, petite woman sat in a comfortable, high-backed chair on the second floor of the Athenaeum Club in central London, looking out a window at a ceremonial unveiling in Waterloo Place. Jane, Lady Franklin, her thinning white hair hidden beneath a fashionable bonnet, watched as politicians and senior naval officers clustered around a larger-than-life statue of her dead husband. Created by the well-known sculptor Matthew Noble, the monument identified Sir John Franklin as the discoverer of the Northwest Passage—a circumstance most women would have regarded as a final vindication.

"The moment selected for representation," the *Times* would report the next day, "is that in which Franklin has at length the satisfaction of informing his officers and crew that the North West Passage has been discovered. In his hand he grasps the telescope, chart and compasses, and over the full uniform of a naval commander assumed in connection with the important announcement he is in the act of making, he wears a loose overcoat of fur."

Having herself created that perfect moment, Jane Franklin knew it to be a fiction, and so vulnerable to challenge and contradiction. That was why she had taken such pains with the memorial. Having spent two decades and a small fortune establishing the appropriate mythology—the legend of Sir John Franklin as Discoverer—Jane had left no detail to chance. She had hired the sculptor and stipulated the pose. She had positioned the statue precisely, insisting, after checking the view from this gentlemen's club, that it be moved back from the street eighteen inches.

Jane Franklin had also supervised the creation of the bas-relief beneath the figure of Franklin, a panel that depicted his second-in-command reading the burial service over a coffin mounted on a sledge. In the background, obscured by mounds of ice, arise the masts of Franklin's ships, the *Erebus* and the *Terror*. Jane had required that the flags be altered to reflect the effects of freezing-cold temperatures. At the base of the statue, she had inscribed the names of the officers and crew of both ships and, in larger letters, the evocative phrase coined by her friend Sir John Richardson: "They forged the last link with their lives."

Richardson was extrapolating from the work of Leopold McClintock. "Had Sir John Franklin known that a channel existed eastward of King William Land (so named by John Ross)," McClintock wrote, "I do not think that he would have risked the besetment of his ships in such very heavy ice to the westward of it. Had he attempted the north-west passage by the eastern route he would probably have carried his ships through to Behring's Straits. But Franklin was furnished with charts which indicated no passage to the eastward of King William Land, and he made that land (since discovered by Rae to be an island) a peninsula, attached to the continent of North America; and he consequently had but one course open to him, and that [was] the one he adopted."

McClintock added that "perhaps some future voyager, profiting by the experience so fearfully and fatally acquired by the Franklin expedition, and the observations of Rae, [Richard] Collinson, and myself, may succeed in carrying his ship through from sea to sea; at least he will be enabled to direct all his efforts in the true and only direction." In this surmise, McClintock anticipated Roald Amundsen, who would become the first to navigate the Passage in 1903–1906.

But the British naval officer also thought to add, "In the mean time, to Franklin must be assigned the earliest discovery of the Northwest Passage, though not the actual accomplishment of it in his ships." McClintock was following the line laid down by Lady Franklin. Francis Beaufort, another of the lady's friends, summarized the cabal's position: "Let due honours and rewards be showered on the heads of those who have nobly toiled in deciphering the puzzling Arctic labyrinth, and who have each contributed to their hard-earned quota; but let the name of Discoverer of the North-West Passage be forever linked to that of Sir John Franklin."

Franklin apologists would carry this notion through the twentieth century. And some scholars who recognized its dubiousness would, in effect, shrug. Canadian historian Leslie Neatby explained, for example, that travelling south from Parry Channel, "the true Passage lies to the left of Cape Felix through Ross and Rae Straits, for, once in Simpson Strait, the navigator can hope for reasonably plain sailing along the continental shore to Alaska. The key, then, to the navigable North West Passage lay in the well-concealed waters which separated King William Island from the Boothia Peninsula." The discovery of the Northwest Passage by John Franklin, Neatby added, "was a point to be judged not by logic, but by sentiment."

In truth, Franklin discovered no Passage. The man himself died a few months after his ships got trapped in the pack ice. And when his crews marched south to seek help, they forged no link in any chain. They struggled along a permanently frozen strait that constituted no navigable passage; none. In *Writing Arctic Disaster*, Adriana Craciun argues convincingly that the Franklin expedition "became a *cause célèbre* because of a preventable disaster, and that in the history of Arctic discoveries Franklin deserves a minor role." No ship would get through Victoria Strait until 1967, when the icebreaker *John A. Macdonald* pounded through en route from Baffin Bay to the Beaufort Sea.

Today, because climate change is opening up the entire Arctic archipelago, conventional vessels can often sail through that channel. Yet in 2014, the pack ice there proved impenetrable to the Victoria Strait Expedition, and so forced those involved to proceed south through Rae Strait to focus on the alternative area off Adelaide Peninsula, where they found the *Erebus*.

Almost alone among her contemporaries, Lady Franklin understood the power of statues, monuments and memorials to shape public opinion and, indeed, to create history. In 1861, she encouraged the Lincolnshire town of Spilsby to erect a statue to her late husband, its most illustrious native son. When a local newspaper suggested an inscription praising Franklin, "who perished in the attempt to discover a North-west Passage," she quickly vetoed that in favour of a more positive identification: "Sir John Franklin / Discoverer of the Northwest Passage."

In London, she failed in an effort to have a Franklin memorial installed in Trafalgar Square, one that would match the famous sky-high monument to Admiral Lord Nelson. She settled in 1866 for that larger-than-life statue at Waterloo Place, adjacent to the Athenaeum Club. She finalized the inscription: "To the great Navigator / And his brave companions / Who sacrificed their lives / Completing the discovery of / The North-West Passage / A.D. 1847–48."

As part of her campaign to make a legend of her husband, Lady Franklin paid for this statue and shipped it to Hobart.

Lady Franklin added an international dimension to the commemoration of Franklin by casting the statue twice. The first copy, a prototype that would reveal any design flaws, she would send to the far side of the world. She had extended this offer to old friends in Tasmania—at last the name "Van Diemen's Land" had been replaced—and they had undertaken to erect the statue in Hobart. The Franklin memorial in downtown Hobart, with its ornamental pool and spray jets of water, stands today as the most attractive of all the monuments that Lady Franklin built.

The Lady's machinations required time, energy, perseverance and attention to detail. In 1866, at the Athenaeum Club, while watching the unveiling of the Waterloo Place statue, Jane Franklin allowed herself to savour a partial victory. This statue encapsulated the climax of Arctic discovery, or at least the official version, proclaiming Franklin an indefatigable explorer who had successfully completed a centuries-long quest at the cost of his life. A less ambitious woman, looking out over the ceremony, smiling to see her various surrogates puffed up and vying for pride of place, would have relished this commemoration as a stunning triumph of female sagacity in a world profoundly male. But Jane Franklin felt that her work was not yet done. What of Westminster Abbey? Surely the discoverer of the Northwest Passage deserved to be memorialized in the Abbey, where he would stand among the greatest figures of British history?

25.

Tookoolito and Hall Gather Inuit Accounts

"While intently occupied in my cabin, writing, I heard a soft, sweet voice say, 'Good morning, sir.' The tone in which it was spoken—musical, lively, and varied— instantly told me that a lady of refinement was there greeting me. I was astonished. Could I be dreaming? No! I was wide awake, and writing. But, had a thunder-clap sounded in my ear, though it was snowing at the time, I could not have been more surprised than I was at the sound of that voice. I raised my head: a lady was indeed before me, and extending an ungloved hand."

The date: November 2, 1860. The location: on board the *George Henry* off the east coast of Baffin Island. The writer: Charles Francis Hall, American explorer. The light prevented Hall from seeing his visitor clearly at first: "But, on turning her face," he wrote, "who should it be but a lady Esquimaux! Whence, thought I, came this civilization refinement?"

Hall was meeting Tookoolito, the younger sister of Eenoolooapik, the Inuk who had visited Scotland in 1839 and helped launch the Baffin Island whale fishery. "She spoke my own language fluently," Hall wrote, "and there, seated at my right in the main cabin, I had a long and interesting conversation with her. Ebierbing, her husband—a fine, and also intelligent-looking man—was introduced to me, and, though not speaking English so well as his wife, yet I could talk with him tolerably well."

Together, Tookoolito and Ebierbing—who had spent two years in England and were often called Hannah and Joe—would make one of the most important of all contributions to understanding what had happened to the lost expedition of Sir John Franklin, who was yet to be memorialized even at Waterloo Place. They would teach Hall to adapt to the Arctic, and help him collect Inuit testimony that would finally be recognized as especially crucial after the 2014 discovery of *Erebus*.

Tookoolito and Ebierbing, shown flanking Charles Francis Hall, made crucial contributions to our understanding of what had happened to the lost expedition of John Franklin.

Tookoolito had been born in 1838 at Cape Searle in Cumberland Sound. In 1853, with her husband Ebierbing, and emulating her brother Eenoolooapik, she sailed to England with a whaling captain named John Bowlby. Exhibited at several locations over a period of twenty months, and thanks mainly to Tookoolito's linguistic abilities, they became a sensation. The Inuit couple dined with Queen Victoria and Prince Albert at Windsor Castle, which, according to Tookoolito, was "a fine place, I assure you, sir."

Bowlby had kept his promise to return the Inuit to Baffin Island. And in 1860, Hall wrote of Tookoolito, "I could not help admiring the exceeding gracefulness and modesty of her demeanor. Simple and gentle in her way, there was a degree of calm intellectual power about her that more and more astonished me." At first meeting, Hall had asked Tookoolito how she would like to live in England. She answered that she would like that very well. "'Would you like to go to America with me?' said I. 'I would indeed, sir,' was the ready reply."

With her husband, Tookoolito would transform the unpromising Hall into a significant figure. In the late 1850s, soon after it appeared, Hall had read *Arctic Explorations*, Elisha Kent Kane's two-volume work about his second expedition. Hall, who had apprenticed as a blacksmith before turning to printing two small newspapers in Cincinnati, became convinced that some of Franklin's men had survived and taken refuge among the Inuit. He felt a sense of vocation, and that God was calling him to go north and rescue those survivors. To do so, he would abandon his pregnant wife and small child.

The man was nearing forty years of age. He had no experience in the North and no qualifications to lead an expedition. But he was bent on searching the area around King William Island and, incredibly, managed to get some financial backing from Henry Grinnell, who had sponsored Kane. Unable to afford a ship, Hall secured free passage to Baffin Island on a whaling vessel, the *George Henry*. He brought a specially built boat, which he intended to sail west through what he called "Frobisher Strait" as far as he could. Then, having hired Inuit guides, he would continue west by sledge.

Hall left his family and, on May 29, 1860, sailed north out of New London, Connecticut. The ship called at Holsteinborg, Greenland, known today as Sisimiut, and then crossed Davis Strait to Baffin Island, putting in at Cyrus Field Bay on the east coast just north of

Frobisher Bay. Now came one of the great synchronicities of exploration history. During that first winter on Baffin, Hall met Tookoolito and her husband, Ebierbing, who began working with him as guides and interpreters.

During the winter of 1861, Hall joined these two and others on a forty-two-day hunting trip, so getting a first taste of building snow huts and driving dogs. Back at camp, Ebierbing's grandmother—the remarkable Ookijoxy Ninoo, who lived for more than one hundred years—relayed enduring oral stories of white men visiting their lands three years in a row. She described how five of them had spent a winter nearby and then built a boat in which they set out to sail home.

Late the following summer, Hall investigated the location she specified, Kodlunarn Island. He found relics and the foundations of a house dating back to the 1570s and Martin Frobisher. He revisited the island the next summer, and acquired more relics. He made no tangible progress towards his primary objective, but if the Inuit could accurately report events almost three centuries old, surely they could be relied upon to advance the search for Franklin.

In the autumn of 1862, Tookoolito and Ebierbing travelled south with Hall to the United States, where they appeared at his lectures, helping him raise money for another expedition in search of Franklin survivors. Barnum's American Museum in New York City advertised them as "those wonderful Esquimaux Indians which have arrived from the arctic regions . . . the first and only inhabitants of these frozen regions to visit this country."

Early in 1863, during an east coast tour, Tookoolito suffered the devastating loss of a new-born son—Tukelieta, Little Butterfly—to pneumonia. She recovered slowly and, in 1864, returned to the Arctic with Hall and her husband. They sailed north in another whaler, the *Monticello*, bent on launching their search from Repulse

In 1861, during a forty-two-day hunting trip, Charles Francis Hall got his first taste of building snow huts and driving sled dogs.

Bay, where John Rae had sojourned. Because he debarked too far south, Hall did not reach that destination until June 1865. He set up camp at Fort Hope, where Rae had first wintered almost two decades before.

The team spent three bizarrely frustrating years chasing one false lead after another. In 1866, during a failed expeditionary attempt to reach King William Island, Tookoolito lost a second child—a male

Hall had named King William. Finally, in April 1869—after travelling with eight Inuit, among them Tookoolito and her newly adopted daughter, Punna (also known as Punny)—Hall reached Rae Strait and the west coast of Boothia Peninsula. There, with Tookoolito's help, he interviewed some Inuit who had personally encountered Franklin survivors trekking south, and others who had later discovered dead bodies. From them, he acquired several relics, among them a spoon bearing Franklin's initials and part of a writing desk.

Hall crossed Rae Strait to King William Island, and in the south, on one of the Todd Islets, he found a complete skeleton. Later, he would send this to England, where leading biologists misidentified it as belonging to Lieutenant Henry Le Vesconte. Recent forensic studies indicate that the remains are those of Harry Goodsir, the Franklin expedition's physician and scientist. In 1869, Hall wanted desperately to remain on the island into the summer, when disappearing snow might reveal undiscovered relics. But the Inuit hunters had other priorities. The explorer was back at Repulse Bay by June 20, and sailing south soon afterwards, again with Tookoolito and Ebierbing.

Hall's crucial contribution lies in the accounts he gathered, mainly through Tookoolito, from the Inuit eyewitnesses. These stories, preserved in notebooks and the published *Narrative of the Second Arctic Expedition Made by Charles F. Hall*, constitute the single most extensive archive of Inuit testimony about the Franklin expedition. Hall was not a clear thinker, nor was he a good writer, but with Tookoolito's help, he did collect and compile an encyclopedia of material that vindicates John Rae's reports of cannibalism, and also anticipates and clarifies the recent discovery of *Erebus*.

Here we encounter horrific tales whose details are so vivid as to be incontrovertible, including references to human flesh cut to facilitate boiling in pots and kettles: "One man's body when found by the Innuits flesh all on & not mutilated except the hands sawed off at the wrists—the rest a great many had their flesh cut off as if some one or other had cut it off to eat."

Without the help of Tookoolito, who did most of the translating, Charles Francis Hall would never have gleaned a single word about the fate of the Franklin expedition.

Some Inuit spoke of finding numerous bodies in a tent at what is now called Terror Bay on the west coast of King William Island. One described a woman using a heavy, sharp stone to dig into the ice and retrieve a watch from the body of a corpse: "[The woman] could never forget the dreadful, fearful feelings she had all the time while engaged doing this; for, besides the tent being filled with frozen corpses—some entire and others mutilated by some of the starving companions, who had cut off much of the flesh with their knives and hatchets and eaten it—this man who had the watch she sought seemed to her to have been the last that died, and his face was just as though he was only asleep."

Hall multiplied gruesome examples, recording tales of finding bones that had been severed with a saw and of skulls with holes in them through which brains had been removed "to prolong the lives of the living." Hall also met In-nook-poo-zhe-jook, John Rae's most articulate informant. After talking with Rae, and then learning of

McClintock's visit to the region, this hunter had personally explored King William Island. Hall described him as "very finicky to tell the facts . . . In-nook-poo-zhe-jook has a noble bearing. His whole face is an index that he has a heart kind & true. I delight in his companionship." Later, the capricious Hall would suggest that "he speaks truth & falsehood all intermingled," though as David C. Woodman suggests, In-nook-poo-zhe-jook "probably never intentionally told Hall a falsehood."

At Erebus Bay, the Inuk had located not only a pillaged boat—the one Hobson and McClintock had ransacked for relics—but a second boat, untouched, about one kilometre away. Here, too, he discovered "one whole skeleton with clothes on—this with flesh all on but dried, as well as a big pile of skeleton bones near the fire place & skulls among them." Bones had been broken up for their marrow, and some long boots that came up as high as the knees contained "cooked human flesh—that is human flesh that had been boiled."

Late in the twentieth century, while researching *Unravelling the Franklin Mystery*, Woodman perused Hall's unpublished field notes. In them, he found testimony elaborating on stories about a shipwreck at the location that McClintock had called Oot-loo-lik, and which Hall transcribed as Ook-joo-lik. According to a local named Ek-kee-pee-ree-a, the ship "had 4 boats hanging at the sides and 1 of them was above the quarter deck. The ice about the ship one winter's make, all smooth flow, and a plank was found extending from the ship down to the ice. The Innuits were sure some white men must have lived there through the winter. Heard of tracks of 4 strangers, not Innuits, being seen on land adjacent to the ship."

A woman named Koo-nik, identified as the wife of Seeuteetuar, described the finding of a dead white man on a ship. She reported that several Inuit "were out sealing when they saw a large ship—all very much afraid but Nuk-kee-che-uk who went to the vessel while the others went to their Ig-loo. Nuk-kee-che-uk looked all around and saw nobody & finally Lik-lee-poo-nik-kee-look-oo-loo (stole a very little or few things) & then made for the Ig-loos. Then all the Innuits went to the ship & stole a good deal—broke into a place that was fastened up & there found a very large white man who was dead, very tall man. There was flesh about this dead man, that is, his remains quite perfect—it took 5 men to lift him. The place smelt very bad. His clothes all on. Found dead on the floor—not in a sleeping place or birth (sic)."

Hall asked Koo-nik if she knew "anything about the tracks of strangers seen at Ook-joo-lik?" Some other Inuit had mentioned "walking along the tracks of 3 men Kob-loo-nas & those of a dog with them . . . says she has never seen the exact place not having been further w or w & south than Point C. Grant, which is the Pt. NE of O'Rialy [O'Reilly] Island. She indicates on Rae's chart the places, recognizing them readily."

With the help of Tookoolito, Charles Francis Hall gathered a wealth of new information. But he lacked the analytical and imaginative abilities required to develop a coherent revision of the "standard reconstruction" that had evolved from the findings of Rae and McClintock and the one-page Victory Point record.

On September 28, 1869, the *Times* reported that, after five years in the Arctic, explorer Charles Francis Hall had arrived in New Bedford, Massachusetts. He had discovered the skeletons of several of Sir John Franklin's party and had returned with relics from the lost expedition. Jane Franklin immediately sent a telegram to Henry Grinnell, asking whether Hall had discovered any writings, journals or letters—any written evidence that her husband had indeed completed a northwest passage. The shipping magnate quickly replied, "None."

Grinnell sent Lady Franklin a copy of Hall's report. She found it "so devoid of order and dates as to leave much confusion and perplexity in the mind." She wished to interview the explorer—in England, if he could be persuaded to visit at her expense, or else in America. She wrote, "If the journals of my husband's expedition should be brought to light, nothing that reflects on the character of another should be published—nothing that would give sharp pain to any individuals living."

Leopold McClintock, who considered the fate of Franklin settled to his own everlasting credit, and who feared sensational revelations, wrote to Sophy Cracroft, knowing she would relay his opinion: "I do not see what Lady Franklin can want to see Hall for . . . His report has been moderate for him and I think he is better left alone."

Lady Franklin would not be deterred. When Hall had returned home to Cincinnati, Ohio, to write a book about his quest, she decided to make an adventure of what would probably be her final trip to North America. In January 1870, Jane Franklin and her niece, Sophy Cracroft, sailed not for New York City but San Francisco, proceeding yet once more around the bottom of South America. Besides the usual maid, they travelled with an efficient manservant named Lawrence, who made this journey—and several that followed—far easier.

In San Francisco, the women boarded a ship sailing north to Sitka, Alaska. That seaside village, situated at latitude 58°, was closer to the Northwest Passage than Jane Franklin had ever come. She and Sophy spent two months in the village—a sojourn that would later be memorialized in *Lady Franklin Visits Sitka, Alaska 1870*, a 134-page book made up of quotations from Sophy's journal and contextual articles and appendices.

At last the women journeyed south to Salt Lake City and east to

Cincinnati. There, on August 13, 1870, Lady Franklin met Charles Francis Hall. Neither she nor Sophy left any permanent record of this visit—a predictable elision. Jane had already gone on record as believing that, with regard to cannibalism among final survivors of the Franklin expedition, nobody should ever have written a word.

Now, having interviewed the Inuit who discovered the most horrific of the campsites, Hall had recorded many detailed and irrefutable eyewitness accounts. When Lady Franklin arrived, he was compiling these into his soon-to-be published book *Life with the Esquimaux: A Narrative of Arctic Experience in Search of Survivors of Sir John Franklin's Expedition*. How much detail did the explorer share with Lady Franklin? Hall had been counselled by his sponsor, Henry Grinnell, to show sensitivity. And he needed Grinnell's backing for a proposed expedition to the North Pole. Still, Hall would have revealed as much truth to Lady Franklin as he thought she could handle. The truth was that John Rae had been right all along. The final survivors of the Franklin expedition had resorted to eating their dead comrades.

Later, in a letter to Lady Franklin dated January 9, 1871, Hall addressed only tangential issues. The explorer, apologetic, explained that he had lost faith in that "almost holy mission to which I have devoted about twelve years of my life . . . eight of these in the icy regions of the North. What burned with my soul like a living fire, all the time, was the full faith that I should find some survivors of Sir John's remarkable expedition, and that I would be the instrument in the hands of Heaven, of the solution, but when I heard the sad tale from living witnesses . . . how many survivors in the fall of 1848 had been abandoned to die, my faith till then so strong, was shaken and ultimately was extinguished."

About this "abandonment": Hall had interviewed and harshly

judged two Inuit hunters, Teekeeta and Ow-wer, who had encountered forty starving men trekking south near Washington Bay on the west coast of King William Island. These two had slipped away instead of somehow rescuing the marchers—as if, in one of the most desolate, animal-empty areas in the Arctic, they could have miraculously produced enough food to sustain so large a party.

As for finding written records, Hall professed hope. He believed that Franklin's officers had buried them on King William Island before abandoning their ships: "God willing, I will make two more voyages to the North—first for the discovery of the regions about the Pole—and then to obtain the records of Sir John Franklin's expedition to obtain other information than what I already possess in relation to it."

For Lady Franklin, this misfit American explorer had already delivered a revelation. At age seventy-eight, and after a lifetime of bending the world to her indomitable will, she had come up against a rock-hard reality she could not reshape. Faced with the detailed narratives of Charles Francis Hall, she could deny the truth no longer. Even the best of Christian men, in order to stay alive, would jettison any religious teaching, cross any moral boundary and resort to any horror. Such was the truth of human nature.

The following January, in response to her request, the explorer sent Lady Franklin two of the original notebooks he had used in preparing his book. Long before those notebooks arrived—indeed, virtually as soon as she spoke with Hall—Jane would have known what they confirmed. And yet, undaunted, she urged the explorer to travel north again and to resume the search for written records.

26.

Inuit Hunters Keep Castaways Alive

"It was blowing a terrific gale from the northwest," the Inuk Hans Hendrik tells us in a dramatized narrative, "and about six o'clock in the evening we were nipped in the ice. The ice crushed down on us with tremendous pressure, and if the *Polaris* had not been surprisingly strong she would have sunk at once." This happened on October 15, 1872, during an expedition that had set out under the command of Charles Francis Hall, bent now on becoming the first explorer to reach the North Pole.

Most of the men on board the *Polaris*, we learn, were gathered in the waist of the vessel, looking over the rail at the floe to which we were made fast. The ship was rising somewhat to the pressure. Now the engineer came running up from below, and shouted that the vessel had started a leak aft and that the water was gaining on the pumps."

The ship had sprung no leak, Hendrik adds in *Hans the Eskimo* by Edwin Gile Rich, which is based on *Memoirs of Hans Hendrik, the Arctic Traveller*. But the engineer "was too scared to know exactly what was happening." When Captain Sidney Budington (also spelled Buddington) heard of the supposed leak, he "threw up his hands in excitement, and shouted, 'Throw everything on the ice.' He must have thought the *Polaris* was sinking with all hands."

In the memoir, published in 1878, Hans Hendrik—who had first sailed far north twenty-five years earlier with Elisha Kent Kane—declares simply that "the movement of the frozen mass in a heavy gale caused the ship's crew to land boats and provisions on the ice, to be prepared for the worst. In the following night the accident occurred which separated the ship's company." He then lists the nineteen persons "left upon the ice," and the fourteen who "were drifted off with the ship."

In the dramatized version quoted above, which surfaced in 1934, the ice commenced cracking and "exploded under our very feet and broke in many places. The ship broke away in the darkness and we lost all sight of her in a moment." Snow was falling and a stiff gale was blowing from the southeast: "So bad were the snow and sleet, that one could not even look to windward."

In addition to Hans Hendrick and his family, three more Inuit—Tookoolito, Ebierbing and their adopted daughter, Punna—were among the nineteen people stranded on the ice floe. Without that Inuit presence, all of the castaways would almost certainly have died.

In June 1871, Tookoolito and Ebierbing had accompanied Hall in sailing from New York for the North Pole on the *Polaris*, intent on extending the route discovered by Kane. At Proven on the west coast of Greenland, just south of Upernavik, Hall met Hans Hendrik. That resourceful Inuk had spent the past decade working in this area for the Greenland Trading Company. At Hall's invitation, Hans joined the expedition aboard the *Polaris*, bringing his wife, Mersuk—whom he had met while voyaging with Kane—and their three children.

The ship was not a happy one. Two men accustomed to captaincy—George Tyson and Sidney O. Budington—soon came to detest each other. And Hall and the chief scientist, Dr. Emil Bessels, fell out over who controlled the scientific staff. A large contingent on the ship, resenting Hall's micro-managing, sided with Bessels. Amidst

acrimonious exchanges, the *Polaris* proceeded north into Smith Sound. By September, it had reached a latitude (82°29′ north) some distance beyond that attained by Kane—a new "farthest north by ship." Tensions flared over whether to go still farther, so risking the ship to reduce the length of the projected dogsled journey. But on September 10, 1871, the ship settled where it was, in "Thank God Harbour" in northern Greenland.

Charles Francis Hall in his grave. In 1968, almost one hundred years after the explorer died, biographer Chauncey C. Loomis exhumed the body and determined that Hall had died of arsenic poisoning.

The following month, as the dark winter took hold, Charles Francis Hall became ill. Emil Bessels maintained a vigil by his bedside, ostensibly to treat him. Hall accused the doctor of poisoning him and refused further treatment. On November 8, 1871, he died, possibly the victim of deliberate poisoning. An official investigation would rule that Hall had died of apoplexy. In 1968, the scholar Chauncey C. Loomis, while writing a biography of Hall, travelled to Greenland and exhumed the explorer's body, which was well preserved by permafrost. Forensic testing showed that Hall had indeed died of arsenic poisoning. This might have been accidental, although Loomis doubted it. No charges were ever laid. Tookoolito strongly suspected that Hall had been poisoned, and spoke of coffee provided to him by Bessels: "He [Hall] said the coffee made him sick. Too sweet for him." She quoted the explorer's words: "It made me sick and [want] to vomit." The inquest discounted her evidence. Some pointed to Bessels, while George Tyson was convinced that Budington was the guilty party. In a 2001 book called *Trial by Ice*, surgeon-author Richard Parry suggests that Budington was an accomplice who "knew or suspected more than he let on." In the present work, we must content ourselves with noting the controversy.

Now, in June 1872, with Hall dead and buried, Budington dispatched a party to try for the North Pole in a whaleboat. A few kilometres out, ice crushed this craft. Budington tried again, sending out both a collapsible boat and a second whaleboat. But then the *Polaris* floated free, and he sent Ebierbing north to summon the men. When they arrived, determined to avoid another Arctic winter, Budington turned the ship around and started south.

On October 15, while opposite Humboldt Glacier, *Polaris* ran up onto a shallow iceberg and got stuck. When a second iceberg threatened to demolish the ship, men began throwing cargo overboard to lighten and free the vessel. This was when those nineteen people, having been ordered off the ship, found themselves out on the ice when the pack began to break up. The two Inuit families were among them. As the castaways watched the ship drift farther away, and then disappear into the distance, the hunters turned to building igloos on what they now determined was a massive ice floe.

Those fourteen men still on the damaged *Polaris* would run ashore near Etah, Greenland, within a couple of weeks of the accident. They would survive a harsh winter thanks to the Inuit who lived nearby, and after starting south in two rough-built boats, would be rescued the following July by the whaler *Ravenscraig*.

The more dramatic struggle for survival played out on the ice floe. The jettisoned supplies included 1,900 pounds of food. For the rest, those stranded looked to the Inuit hunters, Ebierbing and Hendrik. They kept everyone alive as, during the next six months, the ice floe shrank in diameter from a few kilometres to not more than one hundred metres. The ice carried them, drifting, more than 2,900 kilometres south. George Tyson, the ranking officer on the floe, wrote: "We survive through God's mercy and Joe's [Ebierbing's] ability as a hunter."

Finally, on April 30, 1873, off the coast of Newfoundland, sealers aboard a ship called the *Tigress* spotted and rescued the castaways. They had survived thanks to the survival skills of Ebierbing, Hendrik and Tookoolito, though official reports and newspaper scarcely mentioned this. Hans Hendrik did undertake a modest speaking tour of several American cities. Then, back at Upernavik, he resumed working for the Greenland Trading Company.

In 1875, Hendrik joined a British expedition led by George Nares and sailed on the *Discovery* to the northeast coast of Ellesmere Island. Nares wrote later that "all speak in the highest terms of Hans . . . who was untiring in his exertions with the dog-sledge, and in procuring game."

After the debacle of the *Polaris* expedition, Tookoolito and Ebierbing returned to Groton, Connecticut, where with the help of Hall and Budington, they had established a home. Ebierbing revisited the Arctic several times as a guide, while Tookoolito stayed in Groton, working as a seamstress and caring for their daughter, who had not been well since those months on the ice floe. When Punna died at age nine, Tookoolito fell into declining health. Ebierbing was with her when, at thirty-eight, she died on December 31, 1876. She was buried in Groton.

Her death meant that Ebierbing was alone two years later when Lieutenant Frederick Schwatka invited him to travel north to renew the search for records from the lost Franklin expedition. Over the next two years, as the guide and main interpreter on the longest sledge journey recorded to that date—4,360 kilometres—he would play a crucial role in unearthing still more Inuit testimony. And in 1880, when Schwatka sailed home, Ebierbing would remain in the Arctic.

27.

Ebierbing and Tulugaq Work Magic for Schwatka

S ince the mid-nineteenth century, countless investigators—fur
traders, sailors, scientists, obsessive amateurs—have added
detail and nuance to John Rae's original report on the fate of
the Franklin expedition. In *Unravelling the Franklin Mystery*, Canadian historian David C. Woodman summed up succinctly: "For one
hundred and forty years the account of the tragedy given to Rae
by In-nook-poo-zhe-jook and See-u-ti-chu has been accepted and
endorsed. As we shall see, it was a remarkably accurate recital of
events. But it was not the whole story."

After 1875, prompted by the death of Lady Franklin, the American Geographical Society decided to send another expedition in
search of relics and documents pertaining to the Franklin expedition.
Frederick Schwatka, an ambitious lieutenant with the Third United
States Cavalry, volunteered to lead it. Born in 1849, Schwatka had
been too young to play a role in the American Civil War. When he
graduated from West Point in 1871, the military was shedding men.

Schwatka served as a fighting officer in the west, and devoted
considerable time to studying the native peoples, ranging among the

Apache in the Arizona Territory to the Sioux of the northern plains. He was admitted to the Nebraska bar in 1875 and, the following year, earned his medical degree in New York City.

He was brilliant and practical and, despite his lack of Arctic experience, he won the appointment and sailed from New York on June 19, 1878. His five-man party included "Joe" Ebierbing, the Inuk

With Tookoolito dead, Ebierbing sailed north out of New York City with Frederick Schwatka.

interpreter who had sailed with Charles Francis Hall and others; an experienced Arctic hand named Frank Melms; and two men who would write books about the expedition—William Henry Gilder of the *New York Herald*, and Heinrich (Henry) Klutschak, a German artist and surveyor who had emigrated to the United States in 1871.

The party set up base camp and spent the winter near Daly Bay, north of Chesterfield Inlet on the coast of Hudson Bay. On April 1, 1879, accompanied by a dozen local Inuit, and with three sledges drawn by more than forty dogs, Schwatka and his men set out for the west coast of King William Island. Over the next year, while relying on an Inuit diet and travel methods, they reached their target destination by accomplishing the longest sledge journey on record: 4,360 kilometres.

Schwatka spent the summer searching the area from the mouth

of the Back River to Cape Felix at the northern tip of King William Island. He found bones and relics that would in winter have been covered by snow. William Ouligbuck Jr. had joined the party, and Gilder would verify what John Rae had asserted—that Ouligbuck spoke all the Inuktitut dialects fluently, and that he "spoke the [English] language like a native—that is to say, like an uneducated native." He and Ebierbing enabled Schwatka to gather an extraordinary amount of crucial Inuit testimony.

But the man who kept the party fed and flourishing was a locally hired Inuk named Tulugaq, a little-known figure who emerges in accounts of the expedition as singular and irreplaceable. As Matonabbee was to Samuel Hearne, so Tulugaq was to Frederick Schwatka: he was the man who made the journey happen. A superlative dogsled driver, he was also, above all, a peerless hunter. When the party located a herd of caribou and Ebierbing, that excellent shot, killed eight of them, Tulugaq bagged twelve.

Eight times, during this year-long Arctic odyssey, Tulugaq killed two caribou with a single shot. At one point, according to Klutschak, he was set upon by a pack of thirty wolves. He leapt onto a high rock and, knowing that wolves will halt any attack to consume their own dead, "with his magazine rifle began providing food for the wolves from their own midst." When they were distracted, he made his escape.

But Tulugaq's courage and skill register most memorably in his dealings with polar bears. At Cape Felix, at the northernmost tip of King William Island, Tulugaq used his telescope to locate a bear on the ice roughly nine kilometres away. He hitched up twelve dogs and, with Frank Melms and a youth, set off at a furious pace. When he drew within five hundred paces of the polar bear, the creature turned and fled, making for open water. But Tulugaq had already

Crossing Simpson Strait in kayaks. This image of Schwatka and some of his men appeared in The Illustrated London News *in 1881.*

unleashed three dogs. He then freed three more, and finally the bear had to stand and fight to keep the six dogs at bay.

From twenty-five paces, Tulugaq fired one shot and then another, but the bear, which stood more than ten feet tall, scratched at his head, whirled and came charging at him. Tulugaq's third shot hit the bear in the heart and brought him down. The hunter dug his first bullet from the bear's head. Despite the close range, Klutschak writes, "it had not penetrated the bone but had been completely flattened."

Not long afterwards, when the expedition had finished searching Terror Bay and had travelled more than eighty kilometres south, Tulugaq took a dog team to retrieve some goods left behind at the camp. While travelling, he spotted three bears and gave chase as they fled for open water. As they reached it, Tulugaq shot and killed all three of them with five shots. To take their hides, he then led his female travelling companion in hauling the bears out of the water, each of them weighing at least eight hundred pounds. "For Tulugaq," Klutschak writes, "nothing was impossible—except transporting the skull of an Inuk."

On another occasion, Tulugaq spotted a large piece of driftwood in the water. He took some dogs to help him fetch it but, unusually, left his rifle behind. Near the shore, he chanced upon a large female polar bear with a cub three or four months old. He loosed all his dogs and pelted the mother to separate her from her cub. With the dogs at her heels, she took to the water, and Tulugaq used his knife to finish the cub. "Apart from its tenderness," Klutschak writes, "the cub's meat had a particularly piquant taste, and we greatly regretted that the old bear had not had twins."

Tulugaq was also remarkable for his good humour, his willpower and his perseverance, and when Klutschak writes of sadly parting from him, he freely admits that "for a full year we had been indebted to this man for the fact that the execution of our plans had proceeded so well." What did the expedition accomplish? For starters, on the west coast of King William Island, at a place known as Camp Crozier, Schwatka discovered the remains of Lieutenant John Irving of the *Terror*, identifiable by the presence of a silver medal for mathematics. He built a cairn at this location and eventually sent the remains to Edinburgh, where they were reburied at an elaborate public ceremony.

At Terror Bay on that same island, where the *Terror* was coincidentally found, and at Starvation Cove on the mainland near Chantrey Bay, Schwatka found more remains and evidence of cannibalism. With Ebierbing and William Ouligbuck Jr., he interviewed a number of Inuit, eliciting first-person accounts whose crucial importance is emerging only now, in light of the 2014 discovery of the *Erebus*.

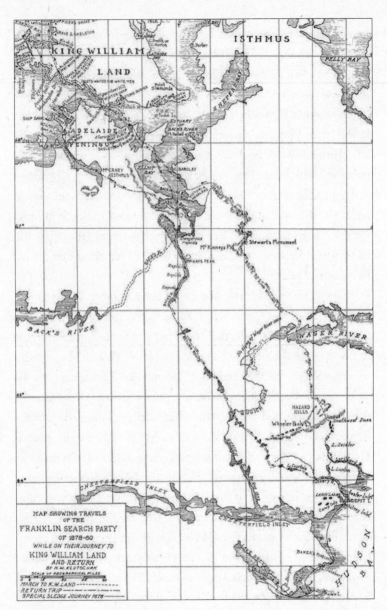

Journey of the Schwatka expedition to the northern coast of King William Island.

Schwatka heard tales of Inuit entering an abandoned ship and accidentally sinking it by cutting a hole in the side, and of papers being distributed among children, buried in sand and blown away by the wind. He gathered complete accounts from several Inuit of their discoveries at Terror Bay, Starvation Cove and Ootjoolik. Gilder's florid newspaper articles about this expedition, including one that appeared in the *New York Herald* of October 29, 1880, included headlines such as "Franklin's Fate Determined"—as if, at last, this expedition had finally finished the job.

Given the 2014 discovery of the *Erebus* at Ootjoolik (in Wilmot and Crampton Bay, off Grant Point and Adelaide Peninsula), we recognize the special relevance of Schwatka's interview with Puhtoorak, who went aboard the ship before it sank. We have three accounts of that interview.

According to Gilder, Puhtoorak—"now about sixty-five or seventy"—had only once seen white men alive. As a boy, while fishing on the Back River, "they came along in a boat and shook hands with him. There were ten men. The leader was called "Tos-ard-e-roak," which Joe [Ebierbing] says, from the sound, he thinks means Lieutenant Back. The next white man he saw was dead in a bunk of a big ship which was frozen in the ice near an island about eight kilometres due west of Grant Point, on Adelaide Peninsula. They had to walk out about three miles on smooth ice to reach the ship."

Around this time, which Gilder estimated to be 1851 or 1852, Puhtoorak saw the tracks of white men on the mainland. Gilder writes that when he first saw them there were four, and afterward only three:

This was when the spring snows were falling. When his people saw the ship so long without any one around, they used to go on board and steal pieces of wood and iron. They did not know how to get inside by the doors, and cut a hole in the side of the ship, on a level with the ice, so that when the ice broke up during the following summer the ship filled and sunk. No tracks were seen in the salt-water ice or on the ship, which also was covered with snow, but they saw scrapings and sweepings alongside, which seemed to have been brushed off by people who had been living on board. They found some red cans of fresh meat, with plenty of what looked like tallow mixed with it. A great many had been opened, and four were still unopened. They saw no bread. They found plenty of knives, forks, spoons, pans, cups, and plates on board, and afterward found a few such things on shore after the vessel had gone down. They also saw books on board, and left them there. They only took knives, forks, spoons, and pans; the other things they had no use for.

Klutschak reprised the story. He wrote that Puhtoorak "was one of the first people to visit a ship which, beset in ice, drifted with wind and current to a spot west of Grant Point on Adelaide Peninsula, where some islands halted its drift." According to Puhtoorak, then, the ship did not sail to its final location, but was carried there while frozen in the ice. Klutschak notes that "on their first visit [in the autumn] the people thought they saw whites on board; from the tracks in the snow they concluded there were four of them."

He reiterates how, the following spring, when the whites were gone, the Inuit "found a corpse in one of the bunks and they found meat in cans in the cabin." He added that "the body was in a bunk inside the ship in the back part." The Inuit also found "a small boat in Wilmot Bay which, however, might have drifted to that spot after the ship sank." That boat might also have been left by sailors making a final bid to escape overland.

In Schwatka's rendition, the Inuit found the tracks first of four white men, and later of only three. Puhtoorak "never saw the white men. He thinks that the white men lived in the ship until the fall and then moved onto the mainland." When he went on board the ship, Puhtoorak "saw a pile of dirt on one side of the cabin door showing that some white man had recently swept out the cabin. He found on board the ship four red tin cans filled with meat and many that had been opened. The meat was full of fat. The natives went all over and through the ship and found also many empty casks. They found iron chains and anchors on deck, and spoons, knives, forks, tin plates, china plates, etc." According to Schwatka, Puhtoorak "also saw books on board the ship but the natives did not take them. He afterwards saw some that had washed ashore."

This Inuit testimony takes on special resonance, obviously, in light of the discovery of *Erebus*. That was the ship Puhtoorak visited, and these were the stories to which it gave rise. Frederick Schwatka could gather this oral history because he established a rapport with his Inuit informants. Without Ebierbing, who did most of the translating with Puhtoorak, neither Schwatka nor Gilder nor Klutschak would ever have gleaned a word about the *Erebus*. And without the accounts they relayed, which identified a general location, that ship might never have been found. To the work of Tulugaq, then, must be added that of Ebierbing. Together, those two remarkable Inuit enabled Schwatka to etch his name in the annals of those who elaborated the fate of the Franklin expedition.

28.

Lady Franklin Attains Westminster Abbey

By 1878, when Frederick Schwatka and Ebierbing sailed north to gather still more Inuit testimony, Jane Franklin had been dead for three years. Of her unprecedented travels, which she astutely downplayed, she had remained fiercely proud. And yet, after the vanishment of her sailor-husband, one passion gripped her more strongly even than the desire to travel the world, and that was her yearning to create, out of the tragic tale of Sir John Franklin, an Arctic legend.

Writing in the 1940s, Australian Kathleen Fitzpatrick suggested that even before Franklin disappeared, he "had become a legend in his own lifetime, both for courage and for sheer beauty of character." Well, not quite. By the time he arrived home in England from Van Diemen's Land, Franklin stood nearer to disgrace than to canonization, and only the fear of an enduring ignominy, exacerbated by the urgings of his importunate wife, drove him to undertake that final expedition.

In *A History of Australia*, C. M. H. Clark argues that, because she felt guilty over the ensuing disaster, Jane Franklin spent three decades recreating the reputation of a man "she had pushed beyond his strength." Certainly, whether driven by guilt or ambition, Jane Franklin displayed exceptional perseverance in establishing the fate of her husband's expedition. Having created a suitable narrative, she showed an equal enthusiasm for memorializing Sir John—seeing this latter quest as an extension of the former.

In seeking to turn her dead husband into an Arctic hero, Jane Franklin did not begin with promising material. On his first expedition, as a result of his poor decision-making, Franklin lost more than half his men; on his last, which culminated in disaster, he lost all his men and also his own life. Sir John can be credited with having charted more than 2,700 kilometres of previously unknown coastline—but only if we include the 1,600 kilometres contributed by John Richardson, his second-in-command.

Of significant geographical features, Franklin discovered none. In *The Friendly Arctic*, Vilhjalmur Stefansson would observe, "It is a commonplace in the history of polar exploration that the greatest advance in our knowledge of the region to the north of Canada resulted not from the life work of Sir John Franklin, but from his mysterious disappearance and the long series of expeditions that went out in search of him."

Jane Franklin drove that endeavour. She not only brought pressure to bear on Parliament and the Admiralty, but financed and organized key expeditions and inspired the American Henry Grinnell to dispatch still others. But for her, the opening up of the Arctic would have required additional decades. In Victorian England, of course, that patriarchal bastion, nobody would dream of advancing such a claim. But, having identified herself with her husband, Jane Franklin could embark on a quest to create a legend, and to shape future understanding of Arctic history. Her husband had lost his life in the Arctic. She would portray him as having sacrificed that

The myth of Franklin as Arctic hero, initiated by Lady Franklin and supported by the British naval establishment, became central to the orthodox version of exploration history.

life not to escape disgrace, and much less in an effort to satisfy his insatiable wife, but in a quest far greater than himself—indeed, in a national cause.

Nobody better understood the creative power of public memorials to shape historical perception than this adventure traveller who had spent so much of her life visiting historic sites. Jane Franklin grasped that monuments create history. So she had led the creation of statues in Waterloo Place, Lincolnshire and Tasmania. For most, these memorials would have sufficed. But her husband's reputation was synonymous with her own, and Jane Franklin craved heroic status. She wanted Westminster Abbey—and, in the late 1860s and early 1870s, she set about getting it.

To the dean of Westminster, she offered to supply a suitable bust of Sir John, complete with an inscription by poet laureate Alfred Lord Tennyson, yet another relative. Initially the dean balked. He proposed a modest stained-glass window. Lady Franklin remained adamant, and with backing by friends in high places, she carried the day.

She hired Matthew Noble, sculptor of the Waterloo Place statue, to create a suitable bust. Then, feeling that a bust was insufficiently grand, she conceived of adding first a canopy and then a base, so transforming the bust into a full-blown, stand-alone monument, complete with bas-relief, that easily exceeds six feet in height. To create the canopy and base, she enlisted Sir George Gilbert Scott, a prominent architect. And then she kept close watch.

Late in December 1874, as the memorial neared completion, Jane Franklin realized with a shock that, in the bas-relief at the front of the base, the sculptor had placed a flag at half-mast. This contradicted the revised myth she was elaborating—that Franklin had discovered the Northwest Passage and knew it before he died. At Jane's urgent command, Sophy "went to Mr. Noble and explained that the placing of the flag at half mast would be inconsistent with the circumstances intended to be set forth, namely, the Discovery of the North West Passage, my uncle's death having as we judge by the date, followed the return of [Lieutenant] Graham Gore's party which would undoubtedly ascertain the fact of the continuous channel to the coast."

Having realized that Franklin's ships had got trapped on the wrong side of King William Island, Lady Franklin had made one final amendment to the official version of his supposed discovery. She now asserted, without a shred of evidence, that Franklin's men had found the final link in the Passage—in fact, the channel John Rae discovered in 1854. Jane Franklin tacitly admitted that Rae Strait was indeed the key to the Passage. Sculptor Matthew Noble deferred and raised the flag.

There remained a few small problems. Skeptics wondered if a geographical discovery that nobody survived to report could rightly be designated a discovery? Lady Franklin asserted that, yes, it most certainly could. And if anybody thought otherwise, she would demand that a parliamentary committee be raised to investigate the matter. Could anybody doubt what such a committee would conclude?

In June 1875, British newspapers reported that, at age eighty-three, Lady Franklin was sinking. The Prince and Princess of Wales enquired after her health. Churches throughout the English-speaking world began offering up prayers. The invalid rallied but lasted only three more weeks. On July 18, 1875, with Sophy Cracroft at her side, Jane Franklin passed away.

The following day, the *Times* published a two-column obituary that situated her as "among the gifted woman of her time." It went on to observe that, "remarkable as her life had been in many respects, she is chiefly known in having taken a prominent and distinguished part in the cause of Arctic discovery. A generation has elapsed since her gallant husband, with a small band, the flower of the British navy, under his command, sailed as the leader of a great expedition, sent to accomplish the North-West Passage."

On July 29, 1875, the funeral procession included ten mourning coaches and almost that many private carriages. Numerous prominent Victorians attended, and dignitaries, knights and admirals served as pallbearers. Two days later, the faithful Sophy Cracroft organized an event at Westminster Abbey. In the crowded chapel of St. John the Evangelist, immediately to the left as one enters the world-famous shrine, friends and relations gathered to witness the unveiling of Jane Franklin's final testament. Sir George Back, Franklin's old rival, stepped forward and, according to a family eyewitness, silently "drew off the white cloth that had covered the monument to reveal a most beautifully represented Bust in bas-relief."

Those who had known Franklin could not help remarking discrepancies—the marble chin looked far too strong—and George Back spoke for all when he declared it "a fine Historic Bust but not a perfect likeness." Soon after the unveiling, the Dean of Westminster added an inscription hailing Franklin for "completing the discovery of the North-West Passage," and noting, "This monument is erected by Jane, his widow, who, after long waiting and sending many in search of him, herself departed to find him in the realms of Life, July 18th, 1875, aged 83 years."

Yet even then, Lady Franklin was not finished. Decades after her death, asserting her formidable will through Sophy Cracroft, Jane Franklin made one final gesture. At Westminster Abbey, acting as if from beyond the grave—and just in case anyone should advance an unconscionable claim on behalf of John Rae—she provided through Sophy for the addition to the monument of one last inscription: "Here also is commemorated Admiral Sir Leopold McClintock, 1819–1907, discoverer of the fate of Franklin in 1859."

With the help of her niece, Jane Franklin had put the finishing touches on an exploration legend, a fanciful narrative that would endure as "historical truth" through the twentieth century. Only now, in the twenty-first century, does the woman shine forth as a peerless mythologizer. Only now does her elaborate fable stand revealed as wishful thinking writ large.

Part Seven

SETTING THE
RECORD STRAIGHT

29.

The Last Viking in Gjoa Haven

Located in the middle of the Northwest Passage, the hamlet of Gjoa Haven is today home to 1,300 Inuit. In September 1903, when Roald Amundsen put into the bay here in his tiny, one-masted ship, the *Gjoa*, he felt he had entered "the finest little harbour in the world." The Norwegian was bent on becoming the first explorer to navigate the Passage from one ocean to another. He hoped also to pinpoint the north magnetic pole. In 1831, more than seven decades before he arrived, and roughly 160 kilometres northwest of Gjoa Haven, James Clark Ross had caught up with that ever-moving pole on the west coast of Boothia Peninsula. Amundsen wanted to determine how far the pole had shifted, and so enable geophysicists to make a comparison.

To that end, on the high ground overlooking the bay, Amundsen set up an evolving series of stations from which to take magnetic observations. He established friendly relations with Inuit who turned up and settled nearby. And he remained through not one but two cold, dark Arctic winters, delaying his epochal voyage for the sake of the Magnetic Crusade.

A view of Gjoa Haven harbour (Uqsuqtuuq) from the Amundsen memorial. On this high hill, Roald Amundsen set up an evolving series of stations from which to take magnetic observations.

Roald Amundsen was born in July 1872 into a substantial, sea-faring family based near Sarpsborg, about ninety-five kilometres south of Oslo. He grew up on the outskirts of the city, then called Christiania. As a boy, he became enthralled with his fellow Norwegian Fridtjof Nansen, who had made the first crossing of the Greenland ice cap and then crossed the Arctic by exploiting the drift of the pack ice. Amundsen began skiing seriously, honing his abilities by undertaking ambitious (and dangerous) cross-country expeditions.

At the same time, he became intrigued by the lost Franklin expedition. His mother wanted him to become a doctor, but after she died in 1893, Amundsen quit university and took to the sea as an ordinary sailor. He qualified as a mate within two years and obtained his master's licence in 1900. By then he had spent two years as a mate on the *Belgica* Antarctic expedition led by Adrien de Gerlache, during which he developed a lasting friendship with the American doctor Frederick A. Cook.

Influenced by Nansen, Amundsen grew interested in the scientific dimension of Arctic exploration, especially the mystery of the shifting magnetic poles. He consulted a scientist at the meteorological institute in Christiania, who encouraged him to learn the necessary skills and provided a reference letter. Amundsen travelled south to Hamburg to seek instruction from geophysicist Georg von Neumayer, director of the German Marine Observatory, and the world's foremost expert on terrestrial magnetism.

Neumayer had been engaging with the shifting poles for more than three decades. In 1857, steeped in the science of Alexander von Humboldt and encouraged by the British naval establishment, he had sailed to Melbourne, Australia, built the Flagstaff Observatory and conducted extensive magnetic studies. Back in Germany, he had become chair of the International Polar Commission and, in the early 1880s, founded the first International Polar Year.

Amundsen described later how in Hamburg, he "hired a cheap room in the poor part of the city." Next day, "with beating heart," he presented his letter card to Neumayer's assistant and was ushered into the presence of a man of about seventy, with "white hair, benign, clean-shaven face, and gentle eyes." The young man, stammering, said he wanted to go on a voyage and collect scientific data. Neumayer drew him out, and finally Amundsen blurted that he wanted to conquer the Northwest Passage, and also take accurate observations of the north magnetic pole to resolve its mysteries. The white-haired man rose, stepped forward and embraced him. "Young man, if you do that," he said, "you will be the benefactor of mankind for ages to come. This is the great adventure."

For three months, Amundsen studied with Neumayer. The older man treated him to dinners and introduced him to scientists and intellectuals. Then, back in Norway, having secured the backing of the influential Nansen, Amundsen set about preparing his dual-purpose expedition. He used a small inheritance to buy a tiny forty-seven-ton sloop, a fishing boat called the *Gjoa* (seventy feet by twenty). He then devoted two years to training and refurbishing, sailing in the waters east of Greenland while, at the behest of Nansen, conducting oceanographic observations.

Amundsen had difficulty raising enough money to undertake his quest. He borrowed considerable sums. Creditors began threatening to place the *Gjoa* under lien. On June 16, 1903, with six carefully chosen men, he slipped away, sailing out of Oslo under cover of darkness.

On the west coast of Greenland, at Godhavn (Qeqertarsuaq) in Disko Bay, Amundsen brought aboard twenty "Eskimo" dogs. Then, after acquiring additional provisions and kerosene from Scottish whalers, he sailed across Davis Strait into Lancaster Sound. He proceeded past Beechey Island and swung south into Peel Sound. He battled storms, survived an engine-room fire and, in Rae Strait, sailed too close to shore and nearly ran aground on a submerged rock.

In early September, with winter threatening, Amundsen entered the shelter of Gjoa Haven. Here he spent the next nineteen months, taking continuous magnetic readings. Soon after arriving, and as the ice formed, Amundsen put together a magnetic observatory out of shipping crates built in Norway with copper nails to avoid magnetic interference. He covered this with sod to keep the light from impinging on photographic paper, and used oil lamps for heat.

Both Amundsen and his assistant, Gustav Wiik, probably suffered enough carbon monoxide poisoning to damage their hearts. Wiik, who conducted 360 magnetic readings using four different instruments, and so spent by far the most time in the makeshift hut, died on the westward voyage out of the Passage.

Charles Deehr, a space physicist at the University of Alaska Fairbanks' Geophysical Institute, says that the information collected by Amundsen and Wiik is similar to what he collects today from satellites in the so-called "solar wind," the flow of sun radiation that excites the aurora borealis. Those measurements, Deehr says, "offer more than a glimpse of the character of the solar wind 50 years before it was known to exist." Quoted by journalist Ned Rozell in the *Alaska Science Forum*, Deehr said that "Amundsen was the first to demonstrate, without doubt, that the north magnetic (pole) does not have a permanent location, but moves in a fairly regular manner."

Amundsen's results, analyzed in 1929, showed that between 1831 and 1904, the north magnetic pole moved fifty kilometres. In the summer of 1905, as he prepared to sail out of Gjoa Haven, Amundsen buried a few artifacts beneath a cairn. Those artifacts, among them a signed photograph of Neumayer, can today be found in Yellowknife at the Prince of Wales Heritage Centre.

In *The Last Viking: The Life of Roald Amundsen*, Canadian author Stephen R. Bown remarks that most books treat Amundsen in the context of the 1911 race to the South Pole. That race—which ended with Amundsen becoming the first explorer to reach the Earth's southernmost point, while British explorer Robert Falcon Scott died trying—certainly makes for a gripping story. But both writers and readers often overlook one crucial fact: Amundsen succeeded because, in addition to training in Norway, he gleaned practical knowledge from the Netsilik Inuit. In November 1903, not long after he arrived in Gjoa Haven, a hunting party came upon the Norwegian visitors. Amundsen established friendly relations and, when the Inuit settled nearby, shared many hunting adventures with them. Like John Rae before him, Amundsen adopted Inuit clothing and footgear, and learned from experts how to travel across ice using dogs and dogsleds, and how to build a warm shelter using blocks of hard snow.

The Inuit helped Amundsen in countless ways. As he entered his second season of darkness, knowing that whalers habitually wintered in the northern reaches of Hudson Bay at Fullerton Harbour, Amundsen wrote a note asking to purchase eight dogs. Late in November 1904, a hunter named Artungelar set out to deliver this request. He travelled with one companion and four dogs, and encountered harsh conditions. Three dogs died along the way, and then, as he neared Fullerton early in March 1905, the Inuk discharged his rifle accidentally and shattered his right hand. He bandaged it up and acquired ten dogs from an American whaler and two Canadians—J. D. Moodie and Joseph-Elzéar Bernier—attached to the *Arctic*, a Canadian government vessel. Artungelar set out before the end of March and reached Amundsen on May 20, carrying also, from Bernier, some much-appreciated newspaper clippings.

What he learned from the Inuit, notably about dogs, Amundsen brought to his South Pole expedition. By comparison, Robert Falcon Scott could barely ski and, having never met any Inuit, brought ponies to the Antarctic instead of dogs. Thanks to the same quirk of the British psyche that had transformed the plodding, over-

During his two-year sojourn in Gjoa Haven, Roald Amundsen adopted Inuit clothing and learned from experts how to build snow huts and use dogs and dogsleds.

weight John Franklin into a larger-than-life explorer, Robert Falcon Scott nevertheless became a romantic figure. As Bown writes, he became the embodiment of heroic but doomed struggle, "the man who snatched victory from the jaws of death." Half a century before Scott, the British had convinced themselves that Franklin and his men, tragically lost in an impassable strait, had somehow "forged the last link with their lives."

As to actually navigating the labyrinthian Northwest Passage, how did the Norwegian determine which way to sail? Amundsen credited John Rae: "His work was of incalculable value to the *Gjoa* expedition. He discovered Rae Strait, which separates King William Land from the mainland. In all probability through this strait is the only navigable route for the voyage . . . This is the only passage which is free from destructive pack ice."

History proved Amundsen correct. As late as 1940–1942, when the Canadian schooner *St. Roch* became only the second vessel (after the *Gjoa*) to complete the Northwest Passage, and the first to do so from west to east, Captain Henry Larsen sailed through Rae Strait. And when, in 1944, Larsen managed to return westward through Lancaster Sound and Parry Channel, far to the north, he relied heavily on twentieth-century technology, in the form of a 300-horsepower diesel engine.

In recognizing the crucial importance of Rae Strait, Amundsen recalled the words of Leopold McClintock, who had long ago suggested that if Franklin followed that route, "he would probably have carried his ships through to Behring's Straits." Indeed, McClintock anticipated Amundsen when he added that, "perhaps some future voyager, profiting by the experience so fearfully and fatally acquired by the Franklin expedition, and the observations of Rae, [Richard] Collinson, and myself, may succeed in carrying his ship through from sea to sea; at least he will be enabled to direct all his efforts in the true and only direction."

On August 17, 1905, Roald Amundsen reached Cape Colborne near Cambridge Bay, the easternmost point attained by a ship from the west. By sailing there—almost three hundred kilometres west of where Franklin's *Terror* would eventually be found—he had established the viability of the Northwest Passage. A few days later, he encountered a ship, the *Charles Hansson* out of San Francisco. He hoped to continue into Bering Strait, but ice halted his progress at King Point near Herschel Island. He took magnetic recordings and, over the winter, trekked over the ice to Eagle, Alaska, to send telegrams announcing his accomplishment. He resumed sailing in mid-August 1906, and reached Nome, Alaska, on the thirty-first.

Roald Amundsen achieved more in the Arctic than in the Antarctic. He led the way through the Northwest Passage, and later traversed the Northeast Passage along the Russian coast. In May 1926, he flew an airship over the North Pole, so becoming the first expeditionary leader indisputably to reach it. Amundsen was living at Uranienborg, preparing to marry, when in 1928, at age fifty-five, he flew north to rescue an Italian explorer, Umberto Nobile. He disappeared into the Arctic and was never seen again.

30.

"Give Me My Father's Body"

Today, from a ridge at Cape York on the west coast of Greenland, visitors can gaze out over crescent-shaped Melville Bay, which sweeps southward for 240 kilometres. Directly west of this massive bay, all through the nineteenth century, whalers and explorers dreaded to challenge the Middle Ice. Today, that Middle Ice is just an historical memory: for months every summer, the waters of Baffin Bay lie open. From Cape York, turning and facing inland, visitors can see a twenty-eight-metre-high monument dedicated to American explorer Robert E. Peary, essentially a grotesque obelisk jutting skyward, and topped by a giant "P."

In August 1897, Peary had arrived at this cape on a mission. During a previous expedition, three years before, he had learned the location of three ten-thousand-year-old meteorites from which the polar Inuit had been extracting metal since before 1818, when John Ross found them using metal implements. In 1895, Peary had taken the two smaller chunks, called "the woman" and "the dog," to New York. Now, he hired all the able-bodied Inuit in the area and steamed six hours south to Bushnan Island. There, the people helped him load the largest piece onto his ship—the so-called "Ahnighito fragment," also called "the tent," which weighed almost thirty-five tons. Peary then returned to Cape York. "I sent my faithful Eskimos ashore," he wrote later, "accompanied by several barrels of biscuit, and loaded with guns, knives, ammunition, and numerous other articles which I had brought to reward them for their faithful service."

But as Kenn Harper writes in *Give Me My Father's Body*, six Inuit remained on board his ship the *Hope*, among them a hunter-guide named Qisuk and his young son, Minik or Mene (born at Etah around 1890). On October 2, 1897, when the ship reached the Brooklyn Naval Yard in New York City, twenty thousand people paid twenty-five cents each to visit the ship and see what the *Boston Post* had described as "the strange cargo."

The Inuit were brought to the Museum of Natural History, where according to Minik, "we were quartered in a damp cellar most unfavorable to people from the dry air of the north." Two anthropologists studied the new arrivals, but then came a New York heat wave. Soon all six of the Inuit, lacking immunity to local diseases, were suffering from tuberculosis.

The first to die was Minik's father. "He was dearer to me than anything else in the world—especially when we were brought to New York, strangers in a strange land. You can imagine how closely that brought us together; how our disease and suffering and lack of understanding of all the strange things around us . . . made us sit tremblingly waiting our turn to go . . . we grew to depend on one another, and to love each other as no father and son under ordinary conditions could possibly love."

Robert Peary washed his hands of the Inuit he had brought south. Within eight months three more were dead. A young adult, Uisaakassak, was then sent back to Greenland, leaving Minik alone among strangers. The boy had pleaded to see his father buried with proper Inuit ceremony. Museum staff were bent on studying the dead bodies, so they mounted a make-believe funeral. As Harper writes, "They got an old log about the length of a human corpse. This was wrapped in a cloth, a mask attached to one end." With Minik present to say his ritual goodbye, they buried the lot by lantern light.

William Wallace, the museum's chief custodian, brought Minik to live with his family in New York City and, in summer, upstate New York. The boy attended school, learned to read and write, and became "Minik Wallace." Meanwhile, his father's body was defleshed. Mounted on an armature, the skeleton was put on display at the museum. As William Wallace wrote later, Minik found out the hard way. The New York newspapers had got wind of the display. At school, from other children, he learned of the reports.

The family noticed a change in the boy, Wallace wrote later: "He was coming home from school with my son Willie one snowy afternoon when he suddenly began to cry. 'My father is not in his grave,' he said. 'His bones are in the museum.'" Minik had realized the truth. "But after that," Wallace wrote, "He was never the same boy.... Often we would see him crying, and sometimes he would not speak for days. We did our best to cheer him up, but it was no use. His heart was broken. He had lost faith in the new people he had come among."

William Wallace deeply regretted what had transpired. He supported Minik in a push to get the American Museum of Natural History to release the bones so they could be given a proper burial. On January 6, 1907, in a magazine supplement, the *New York World* published the first article to make his case. The headline gave Kenn Harper his book title: "Give Me My Father's Body."

When that campaign faltered, young Minik turned his energies to getting Robert Peary to send him home. On May 9, 1909, the *San Francisco Examiner* offered a sensational treatment under the

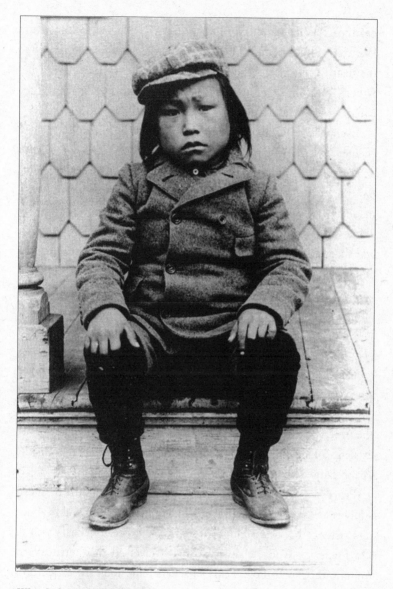

When he learned that his father's bones were on display in the American Museum of Natural History, Minik Wallace lost faith in the people he had come among.

headline, "Why Arctic Explorer Peary's Neglected Eskimo Boy Wants to Shoot Him." The story described how, set adrift after the death of his relatives, "Little Mene Wallace . . . had seen his father's skeleton grin at him from a glass case in the New York Museum of Natural History."

Eventually, Peary's people decided to cut their losses. Later, they claimed that they sent Minik north with many gifts, but Harper determined that the young man arrived in northern Greenland with only the clothes on his back. In August 1909, he came ashore at Uummannaq, an Inuit camp in North Star Bay at the site of present-day Thule. He wore a light sweater, a thin overcoat, a pair of short socks, and shoes fit for New York City. He had his medical and dental kits and nothing else.

Minik had forgotten much of his first language, but picked it up quickly. He also became a notable hunter. He worked as a handyman for Knud Rasmussen and Peter Freuchen, who set up a trading post nearby, Thule Station. For a time, he was married. Even so, he remained an outsider, and a teller of tall tales, and he felt happiest when Qallunaat visited from the south, white men for whom he could work as a guide and translator. In 1913, at age twenty-three, he joined the American Crocker Land Expedition, which set out to confirm the existence of a huge island north of Ellesmere Island—one that Robert Peary claimed he had seen from the far north in 1906.

Peary had invented this island in hopes of securing the financial support of a wealthy banker named George Crocker. Doubts about its existence became significant after 1909, because Peary's rival, Dr. Frederick Cook, claimed to have traversed that territory en route to the North Pole. Peary's backers undertook the expedition to prove Cook a fraud, but they ended up demonstrating that their own man was the scam artist.

In April 1909, and after supposedly completing a twenty-three-year quest to reach that same Pole, Robert E. Peary had refused a congratulatory handshake from his right-hand man, Matthew Henson. On April 6, after taking an astronomical reading in foggy conditions, Peary planted an American flag and ordered Henson to lead their four Inuit companions in three cheers. He then snapped a few photos.

Yet when Henson removed his glove and offered his hand, Peary turned and walked away—perhaps, the all-too-generous Henson wrote later, because "a gust of wind blew something into his eye." A few days previously, on March 31, Peary had sent the expert navigator Bob Bartlett, a Newfoundlander, back to base camp on the north coast of Ellesmere Island—despite his protests. Before leaving, Bartlett—the last of the party who, besides Peary, could take astronomical readings—situated the expedition at latitude 87°46′ north or 134 miles (215 kilometres) from the Pole.

During the next five days, Henson had led the two-dog-team charge. And Peary, disabled by the years-ago loss of eight toes, rode on the second sledge. On April 5, Peary took a reading and declared the party to be within thirty-five miles (fifty-six kilometres) of the Pole. Next morning, Henson "dashed out early," drove hard and eventually stopped and built two igloos.

When Peary arrived, Henson said, "We are now at the Pole, are we not?" And Peary said, "I do not suppose we can swear that we are exactly at the Pole." Yet the next day, as Henson innocently reported, "when the flag was hoisted over the geographical centre of the earth, it was located just behind our igloos."

During the return journey, Henson wrote, the dazed Peary proved "practically a dead weight." On April 27, when the men reached the *Roosevelt*, Bartlett rushed out to greet him: "I congratulate you, sir, on the discovery of the Pole." Peary responded without enthusiasm: "How did you guess it?'

He then withdrew to his cabin and stayed there. No cheering. No celebrating. "From the time we were at the Pole," Henson wrote later, "Commander Peary barely spoke to me. Probably he did not speak to me four times on the whole return journey to the ship . . . On board the ship he addressed me a very few times . . . [And he said] not a word about the North Pole or anything connected with it." Peary would appear to have been in a terrible funk—hardly the mood of a man who had achieved success in a life-long quest.

Four years later, in 1913, Minik Wallace signed on with the American Crocker Land Expedition, which set out to confirm the existence of a huge island Robert Peary claimed he had seen from the northern reaches of Ellesmere Island. On March 11, 1914, Wallace, three Americans and six other Inuit eventually set off from Etah on the 1,900 kilometres journey to "Crocker Land." In freezing-cold conditions, they reached and climbed the 4,700-foot Beitstadt Glacier. One of the Americans suffered frostbite and had to be evacuated. By April 11, only two Americans and two Inuit continued to advance.

Now came another instance of Fata Morgana—the kind of elaborate mirage that, almost one century earlier, had ruined Captain John Ross. Organizer Donald Baxter MacMillan saw, as he said later, "hills, valleys, snow-capped peaks extending through at least one hundred and twenty degrees of the horizon." Piugaattoq, an Inuit hunter with twenty years of experience of the area, told him this was an illusion. MacMillan insisted on chasing the mirage for five days, trekking across two hundred kilometres of threatening sea ice before he admitted that the Inuk was right and turned back. Robert Peary had invented "Crocker Land." His contemptible ruse had failed because in response to the San Francisco Earthquake of 1906, George Crocker turned to rebuilding his devastated hometown.

In 1916, having sought to return south several times, Minik Wallace took passage in the *George B. Cluett*, bound for New York. For a while, he was a curiosity quoted in newspapers. Minik described his seven years in Greenland with good humour, while admitting that he felt like a man without a home: "I still have the impression that it would have been better for me had I never been brought to civilization and educated. It leaves me between two extremes, where it would seem that I can get nowhere. It would have been better if I had never been educated . . . It's like rotting in a cellar to go back there after living in a civilized country."

Minik took a job working in a lumber camp in New Hampshire, and became friends with a fellow worker, a local man named Afton Hall. When winter shut the camp down, Minik accepted Hall's invitation to live with his family on a nearby farm, where he could help out. But then, in autumn 1918, an influenza pandemic swept the area. It killed members of Hall's family and also many itinerant workers who worked seasonally in the lumber camps—among them Minik Wallace, who at twenty-eight died of bronchial pneumonia. He was buried in the Indian Stream Cemetery in Pittsburg, New Hampshire.

Decades later, author Kenn Harper took up the campaign to retrieve the remains of Minik's father, Qisuk, and the other three Inuit who had died in New York, and to accord them a proper burial. In 1993, thanks to his advocacy, and also the backing of the Cape York Inuit and William Wallace's great-granddaughter, the American Museum of Natural History sent the remains to Qaanaaq, formerly Thule, where they were buried with due ceremony. The Cape York meteorites, brought south by Robert Peary, are still on display at the New York City museum.

As for Frederick Cook, he and Peary embodied different attitudes towards the Inuit. Cook was compassionate and gentlemanly; Peary, who was harsh and abrasive, fathered two Inuit sons and abandoned them both. By 1911, Peary had discredited Cook as a fraud, and had convinced Congress to honour him, Peary, as the first man to have attained the Pole.

During the second half of the twentieth century, most Arctic historians concluded that neither Peary nor Cook reached the North Pole. And yet, as we entered the twenty-first century, some people began to wonder: What if Frederick Cook really did reach the Pole? What if, as he claimed, he had pointed at low-lying clouds to reassure his frightened travelling companions that they remained always within reach of land? Later, the two young hunters would recall how Cook had "jumped and danced like an *angacock* (witch doctor)" when he looked at his "sun glass" and realized that they were only a day's march from the Big Nail. In *True North*, published in 2005, author Bruce Henderson argues that Cook's story rings true. Cook, a master of Inuit travel methods, completed several remarkable sledge journeys. And his unprecedented reports, including one of a westward ice-drift, have since been vindicated.

Henderson also rebuts fraud charges levelled against the doctor-explorer by his enemies, and repudiates allegations—this will surprise some—that Cook made false claims about climbing Mount McKinley in Alaska. He offers telling evidence that a fellow climber was bribed to offer false testimony. He reveals that the first verified summiteer supported Cook's description of the climb. And he shows that Cook never claimed that a photo taken on Mount McKinley had been taken at the summit. If Henderson is correct, then Peary not only abused the Greenlandic Inuit and betrayed Minik Wallace but, having failed to reach the North Pole, destroyed the man who first succeeded.

31.

Rasmussen Establishes Unity of Inuit Culture

The colourful Greenlandic town of Ilulissat, formerly known as Jacobshavn, faces east towards Disko Island, where in 1845 John Franklin took on fresh water and supplies. At Disko, according to letters sent home to England, Franklin banned swearing and drunkenness. He discharged 5 men and sent them home on supply ships, so reducing his expedition numbers to 129, including himself.

With a population of 4,500, Ilulissat is home to 6,000 sled dogs, many of them noisily in evidence along a boardwalk that leads to spectacular vistas of ice. From a hilltop vantage point at the end of the boardwalk, visitors can look out over the Ilulissat Icefjord, an ice-river that is the largest producer of icebergs in the northern hemisphere. It spawned the iceberg that sank the *Titanic*, and before that, in the nineteenth century, produced the Middle Ice that gave whalers and explorers so much misery.

The third-largest town in Greenland, Ilulissat is also the most visitor-friendly, and features a multitude of shops. The major in-town attraction is the three-storey Rasmussen museum, originally a vicarage in which Knud Rasmussen was born (in 1879) and

Born in 1879, Knud Rasmussen grew up in this house (then a vicarage) in Ilulissat, Greenland. Today, the house is a museum devoted to Rasmussen, the greatest polar ethnographer of all time.

spent the first twelve years of his life. Hailed as "the father of Eskimology," Rasmussen was brave, adventurous, intelligent, efficient, charismatic and persevering. In the history of polar exploration, he is a singular figure: the greatest polar ethnographer of all time. In Ilulissat, numerous exhibits celebrate the man, at once an explorer, a cultural anthropologist and a storyteller who demonstrated, on his Fifth Thule Expedition, that Inuit culture extends from eastern Greenland to Alaska, and also encompasses Siberia.

The son of a Danish missionary and an Inuit-Danish mother, Rasmussen grew up among the Kalaallit (Greenlandic Inuit). As a child he learned to speak Kalaallisut, which is closely related to the Inuktitut spoken by most Canadian Inuit. This would enable him eventually to add to the stock of Inuit stories pertaining to the Franklin expedition. But first, at age seven, he took to driving a dog sledge. "My playmates were native Greenlanders," he wrote later. "From the earliest boyhood I played and worked with the hunters, so even the hardships of the most strenuous sledge-trips became pleasant routine for me."

While still a boy, and like his older contemporary Roald Amundsen, he found a hero in explorer Fridtjof Nansen, who had set out from Ilulissat on one of his expeditions. Later, Rasmussen went to Denmark for his education, attending school in the town of Lynge, thirty kilometres north of Copenhagen. At nineteen and twenty, he dabbled without success in acting and singing opera, but then he gravitated to ethnology and the outdoors. In 1902, at age twenty-three, with three fellow Danes, he undertook the so-called Danish Literary Expedition to travel around Greenland studying Inuit culture.

He started by travelling to Kristiania (Oslo) to seek help from Fridtjof Nansen in cutting through red tape. That celebrated explorer recognized Rasmussen's potential and told him: "Of course, your work does not end with a description of West Greenland and the Smith Sound Eskimos—you must go on to Cumberland and Alaska, and you have benefits like no other researcher before you."

Because Rasmussen was part Inuit and spoke Kalaallisut, he achieved unprecedented access to Inuit stories and traditions. Ranging throughout the far north Rasmussen would collect stories of fantastical trips to the moon, biographer Stephen Bown tells us—tales

As a young man, Rasmussen organized the Danish Literary Expedition. With three fellow Danes, he travelled around Greenland studying Inuit culture.

"of flesh-eating giants and bears the size of mountains, of evil storm birds and ravenous, human-hunting dogs." As a "butterfly ethnographer," Bown notes, Rasmussen evoked "the rich inner world" of a people who stretch across the entire Canadian Arctic.

He also detailed one remarkable migration. In 1903, Rasmussen interviewed, for the first time, Merqusaq—one of the last remaining Inuit to have emigrated to Greenland from Baffin Island half a century before. Merqusaq, who had lost one eye, had been born around 1850 in the vicinity of Pond Inlet at the north end of Baffin Island.

His extended family of about forty people had arrived there a decade before from Tenudiakbeek or Cumberland Sound, the same whale-rich area that had produced Eenoolooapik and Tookoolito. Pursued by enemies, and led by his uncle Qitlaq, his people crossed Lancaster Sound northward in 1851.

Two years later, at Dundas Harbour on the south coast of Devon Island, they encountered Edward Inglefield, who was searching for John Franklin. Inglefield told them he had seen Inuit on the coast of Greenland, after which, Merqusaq said, Qitlaq "could never settle to anything again." By 1858, when McClintock passed this way, the charismatic shaman had taken his people still farther north. Despite some defections, Qitlaq then led his family across Smith Sound to Greenland, where in the early 1860s they settled near Etah. Here they met the polar Inuit who had saved Elisha Kent Kane, and who introduced them to the kayak, in which they soon became expert.

Qitlaq died while leading twenty people in an attempted return to Baffin Island. Back on what is now the Canadian side of Davis Strait, his followers were starving when Merqusaq, by then a young married man, came under surprise attack by two men who had gone rogue and become cannibals. One of them gouged out his right eye before he was driven off. Merqusaq and his four closest relatives, fearful of further aggression, fled and eventually made it back to Greenland, where they settled permanently among the polar Inuit. Merqusaq's granddaughter, Navarana, married Peter Freuchen, Rasmussen's friend and fellow traveller.

Merqusaq lived with those two during his last years, and Rasmussen would report that, "although old now and somewhat bowed from rheumatism, he continues his journeys of several hundred miles a year on arduous fishing and hunting expeditions." The ethnographer would quote the renowned hunter: "Look at my body: it is covered with deep scars; those are the marks of bears' claws. Death has been near me many times . . . but as long as I can hold a walrus and kill a bear, I shall still be glad to live." Merqusaq died in 1916.

Meanwhile, back in Denmark after his first expedition, Rasmussen gave lectures and wrote *The People of the Polar North* (1908), which combined a travel narrative with a study of Inuit folklore. In 1910, Rasmussen and Freuchen built the Thule Trading Station at Cape York (Uummannaq), Greenland. From this fur-trading outpost, between 1912 and 1933. Rasmussen organized and launched a series of seven expeditions known as the Thule Expeditions.

On the first of these, Rasmussen and Freuchen set out to test Robert Peary's claim that a channel divided "Peary Land" from Greenland. By travelling a thousand kilometres over the ice, they proved that this alleged waterway does not exist. Clements Markham, president of Britain's Royal Geographical Society, hailed this journey as the "finest ever performed by [men using] dogs." Freuchen would write of it in *Vagrant Viking* (1953) and *I Sailed with Rasmussen* (1958).

Starting in 1916, Rasmussen spent two years leading seven men on the Second Thule Expedition, which mapped part of Greenland's northern coast, and fuelled his book *Greenland by the Polar Sea* (1921). In 1919, he led the Third Thule Expedition in depot-laying for Amundsen's polar drift in the *Maud*. And on the fourth sortie in the series, he spent several months collecting ethnographic data on Greenland's east coast. All this set the stage for the epochal Fifth Thule Expedition (1921–1924).

On March 10, 1923, from the northern reaches of Hudson Bay, Rasmussen embarked on the longest dogsled expedition in polar history. With two Inuit companions, twenty-four dogs and two narrow sleds, each piled high with a thousand pounds of gear, the

Greenlandic Dane set out on the final leg of a 32,000-kilometre trek that would, in his words, "attack the great primary problem of the origins of the Eskimo race."

Rasmussen had just spent eighteen months exploring parts of Canada west of Hudson Bay. Now, he would spend sixteen months journeying to the east coast of Siberia, where the Russians would deny further access. No matter. On this expedition, Rasmussen became the first explorer to travel through the Northwest Passage by dogsled. The undertaking generated ten volumes of ethnographic, archaeological and biological data, and later inspired the 2006 movie *The Journals of Knud Rasmussen*. Rasmussen demonstrated that the Inuit, scattered now from Greenland to western Canada and beyond, even into Siberia, constitute a single people.

After leading a seven-person team in doing interviews and excavations on Baffin Island, Rasmussen spent sixteen months with two Inuit hunters, crossing the Arctic to Nome, Alaska. He tells that story in his classic work *Across Arctic America* (1927). Rasmussen also published numerous articles about his expeditions, and one of them has become especially interesting in light of the 2016 discovery of *Terror*.

In a 1931 book, *The Netsilik Eskimos: Social Life and Spiritual Culture*, Rasmussen wrote of interviewing "an old man named Iggiararjuk" who came from Pelly Bay, and told him of a meeting with some of Franklin's men, probably in the vicinity of Terror Bay, northwest of Gjoa Haven.

> My father Mangaq was with Tetqatsaq and Qablut on a seal hunt on the west side of King William's Land when they heard shouts, and discovered three white men who stood on the shore waving to them. This was in spring; there was already open water along the land, and it was not possible

to get in to them before low tide. The white men were very thin, hollow-cheeked, and looked ill. They were dressed in white man's clothes, had no dogs and were travelling with sledges which they drew themselves.

They bought seal meat and blubber, and paid with a knife. There was great joy on both sides at this bargain, and the white men cooked the meat at once with the aid of the blubber, and ate it. Later one of the strangers went along to my father's tent camp before returning to their own little tent, which was not of animal skins but of something that was white like snow. At that time there were already caribou on King William's Land, but the strangers only seemed to hunt wildfowl; in particular there were many eider ducks and ptarmigan then.

The earth was not yet alive and the swans had not come to the country. Father and his people would willingly have helped the white men, but could not understand them; they tried to explain themselves by signs, and in fact learned to know a lot by this means. They had once been many, they said; now they were only few, and they had left their ship out in the pack-ice. They pointed to the south, and it was understood that they wanted to go home overland. They were not met again, and no one knows where they went to.

Rasmussen interviewed several other older men, who added what he called "interesting details of the lost expedition." Faced with testimony that Louie Kamookak has referred to as "mixed stories," Rasmussen combined accounts and presented them in the words of one man, Qaqortingneq. He elicited a story that appears to derive mainly from Franklin's second ship, the *Terror*. Thanks to a tip from

Gjoa Haven resident Sammy Kogvik, who had chanced upon a mast protruding from the winter ice of Terror Bay, that vessel was located in 2016—and has yet to be thoroughly investigated. Rasmussen wrote that two brothers were once out sealing in that vicinity. "It was in spring, at the time when the snow melts away round the breathing holes of the seals. Far out on the ice they saw something black, a large black mass that could be no animal. They looked more closely and found that it was a great ship. They ran home at once and told their fellow villagers of it, and next day they all went out to it. They saw nobody, the ship was deserted, and so they made up their minds to plunder it of everything they could get hold of. But none of them had ever met white men, and they had no idea what all the things they saw could be used for."

They found guns in the ship, for example, "and as they had no suspicion of what they were, they knocked the steel barrels off and hammered them out for harpoons. In fact, so ignorant were they about guns that they said a quantity of percussion caps they found were 'little thimbles,' and they really thought that among the white men there lived a dwarf people who could use them.

"At first they dared not go down into the ship itself," Rasmussen relates, "but soon they became bolder and even ventured into the houses that were under the deck. There they found many dead men lying in their beds. At last they also risked going down into the enormous room in the middle of the ship. It was dark there." Now the explorer relays an anecdote that has sometimes been ascribed to the other ship, *Erebus*. Rasmussen writes that the Inuit "found tools and would make a hole in order to let light in. And the foolish people, not understanding white man's things, hewed a hole just on the water-line so the water poured in and the ship sank. And it went to the bottom with all the valuable things, of which they barely rescued any."

According to Rasmussen, Qaqortingneq also described Inuit finding human remains, citing three men who "were on their way from King William's Land to Adelaide Peninsula to hunt for caribou calves. There they found a boat with the bodies of six men. In the boat were guns, knives and some provisions, showing that they had perished of sickness."

Rasmussen also describes visiting the mainland that looks out on Wilmot and Crampton Bay, where searchers found *Erebus* in 2014:

One day in the late autumn," he writes, "just before the ice formed, I sailed with Peter Norberg and Qaqortingneq up to Qavdlunârsiorfik on the east coast of Adelaide Peninsula. There, exactly where the Eskimos had indicated, we found a number of human bones that undoubtedly were the mortal remains of members of the Franklin Expedition; some pieces of cloth and stumps of leather we found at the same place showed that they were of white men. Now, almost eighty years after, wild beasts had scattered the white, sun-bleached bones out over the peninsula and thus removed the sinister traces from the spot where the last struggle had once been fought.

"We had been the first friends that ever visited the place. Now we gathered their bones together, built a cairn over them and hoisted two flags at half mast, the English and the Danish. Thus without many words we did them the last honours. The deep footprints of tired men had once ended in the soft snow here by the low, sandy spit, far from home, from countrymen. But the footprints were not effaced. Others came and carried them on. So does the work of these Franklin men live on to this day wherever the struggle goes on for the exploration and conquest of our globe.

In 1931, after shuttling between Greenland and Denmark for seven years, lecturing and writing, Knud Rasmussen undertook a Sixth Thule Expedition. It aimed to repudiate the claim of a contingent of Norwegians who had occupied an area on the coast of eastern Greenland, calling it Erik the Red's Land. It also demonstrated that Greenland's east coast, long inaccessible, had become reachable between early July and mid-September. In 1933, the Permanent Court of International Justice vindicated Rasmussen and the Danes, and the Norwegians withdrew their claim.

That same year, continuing his work, Rasmussen launched a Seventh Thule Expedition—an ambitious undertaking involving sixty-two members, twenty-five of them Greenlanders in kayaks. Late in 1933, in eastern Greenland, Rasmussen got food poisoning from eating improperly fermented meat. This evolved into a virulent flu and pneumonia. A Danish ship made a special detour to collect Rasmussen and bring him to Copenhagen. Diagnosed as having a rare form of botulism, combined with pneumonia, he rallied for several weeks. But then, in December, at age fifty-four, he succumbed. Denmark accorded him a state funeral, and tributes came from around the world.

32.

Erebus *and* Terror *Validate Inuit Testimony*

During the summer of 2014, while flying home from Yellowknife to Gjoa Haven, Louie Kamookak noticed that the young man sitting beside him was reading about Sir John Franklin. He introduced himself and ended up chatting with Ryan Harris, a senior archaeologist-diver with Parks Canada. Harris and his team were flying north to embark on yet another Franklin-search expedition, commencing off the northwest coast of King William Island. Before going his separate way, Kamookak suggested that they search an area farther south.

When ice prevented the Victoria Strait Expedition, as it was called, from reaching its intended area, the Parks Canada team turned its attention to what had originally been a secondary area—the one Kamookak mentioned. And that southern area, roughly speaking, is where in September 2014 the searchers found the *Erebus*, hidden just eleven metres beneath the surface.

Two years and one day later, on September 3, 2016, a team from the Arctic Research Foundation found *Terror* off southwestern King William Island after acting on a tip from an Inuk crewmember. Sammy Kogvik, like Kamookak from Gjoa Haven, told operations

In 2014, Parks Canada located HMS Erebus off Adelaide Peninsula. Two years later, divers found HMS Terror in Terror Bay.
According to the Victory Point record, the ships had been beset since September 12, 1846. Map by Chris Brackley.

director Adrian Schimnowski that a few winters ago—"six, seven, or eight years"—while out hunting on the ice of Terror Bay, he chanced upon what appeared to be a protruding mast. He kept the find secret because, after snapping photos, he lost his camera and so lacked proof.

The team entered Terror Bay and soon located *Terror* sitting on the ocean floor twenty-four metres below the surface. Schimnowski sent a remotely operated vehicle (ROV) into the ship through an open hatch. "We have successfully entered the mess hall, worked our way into a few cabins and found the food storage room with plates and one can on the shelves," Schimnowski told the *Guardian* newspaper by email. "We spotted two wine bottles, tables and empty shelving. Found a desk with open drawers with something in the back corner of the drawer."

Using the ROV, the men determined that the ship's three masts were still standing, most hatches were closed and everything was neatly stowed. Schimnowski added that the "wreck is sitting level on the sea bed floor not at a list—which means the boat sank gently to the bottom." The presence of a heavy rope line suggests that someone may have deployed an anchor. "This vessel looks like it was buttoned down tight for winter and it sank," Schimnowski told the *Guardian*. "Everything was shut. Even the windows are still intact. If you could lift this boat out of the water, and pump the water out, it would probably float."

Jim Balsillie, former co-leader of Research in Motion (makers of BlackBerry) and co-founder of the Arctic Research Foundation, told the *Guardian*: "Given the location of the find and the state of the wreck, it's almost certain that HMS *Terror* was operationally closed down by the remaining crew who then re-boarded HMS *Erebus* and sailed south where they met their ultimate tragic fate."

These findings speak to one of the two great mysteries of

nineteenth-century Arctic exploration: What happened to John Franklin and his two ships? The discovery of these two ships demonstrate that the demise of the expedition was far more complex and protracted than first thought. And they vindicate both the Inuit and those who relayed their stories.

Let's take it from the top. John Rae relayed Inuit testimony, as translated by William Ouligbuck, that many of Franklin's men had starved to death while trekking south, and that some of the final survivors had been driven to cannibalism. Victorian England refused to believe this and, through Charles Dickens, suggested instead that the Inuit had murdered the weakened white sailors. Lady Franklin decreed that the final survivors had completed the Northwest Passage. Somehow, they had "forged the last link with their lives." This assertion brings us to the second great riddle: Who discovered the Northwest Passage?

Five years after Rae's report of cannibalism exploded in Britain like a bombshell, Leopold McClintock returned from King William Island having found skeletons and a one-page record left in a cairn by expedition officers. Today, most serious analysts lean to the view that this "Victory Point record" has been accorded too much weight.

It did reveal that Franklin spent the winter of 1845–46 at Beechey Island (where he buried three men). The following spring, when Peel Sound opened unexpectedly, Franklin sailed southward. On September 12, 1846, his ships got trapped in pack ice off Cape Felix at the northwest corner of King William Island. On June 11, 1847, Franklin himself died. Over the next several months, many

A Parks Canada diver finds a nineteenth-century plate on HMS Erebus. *The wreck is turning up a multitude of relics.*

others died. Total reported loss: nine officers and fifteen crew. So far, no real contention.

As noted in Chapter 23, McClintock himself, having examined the Victory Point record, launched the "standard reconstruction." The starving crews, he wrote, abandoned the *Erebus* and the *Terror* in April 1848. "The survivors, under Crozier and Fitzjames, numbered in all 105; they proceeded with boats on sledges to the Great Fish River. One of their boats was found by us, untouched by the Esquimaux, and many relics brought from her, as also obtained from the natives of Boothia and the east shore of King William Island."

Today, thanks to the discoveries of *Erebus* and *Terror*, we know that this scenario requires major revision. We know that, while some men trekked south along the coast of King William Island in 1848, some returned to the ships—both now located, neither thoroughly searched. Within the next few years, archaeologists are certain to unearth much new evidence—including, perhaps, even some written documents. This evidence will enable scholars to sift through the extensive Inuit testimony gathered by Charles Francis Hall, Frederick Schwatka and others, and to separate the wheat from the chaff. Doing so will take years.

In 1923, ethnologist-explorer Knud Rasmussen collected stories and, apprised by local Inuit, found bones and skulls at Starvation Point on the Canadian mainland. Subsequent discoveries, such as those of remains found twenty-five kilometres west of Starvation Cove in 1926 and 1936, suggested that instead of marching south in a single body, those later survivors had travelled in smaller groups. In 1931, a Hudson's Bay Company trader, William "Paddy" Gibson, grandfather of Louie Kamookak, found the remains of four skeletons on one of the Todd Islets southwest of Gjoa Haven. Also, on an islet in Douglas Bay off the south coast of King William Island, Gibson found the remains of seven men and buried them beneath a large stone cairn.

Half a century later, a forensic anthropologist, Owen Beattie, discovered and analyzed some skeletal remains from the mainland. They showed evidence of scurvy and such high levels of lead as to suggest lead poisoning. In 1984 and 1986, Beattie excavated three early-expedition graves at Beechey Island, where bodies had been buried in permafrost. His most significant discovery, as described in *Frozen in Time*, which he co-authored with John Geiger, was that the three men had indeed suffered from high lead levels, although this had not killed them.

Beattie theorized that lead poisoning, contracted from the solder used to seal cans of preserved food, affected the entire expedition.

Its symptoms include anorexia, weakness, fatigue, anemia, paranoia and irritability, which matched certain Inuit tales of disoriented sailors. But some researchers have grown skeptical that lead poisoning played a major role in what happened. And others argue that if it did, the lead probably came from the ships' water pipes.

In 2016, after studying the 170-year-old thumbnail of John Hartnell—one of the three crewmen buried on Beechey Island—some Canadian scientists made a case that zinc deficiency caused by malnutrition played a greater role than lead poisoning in the early deaths. Led by TrichAnalytics Inc., scientists from the Universities of Saskatchewan, Victoria and Ottawa used cutting-edge technology to analyze nail tissue for metal exposure and diet. That tissue, provided by the Inuit Heritage Trust and the Canadian Museum of History, showed that until his final few weeks, Hartnell had normal lead levels. Significant lead exposure did not occur during the expedition. Rather, a severe zinc deficiency led to a weakened immune system and then tuberculosis, which led to a release of previously stored lead into Hartnell's bloodstream.

Nor is that the only question that has haunted historians. Why did the deaths of nine officers and fifteen men, which happened while the ships were beset off the northwest coast of King William Island, include such a high percentage of officers: 37 percent, compared with 14 percent of crew members? Some have speculated about accident and injury. Others have suggested that the dead officers ingested something that most seamen did not. But oddly enough, nobody has publicly invoked the calamitous Jens Munk expedition of the early 1600s, which lost sixty-one men out of sixty-four, almost certainly because the sailors ate uncooked polar-bear meat infected with trichinosis. The Munk catastrophe, reprised in Chapter 2, suggests a new hypothesis. While visiting Beechey Island, contemporary voyagers have sometimes been driven off by polar bears, choosing to withdraw rather than shoot the glorious creatures. In the same situation, how would Franklin's men have responded? Undercooked polar-bear meat, unevenly distributed among officers and crew, might well lead to lopsided fatality statistics.

In the mid-1990s, archaeologist Margaret Bertulli and physical anthropologist Anne Keenleyside investigated a grisly discovery in Erebus Bay on the west coast of King William Island. They catalogued more than two hundred identifiable artifacts—nails, buttons, combs, clay pipes, wire gauze from snow goggles—and analyzed more than four hundred bones, the remains of at least eight men. They found high lead levels, supporting Beattie's hypothesis of lead poisoning. Also, using an electron microscope, they discovered cut marks on ninety-two bones—impressions easily distinguished from the marks of animal teeth or stone tools. They occurred "in a pattern consistent with intentional disarticulation." In short, the survivors had dismembered bodies and carved away flesh.

This forensic examination, as British author Roland Huntford observed in *The New York Times Book Review*, proved beyond doubt that starvation reduced the Franklin expedition to cannibalism and "vindicates Dr. John Rae of the Hudson's Bay Company, who, through contact with the Eskimos in 1854, uncovered the first traces of the expedition, including reports of cannibalism. He has been reviled, or ignored, for his pains by apologists for Franklin ever since."

Today's Royal Navy, represented by historian Andrew Lambert, has finally acknowledged the overwhelming evidence of cannibalism. Lambert begins his 2009 biography of Franklin with a prologue vividly describing how sailors from the *Erebus* and *Terror* "began butchering and eating their comrades."

But pass on. The *Erebus* turned up some distance to the south of where, supposedly, Franklin's men abandoned the ship. And that brings us to David C. Woodman, who in 1991 challenged the standard reconstruction with *Unravelling the Franklin Mystery: Inuit Testimony*. Woodman created an alternative scenario, which now stands corroborated in many particulars, by sifting through Inuit accounts as gathered by explorers.

Woodman drew mainly on the work of five of them. John Rae interviewed numerous Inuit, among them In-nook-poo-zhe-jook, in 1854. He reported what he had learned, including the cannibalism, and indicated where the disaster unfolded. Later that decade, dispatched to King William Island by Lady Franklin, Leopold McClintock found skeletons, relics and the Victory Point record.

In the late 1860s, with the help of Ebierbing and Tookoolito, those outstanding Inuit translators, Charles Francis Hall gathered detailed accounts, including reports that a ship had sunk near an island off the west coast of Adelaide Peninsula. (This was *Erebus*.) In 1878–1880, on that same peninsula, Frederick Schwatka conducted interviews and found skeletons in an area he named "Starvation Cove." While traversing the Northwest Passage by dogsled in 1921–1924, Rasmussen was able to add more detail because he spoke fluent Kalaallisut, which is closely related to Inuktitut.

Without the papers, journals and published books of these explorers, crucial accounts would never have survived in the detail that makes them so vivid and utterly convincing. After analyzing the Inuit testimony, Woodman argued that the Victoria Point document found during McClintock's expedition indicated only what the surviving sailors intended to do, not what they did.

Thanks to the finding of *Erebus* and *Terror*, we can see that Woodman was essentially correct. He suggested that in 1848, with Franklin dead, Captain Francis Crozier set out with the bulk of the remaining men to hunt near the mouth of Back's Great Fish River, almost 1,500 kilometres away. Virtually all these men returned to the ice-locked ships, however. One vessel—it could only have been the *Terror*—may have sunk quickly with many sailors on board, trapped, unable to escape. About this we will know more soon enough.

The other ship (*Erebus*) was carried south by ice to Wilmot and Crampton Bay, an area known to the Inuit as Ootjoolik. Woodman suggested that a large group of sailors abandoned that vessel in 1851, while it drifted south in the ice. Some Inuit hunters met this party of men, weak and starving, slogging south along the west coast of King William Island. These were the men In-nook-poo-zhe-jook described to John Rae. A few sailors—probably four, according to Puhtoorak—remained aboard the ice-locked ship, probably until early 1852.

This is not the place for a forty-page analysis of Inuit oral history. But the discoveries of the ships do suggest turning a spotlight on a few key passages that explain why most Franklin aficionados believe archaeologists will discover at least one body aboard the *Erebus*. Not far from where Canadian searchers found the ship, Charles Francis Hall and Tookoolito interviewed a local woman named Koo-nik. She was the one who spoke of finding "a very large white man" dead on the floor inside a ship. In a letter to his sponsor, Henry Grinnell, Hall added details: "The party on getting aboard tried to find out if any one was there, and not seeing or hearing any one, began ransacking the ship. To get into the igloo (cabin), they knocked a hole through because it was locked. They found there a dead man, whose body was very large and heavy, his teeth very long. It took five men to lift this giant Kabloona [Qallunaat or white man]. He was left where they found him. One place in the ship, where a great many things were found, was very dark; they had to find things there by feeling around. Guns were there and a great many very good buckets and boxes. On my asking if they saw anything to eat on board, the reply was there was meat and tood-noo [caribou fat] in cans, the meat fat and like pemmican. The sails, rigging, and boats—everything about the ship—was in complete order."

This same story turns up again in 1879, when with the help of Ebierbing, Frederick Schwatka interviewed Puhtoorak, one of the Inuit who had ventured aboard the *Erebus*. Puhtoorak said that he found a dead white man in a large ship eight miles (thirteen kilometres) off Grant Point (near where *Erebus* was found). He reported that the Inuit found a small boat on the mainland, and many empty casks on the ship. "He also saw books on board the ship but did not take them."

Puhtoorak also said that before discovering the ship, while hunting along the shore with friends, he came across the tracks of four white men and "judged they were hunting for deer." Later, he found the tracks of three men, and suggested "that the white men lived in this ship until the fall and then moved onto the mainland." In so saying, he affirmed the earlier account by Koo-nik, who told Hall that Inuit had seen "the tracks of 3 men Kob-loo-nas & those of a dog with them." Hall added that "there is no such thing as their being mistaken when they come across strange tracks & pronounce them not to be Innuits."

These accounts and others, taken together, suggest that four men were living aboard the *Erebus* when the ice carried it—some suggest they guided it—into Wilmot and Crampton Bay. One of them—a large man?—probably died on board. The other three left the ship in a bid to survive, and were never seen again. Inuit hunters boarded the ship. They made off with a few "treasures" but left a great many more.

Over the next few years, Parks Canada archaeologists will almost certainly produce artifacts and possibly papers that will further clarify what happened to the Franklin expedition. Inuit testimony suggests that they will come across at least one body in *Erebus*, and perhaps several in *Terror*. If the past is any guide, these findings will generate conflicting interpretations. This much is certain: as experts thrash out an all-encompassing revision, they will draw heavily on Inuit testimony.

EPILOGUE

Dead Reckoning in the Northwest Passage

A couple of experienced Arctic hands worried aloud that we might not be able to find the memorial plaque. But I knew that locating it would be no problem: we had precise coordinates and we were sailing in Rae Strait off the west coast of Boothia Peninsula. This was one of those Adventure Canada voyages I mentioned in the prologue. August 2012. Having entered the twenty-two-kilometre-wide strait from the north, as so often before, our captain augmented the electronic instruments of the *Clipper Adventurer*—later renamed the *Sea Adventurer*—by sending out two men in a Zodiac to take soundings by hand. He had then followed a zigzag course to take us within two kilometres of the coast.

Now, as we roared towards shore in the scout-Zodiac, three men and one woman, I kept my worries to myself. What if boulders or a heavy swell prevented us from landing? What if a blizzard or a polar bear had destroyed the plaque? What if some destructive know-nothing had carried it off? Any of these contingencies would upset my plans. I wanted to establish the John Rae memorial as a viable destination.

TOP: *Louie Kamookak in 1999 at the remains of the cairn John Rae built in 1854.*

BOTTOM: *Also 1999: three adventurers—Cameron Treleaven, Louie Kamookak and Ken McGoogan—drink a toast to John Rae, William Ouligbuck and Thomas Mistegan.*

For years I had been urging people to stop obsessing over Sir John Franklin, that unfortunate Englishman, and instead to celebrate John Rae, intrepid champion of native peoples. In 1999, I had erected a plaque at this location with two fellow adventurers: antiquarian Cameron Treleaven and Inuk historian Louie Kamookak. After crossing Rae Strait in Kamookak's twenty-foot boat, we had camped overnight in a dirt-floor tent. Next day, we had hiked for hours across bog and tundra before we found it: the remains of the cairn John Rae built in 1854.

The day after we did so, we lugged the awkward plaque back to that rough circle of rocks. We planted the metal base nearby and heaped stones around it. We drank a toast to Rae and the two men who had reached this point with him, the Inuk William Ouligbuck and the Ojibway Thomas Mistegan. All this I described in the epilogue to my book *Fatal Passage*. Now, as we arrived by Zodiac thirteen years later, with four of us scanning the horizon, our sharp-eyed ornithologist said: "I see it. Twelve o'clock." Sure enough, there it stood on the horizon: the Rae Strait memorial plaque. We drove the Zodiac onto the sand and swung onto the beach.

We would not have been there at all if critics of adventure tourism had their way. They forget that for many who take an Adventure Canada–style voyage into the Arctic, the highlight is not history, archaeology or wildlife, but meeting the people. The Inuit are incredibly warm and welcoming, though they are clearly far from wealthy. A quick ramble through any Northern store reveals that they need the money tourism brings. How else could they afford those prices? The Inuit want and need visiting Qallunaat (white people) to buy their arts and crafts. In this respect, by making the Arctic more accessible, climate change is proving positive: it has increased adventure tourism, much of which is history-oriented.

This development has given rise to serious reflection, but also to over-the-top commentary. In *The Nation*, after taking a single Arctic voyage in 2015, Roy Scranton wrote: "What the Franklin Expedition glorified was the war of Man—white men—against Nature. Franklin was indeed a tragic figure, and the tragic flaw he embodied was a will to power that knew no bounds. He was doomed because 'nature' proved, finally, unconquerable, but in honoring his memory, we were celebrating and carrying on the war he'd waged."

Ah, yes, the war of those awful white men against nature. That would be the same war that gave rise to the steam engine, airplanes, submarines, icebreakers, central heating, air-conditioning, smart phones and the Internet. Having shown no qualms about accepting a free northern experience, complete with airfare, Scranton declared such voyaging "an ethically dubious proposition." He continued: "Built on and often glorifying a tradition of brutal, racialized colonial domination, adventure tourism restages the white-supremacist conquest of 'nature' and 'natives' as a carefully controlled consumer encounter with 'pristine wilderness' and 'indigenous cultures.'"

From nature we have moved to natives. But when Scranton writes of "brutal, racialized colonial domination," surely he is thinking of the Spanish conquest of the Aztec, Mayan and Incan civilizations. He confuses poor old John Franklin, who had a terrible time finding indigenous folk when he needed them, with such conquistadors as Hernán Cortés and Francisco Pizarro, who did indeed wage "brutal, racialized" wars—though some of their victims were not them-selves without sin. Still, let us admit that Franklin was no John Rae, who made a constant practice of learning from the native peoples, and who championed the Inuit against some of the most powerful people of his times.

I would argue that adventure tourism, far from being part of the problem, can be part of the solution. Whether we like it or not, climate change is demanding adjustment and adaptation. In the Canadian Arctic, where an oil spill would wreak environmental havoc, the greatest threat is that of oil tankers sailing willy-nilly through the Passage. Better, I think, to have adventure tourism clogging those waters with small ships and friendly passengers (maximum, say, two hundred per vessel). Such an adaptation would not only help local economies flourish but strengthen Canada's case for establishing environmental controls—and might teach neophytes that John Franklin was not the only explorer to venture north.

In August 2012, at the John Rae site overlooking Rae Strait, we gathered eighty or ninety passengers around the plaque. We snapped photos and I said a few words about Rae and his travelling companions. Their discovery of this strait changed exploration history, ending a centuries-long search for a way through the Northwest Passage. From home I had brought three small flags, and these I wedged into the stones around the base of the plaque—one each representing Nunavut, Canada and Scotland.

In Scotland, meanwhile, and in Britain generally, the struggle to gain recognition for Rae—and, by extension, the First Peoples he championed—had been gaining momentum for years. In July 2004,

Alistair Carmichael, the Scottish member of Parliament for Orkney, had introduced a motion urging the British Parliament to declare that the House "regrets that Dr. Rae was never awarded the public recognition that was his due." The motion failed.

Five years later, Carmichael tried again, urging Parliament to state formally that it "regrets that memorials to Sir John Franklin outside the Admiralty headquarters and inside Westminster Abbey still inaccurately describe Franklin as the first to discover the [Northwest] passage, and calls on the Ministry of Defence and the Abbey authorities to take the necessary steps to clarify the true position." Again, no success.

But four years later still, when Orcadians mounted a 2013 international conference to mark the two-hundredth anniversary of the birth of John Rae, they would also unveil a new statue of the explorer in Stromness. Its inscription, coined by man-of-letters Tom Muir, rightly hailed Rae as "Discoverer of the final link in the first navigable Northwest Passage." At the unveiling, Carmichael expressed confidence that similar wording would appear on a plaque soon to be installed at Westminster Abbey.

But this was not to be. In a book called *Finding Franklin*, American scholar Russell Potter details how a retired geographer contrived to sabotage Carmichael's campaign to gain proper recognition for Rae in the Abbey. In the past, William Barr has done valuable work as an editor and translator. But recently he had developed a fatuous argument to preclude properly recognizing John Rae. Barr suggested that when the explorer found the strait that bears his name, "there was still a substantial section of that particular route [north of Rae Strait] which was yet uncharted and unsailed"—and Rae had not after all found the final, final, final link. In fact, John Franklin himself had sailed directly past that particular stretch of coastline

TOP: *At Westminster Abbey, the author "reflected" on how John Rae had completed the work of John Franklin.*

BOTTOM: *The ledger stone: John Rae / 1813–1893 / Arctic Explorer.*

before getting trapped off King William Island. I demolished Barr's argument in the *Polar Record*, in a rejoinder entitled "Defenders of Arctic Orthodoxy Turn Their Backs on Sir John Franklin." In brief, they were suggesting that by sailing as far south as he did, Franklin had accomplished nothing.

But Barr remained fixated. That's understandable: he had nothing else to offer. And his allies in England, staunch defenders to a person of Victorian orthodoxy, scurried around London to subvert Carmichael's initiative. This was a particularly shameful episode in a tedious tradition of repudiation that dates back to the days of Dickens. As a result of these machinations, the Orcadian campaign failed to garner for John Rae the eight-foot-tall statue that he deserves, or even the promised plaque proclaiming his singular achievement. Instead, on September 30, 2014, a modest ledger stone was unveiled at Westminster Abbey at the base of the grandiose memorial to John Franklin. It reads simply: "John Rae, Arctic explorer."

Dozens of Orcadians came to London to attend the unveiling, and a few Canadians also turned up. Accorded the privilege of offering "a reflection" on the occasion, I spoke of how Rae had completed the work of Franklin and others. Orcadian musician Jennifer Wrigley then performed a dazzling original fiddle tune called "Air for Dr. John Rae," and two Canadian cousins who share an ancestor with the explorer laid a wreath and flowers beside the new ledger stone.

After the ceremony came Evensong in the Abbey, and then a reception at the Scottish Office in nearby Dover House—London home base for Alistair Carmichael. As one woman put it, looking around at the reception, "This is an occasion we will never forget." For me, it brought back our modest Arctic tribute of two years before, when in 2012 voyagers had gathered around the plaque overlooking Rae Strait. One of my Adventure Canada colleagues, Inuk culturalist Miqqusaaq Bernadette Dean, led two young Inuit women

Jenna Anderson, an Inuk from Labrador, celebrated our 2012 visit to the John Rae memorial site. The ruined cairn Rae built in 1854 is to the right of the plaque in this photo.

from Baffin Island in a song of celebration, and then stood aside while they marked the occasion with throat-singing. Another Inuk staffer, Jenna Anderson of Labrador, celebrated by doing a first-ever handstand at this location.

After the photo-taking, I wedged the three flags, and also a small tin canister containing a note, into the stones at the base. And why wouldn't we mark the occasion? We had demonstrated that this site is readily accessible to adventure travellers. We had honoured Rae and his companions at the location of their epochal achievement. While passengers drifted back to the Zodiacs, I remained at the memorial, not wanting to leave, gazing out over Rae Strait. A magic moment.

And I found myself thinking of all those who had lost their lives while making this moment possible—of the scores who had died early in the quest with Henry Hudson and Jens Munk and James Knight, and then in the massacre of innocents at Bloody Falls. I thought of how, on his first overland expedition, John Franklin had lost more than half his party, and of still more men dying with Robert McClure and Elisha Kent Kane and then Franklin again in the ultimate Arctic catastrophe. I thought of Matonabbee hanging himself and of Mary Norton starving to death and of Albert One-Eye vanishing into a whirlpool on the Coppermine River.

I thought, then, of those survivors who had carried on against all odds, of heroic figures like Rae, Ouligbuck and Mistegan, all written out of "official" history. I thought of Thanadelthur and Sakeouse and Tattannoeuck, neglected, virtually forgotten, and of Eenoolooapik, Tookoolito, Ebierbing and Minik, so often treated as footnotes. Looking out over the ice-free strait, I felt a need, suddenly, to write a fifth Arctic book—not a biography this time, but a wide-ranging work that would encompass the forgotten heroes, above all the First Peoples among them. In its rough contours, I envisioned an historical narrative that would steer between extremes, treating the history of exploration from a contemporary perspective, incorporating what we had learned in recent decades, and elaborating a more inclusive position than the one offered by "official history"—in short, a narrative of discovery for the twenty-first century. I wanted to tell the untold story of the Northwest Passage. Someone called my name. The last Zodiac was leaving. Was I coming? And with that, for the moment, the vision faded. Exhilarated, feeling almost high, I hurried down the sandy slope and swung into the Zodiac, eager to resume sailing through the final link in the Northwest Passage.

ACKNOWLEDGEMENTS

At a raucous post-Christmas party some years ago, Margaret Atwood appeared out of nowhere and seized me by the shirt sleeve. "Come with me," she said. "There's someone I want you to meet." She hauled me from a first crowded room into a second, where she introduced me to Matthew Swan, CEO of Adventure Canada (AC). "You two should talk," she said, and vanished. A few weeks later, Matthew called and said that, seeing as how I had published three books about Arctic exploration, maybe I would like to sail as a resource person in the Northwest Passage. So I owe both Atwood and Swan a massive thank you. Since 2007, Sheena Fraser McGoogan and I have gone voyaging with AC at least once a year, and sometimes twice. As a result, I have met and learned from such outstanding figures as Latonia Hartery, Johnny Issaluk, John Houston, Marc St. Onge, Susie Evyagotailak, Mark Mallory, Tagak Curley, Pierre Richard and Susan Aglukark, among many others. That experience informs this work.

Dead Reckoning is my eighth book with HarperCollins, and for that I thank my lucky stars. I can confirm that editor Patrick Crean is rightly renowned throughout the industry: he has an amazing eye and does not hesitate to put his finger on your sacred text and say: "Well, it's your book . . . but this isn't working." And I owe a shout-out to the rest of the team, among them Leo MacDonald, Rob Firing, Colleen Simpson, Alan Jones, Noelle Zitzer, Michael Guy-Haddock, Cory Beatty, Stephanie Nuñez and Maria Golikova. Copyeditor Angelika Glover did excellent work on this book (not hers but mine the occasional flouting of *Chicago Manual* conventions). And my agent, the legendary Beverley Slopen, has long since become a trusted friend and advisor.

Over the past few years, while working on this book, I have received grants from the Canada Council for the Arts, the Ontario Arts Council and the Access Copyright Foundation. For those, believe me, I am grateful. In Orkney, I have learned a great deal from historian Tom Muir, and benefitted from the kindness of Kathleen Ireland and Andrew Appleby, president of the John Rae Society. Among individuals who have contributed to this book, sometimes without knowing it, I think of John Geiger, Cameron Treleaven and Louie Kamookak, and must also single out Kenn Harper, Randall Osczevski, Andres Paredes, Dawn Huck, Fred McCoy and Lee Preston. I want to say hey to members of the Facebook group *Remembering the Franklin Expedition*, who frequently dazzle me with their arcane knowledge. On the home front, I owe sincere thanks to Carlin, Keriann, Sylwia, Travis, James and Veronica. Above all, I do hereby declare that without Sheena Fraser McGoogan, my life partner, first reader, sometime photographer and fellow traveller, this book would not exist—and that is the truth.

SELECTED REFERENCES

In writing *Dead Reckoning: The Untold Story of the Northwest Passage*, I have built on the foundation I laid with my four previous books about Arctic exploration. Their bibliographies include more than two hundred citations, among them all of the standard references. Those seeking further reading material will find much there:

Ancient Mariner: The Amazing Adventures of Samuel Hearne, the Sailor Who Walked to the Arctic Ocean. Toronto: Harper Perennial, 2003.

Fatal Passage: The Untold Story of John Rae, the Arctic Adventurer Who Discovered the Fate of Franklin. Toronto: Harper Perennial, 2001.

Lady Franklin's Revenge: A True Story of Ambition, Obsession and the Remaking of Arctic History. Toronto: HarperCollins Publishers Ltd, 2005.

Race to the Polar Sea: The Heroic Adventures and Romantic Obsessions of Elisha Kent Kane. Toronto: HarperCollins Publishers Ltd, 2008.

In addition, I have incorporated research I did while writing forewords to three books:

A Journey to the Northern Ocean: The Adventures of Samuel Hearne. Victoria: Touchwood Editions, 2007.

John Rae's Arctic Correspondence, 1844–1855. Victoria: Touchstone Editions, 2014.

The Arctic Journals of John Rae. Victoria: Touchstone Editions, 2012.

The present volume also draws on articles and reviews I have published in *Canada's History, Canadian Geographic, Maclean's, Polar Record, Arctic, Literary Review of Canada, Up Here, Alberta Views,* the *Globe and Mail, National Post, Montreal Gazette* and *Calgary Herald,* as well as "travel logs" I wrote while voyaging with Adventure Canada.

A number of publications not cited in my earlier books—either because they were not relevant or were not yet published—round out a short list for further reading:

Barr, William, ed. *From Barrow to Boothia: The Arctic Journal of Chief Factor Peter Warren Dease, 1836–1839.* Montreal and Kingston: McGill-Queen's University Press, 2002.

——— ed. *Overland to Starvation Cove: With the Inuit in Search of Franklin, 1878–1880.* Toronto: University of Toronto Press, 1987.

Botting, Douglas. *Humboldt and the Cosmos.* New York: Harper & Row, 1973.

Bown, Stephen. *The Life of Roald Amundsen.* Vancouver: Douglas & McIntyre, 2012.

——— *White Eskimo: Knud Rasmussen's Fearless Journey into the Heart of the Arctic.* Vancouver: Douglas & McIntyre, 2015.

Burwash, L. T. "The Franklin Search." *Canadian Geographical Journal,* vol. 1, no. 7 (November 1930): 593.

Byers, Michael. *Who Owns the Arctic? Understanding Sovereignty Disputes in the North.* Vancouver: Douglas & McIntyre, 2009.

Craciun, Adriana. *Writing Arctic Disaster: Authorship and Exploration.* Cambridge: Cambridge University Press, 2016.

Cyriax, R. J. *Sir John Franklin's Last Arctic Expedition.* London: Methuen, 1939.

Davis, Richard, ed. *Sir John Franklin's Journals and Correspondence: The First Arctic Land Expedition, 1819–1822.* Toronto: The Champlain Society, 1995.

Davis, Richard, ed. *Sir John Franklin's Journals and Correspondence: The Second Arctic Land Expedition, 1825–1827*. Toronto: The Champlain Society, 1998.

Dodge, Ernest S. *The Polar Rosses: John and James Clark Ross and Their Explorations*. London: Faber & Faber, 1973.

Eber, Dorothy Harley. *Encounters on the Passage*. Toronto: University of Toronto Press, 2008.

Fleming, Fergus. *Barrow's Boys: The Original Extreme Adventurers*. London: Granta Books, 1998.

Geiger, John, and Alanna Mitchell. *Franklin's Lost Ship: The Historic Discovery of* HMS *Erebus*. Toronto: HarperCollins Canada, 2015.

Grant, Shelagh D. *Polar Imperative: A History of Arctic Sovereignty in North America*. Vancouver: Douglas & McIntyre, 2010.

Hansen, Thorkild. *The Way to Hudson Bay: The Life and Times of Jens Munk*. Translated by James McFarlane and John Lynch. New York: Harcourt Brace, 1970.

Harper, Kenn. *Give Me My Father's Body: The Life of Minik the New York Eskimo*. Vermont: Steerforth Press, 2000.

Henderson, Bruce. *True North: Peary, Cook, and the Race to the Pole*. New York: W. W. Norton, 2005.

Holland, Clive. *Arctic Exploration and Development, c. 500 BC to 1915: An Encyclopedia*. New York and London: Garland Publishing, 1994.

Houston, C. Stuart, ed. *Arctic Artist: The Journal and Paintings of George Back, Midshipman with Franklin, 1819–1822*. Kingston and Montreal: McGill-Queen's University Press, 1994.

——— ed. *Arctic Ordeal: The Journal of John Richardson, Surgeon-Naturalist with Franklin, 1820–1822*. Kingston and Montreal: McGill-Queen's University Press, 1984.

Hunter, Douglas. *God's Mercies: Rivalry, Betrayal and the Dream of Discovery*. Toronto: Doubleday Canada, 2007.

Kenyon, W. A. *The Journal of Jens Munk, 1619–1620*. Toronto: Royal Ontario Museum, 1980.

Krupnik, Igor, ed. *Early Inuit Studies: Themes and Transitions, 1850s–1980s*. Washington, D.C.: Smithsonian Institution, 2016.

Lambert, Andrew. *Franklin: Tragic Hero of Polar Navigation*. London: Faber & Faber, 2009.

Mancall, Peter C. *Fatal Journey: The Final Expedition of Henry Hudson*. New York: Basic Books, 2009.

McDermott, James. *Martin Frobisher: Elizabethan Privateer*. New Haven, C.T.: Yale University Press, 2001.

McGhee, Robert. *The Arctic Voyages of Martin Frobisher: An Elizabethan Adventure*. Montreal and Kingston: McGill-Queen's University Press, 2001.

McGoogan, Ken. "Defenders of Arctic Orthodoxy Turn Their Backs on Sir John Franklin." *Polar Record*, vol. 51, no. 2, (March 2015): 220–221. (Published online October 2, 2014.)

Mills, William James. *Exploring Polar Frontiers: A Historical Encyclopedia*. Santa Barbara, C.A.: ABC-CLIO, 2003.

Neatby, Leslie H. *In Quest of the Northwest Passage*. Toronto: Longmans, Green, 1958.

Newman, Peter C. *Company of Adventurers: The Story of the Hudson's Bay Company*. Toronto: Viking, 1985.

Nickerson, Sheila. *Midnight to the North: The Untold Story of the Inuit Woman Who Saved the Polaris Expedition*. New York: Tarcher-Putnam, 2002.

Osborne, S. L. *In the Shadow of the Pole: An Early History of Arctic Expeditions, 1871-1912*. Toronto: Dundurn, 2013.

Parry, Ann. *Parry of the Arctic: The Life Story of Admiral Sir Edward Parry*. London: Chatto & Windus, 1963.

Parry, Edward. *Memoirs of Rear Admiral Sir William Edward Parry, by His Son*. London: Longman, Brown, 1857.

Parry, Richard. *Trial by Ice: The True Story of Murder and Survival on the 1871 Polaris Expedition.* New York: Ballantine Books, 2001.

Parry, William Edward. *Journal of a Voyage for the Discovery of a North-West Passage . . . in the Years 1819–20.* London: John Murray, 1821.

Potter, Russell. *Finding Franklin: The Untold Story of a 165-Year Search.* Montreal and Kingston: McGill-Queen's University Press, 2016.

Rasky, Frank. *The Polar Voyagers.* Toronto: McGraw-Hill Ryerson, 1976.

——— *The North Pole or Bust: Explorers of the North.* Toronto: McGraw-Hill Ryerson, 1977.

Rich, Edwin Gile. *Hans the Eskimo.* Cambridge, M.A.: Riverside Press, 1934.

Ross, John. *Journal of a Voyage for the Discovery of a North-west Passage.* London: John Murray, 1819.

Ross, M. J. *Polar Pioneers: John Ross and James Clark Ross.* Montreal and Kingston: McGill-Queen's University Press, 1994.

Ruby, Robert. *Unknown Shore: The Lost History of England's Arctic Colony.* New York: Henry Holt, 2001.

Scranton, Roy. "What I Learned on a Luxury Cruise Through the Global-Warming Apocalypse." *The Nation*, November. 9, 2015.

Smith, D. Murray. *Arctic Expeditions from British and Foreign Shores.* Southampton: Charles H. Calvert, 1877.

Steele, Peter. *The Man Who Mapped the Arctic: The Intrepid Life of George Back, Franklin's Lieutenant.* Vancouver: Raincoast Books, 2003.

Stein, Glenn M. *Discovering the North-West Passage: The Four-Year Arctic Odyssey of H.M.S. Investigator and the McClure Expedition.* Jefferson, N.C.: McFarland & Company, 2015.

Woodman, David C. *Unravelling the Franklin Mystery: Inuit Testimony*, 2nd ed. Montreal: McGill-Queen's University Press, 2015.

Young, Delbert A. "Killer on the 'Unicorn.'" *The Beaver*, Winter 1973, 9–15.

ILLUSTRATION CREDITS

Images not otherwise credited come from the author's private collection.

Original maps by Dawn Huck: pages i, v [appeared originally in *Race to the Polar Sea*, p. xii], vii [appeared originally in *Ancient Mariner*, p. 80], 50 [appeared originally in *Ancient Mariner*, p. 132], 206 [appeared originally in *Fatal Passage*, p. 87], 236 [appeared originally in *Race to the Polar Sea*, p. 130], 254 [appeared originally in *Fatal Passage*, p. 60].

Photos by Sheena Fraser McGoogan: pages 3, 5, 252, 323, 362, 380, 409 (bottom), 411.

Courtesy of the British Library Board: page 156.

Courtesy of *Canadian Geographic* magazine: page 391.

Courtesy of the Glenbow Museum: page 217 (55.17.1).

Courtesy of Kenn Harper: pages 147, 257.

Courtesy of HBC Archives: pages 42 (32-28026) [appeared originally in *Ancient Mariner*, p. 124], 53 (24-2806), 210.

Courtesy of HBC Corporate Collection: pages 36 (ART-00036), 188 (ART-00032), 264 (ART-00029).

Courtesy of James Grieve Photography: page 183.

Courtesy of Library and Archives Canada: pages 72 (published holding project/C-025238), 104, 119, 134 (nlc 000 707), 232 (C-016105).

Courtesy of Roger McCoy: page 112.

Courtesy of National Galleries of Scotland: page 68 (PG 2488).

Courtesy of the National Library of Norway: page 367.

Courtesy of the New York Public Library: page 163.

Courtesy of Randall Osczevski: page 91.

Courtesy of Parks Canada: page 394.

Courtesy of Lee Preston: pages 144, 339, 348.

Courtesy of the Toronto Public Library, Special collections: pages 89, 128, 140.

Courtesy of Cameron Treleaven: pages 278, 309, 404.

Courtesy of the Dean and Chapter of Westminster: page 409 (top).

Courtesy of Wikimedia Commons, which makes available images in the public domain: pages 10, 19, 26, 57, 65, 83, 84, 93, 133, 157, 185, 281, 286, 297, 303, 326, 331, 344, 346, 373, 382.

INDEX

Note: Page numbers in italics indicate maps and illustrations.

INDEX